SURVIVAL
P.L.A.N.S

All rights reserved

Copyright 2020 by Sabrina C. Nash

SURVIVAL
P.L.A.N.S

Featuring the **P**oems, **L**etters, **A**rt and **N**oteworthy **S**ayings of…

Adeola Adeniya
*Sistah Joy Alford
Anthony Battle
*Clinton Battle
Darcelle Battle
Kim Battle
Sierra Battle
Florence Bert
Ashby Lou Bito
*DeVante "D.C." Capers
Kim Canales
Chanler Crawford
Janet Dinkins
Lisa "Li" Floyd
Mark Gray
*GradaLove
Erica Hall
Kevin Harrison
Veronica Jackson
Zoe C. James Nash
Alan Kahn
Uchenna Kamalu
Barry Barnett Keith
Tiffany Lee
Jason Lippman

Troy Lockett
Mimi Machado-Luces
Margo Mayo
Karen Mayo Hogan
Latoya McCoy
Angela McPherson
Rahim Mitchell
Shantayah Murray
Kayla Nash Jones
Ariyah C. Nash
Dana A. Nash
David Z. Nash
Sabrina C. Nash
Doris Oseghale
*Pamela "P.S." Perkins
Edana J. Perry
Isis Pree
*Menefen "Funzito" Rasberry
*Curtis Scoon
*Taundra Noel Shaw
Chrystal Sterling
T'Nesha "True" Washington
Jason Whiting
Anita Williams
Crystal Williams

Special Reflections & Advice from:

Merrill and Keith Alston
Keyonna Andrews
Christian A. Battle
Tiffany Battle
Karen Burks
Cassandra Creek
Beth Cruz
Jessica Green
Alicia Jackson-Warren
Nicole Jones
Edwin Miller
Anita Nash
Jeanette Riggins
Crystal Smith
Camille Tyson

Special Thanks to Living Legacies…

*The Battle & Wright Families (Battle History)
*Family of Charles B. Hall (Tuskegee Airmen)
*David L. Nash & Nash Family Contributors
*Gail Smith-Howard & Family
*Donna F. Edwards
*Dr. Charlene M. Dukes
*Kayla Ross Perry and KRP Foundation
*Terrance Sterling & Family
*Marion Miller-Wood & Family
*Nikki Giovanni

Cover Art

Sabrina C. Nash

This book is dedicated to the Memory of the loved ones WE lost

P.L.A.N.S by CONTENTS

PRE-PLAN THOUGHTS xiv
LIFE AND TIMES 1
Awakening In Rain x DC Photography 2
The First Creation 3
The Life and Times Collection XX: H I S - S T O R Y 5
Proclamation 6
US Bill of Rights for US Citizens 8
Historical Haikus 9
Every System (quote) 10
Scoon Speaks 11
Tell Us Your Story 12
My Culture 13
Black Man In America 15
Million Man March 16
The Light 17
Sight You Don't See 18
Blinders in the Matrix DC Photography 22
Scoon Speaks 23
Damage Control (quote) 24
Enjoy! Brought To YOU by Coke 25
Popular Culture 26
Entertainment not Culture(quote) 27
The Life and Times Collection XVII: Popular Culture 28
IG Thoughts 29
The Populist Belief System 30
Scoon Speaks 31
Trumped 32
L E T T E R S 33
Corporate Compassion (quote) 36
Whitey on the Moon 37

SURVIVAL PLANS

Scoon Speaks	38
The Electric Suit	39
The Lie and Times Collection XVII: Creating Belief in Barack	42
No Justice? No Change.	43
Conservatively Black American	44
Remembrance x DC Photography	45
Remembering 9/11	46
9/11 Terrance Sterling	47
That Black and Blue	48
Black, White and Blue @ PGCC	51
Black, White and Blue @ PGCC	52
Black Man Down Remembering *Joseph*	53
Nipsey Hussle	61
Scoon Speaks	62
La Vida En Black Ricardo Jason's Historia	63
America's Promise: The 2nd Amendment	68
I Have Feelings Too	79
Romie's Poem	70
Artist Spotlight: GradaLove	72
F.E.M	73
Funzito Collection "Woman"	74
Rosa Parks	75
Her Story (Haiku)	75
Nikki Giovanni- Unity in Poetry	76
We Need Strong Men	77
Batgirl	78
Accessories of Sex-cess	79
Black Girl Magic	80
Funzito Collection "The Runaways"	81
MUVA Speaks Too	82
Socialite (quote)	83
Birkin Bitch	84
Georgetown Social x DC Photography	85
I see You	86

Seeing Holly Exploit Us	87
Funzito Collection "Cabin"	88
Pride and Joy x D.C. Photography	89
Pride and Joy	90
Her	91
No Lives Matter	94
New Age Wharf x DC Photography	95
Something in the Water x DC Photography	97
The Water	98
DARK SKIES---------	99
B.L.M?	100
Before/Be For?	101
Self Centered With No New Growth In Sight	102
2020 Drastically Changed our Lives---------	
Survival 2020-Panicked Out-----A Year to Remember	104
Making I Contact	107
Sista On Board	108
Sounding Off	110
Scoon Speaks	111
Thoughts On Money	112
The Cost of Living	115
James Baldwin (quote)	117
Media Takeout 2020	118
Things that Don't Mix…	119
K.I.N.G.	120
Tired of being a Nigga!	123
Funzito Collection (Untitled)	125
It's not the crack-house (quote)	126
Survival Can be Like…	127
Creativity Boost:	129
Plans for Survival:	130
Spirits Lay Broken	134
The Life and Times Collection XX: America is Still Number 1	136
Triumvirate of the Masses	137

D.C. (Haiku) 138
Malcolm X Park x DC Photography 139
Imanapitup 140
Bringing Collard Greens To The Table 142
Malcolm X Park x DC Photography 147
Dear President Trump, ... 148
The Life and Times Collection XX: Man on Fire! 149
Thoughts on Real Leadership… 150
U.N.I.T.Y. 151
ComUnity 153
The Revolution 156
To Heal A Wounded World 159
Sistah Joy x Reflections Literary & Arts @ PGCC 161
Today 162
Creativity Booster 164
Life and Times - Crossword Puzzle Clues 166

LOVE AND LOSS 167

Love and Loss 168
Mother Dear 169
Mother's Unconditional Love 170
Some Days You Just Can't Forget (8/15/05) 171
Mommy 175
Love Haikus 178
Love Poem 179
Lust Rush Crush 180
Lusting Go 182
Even with Love… 187
Lesson from a Train Wreck 189
A Leap of Faith 193
Starchild the Urban Unicorn 194
Exist 195
Simple Truths about Love 196
Beauty 197

Rare Rose x DC Photography	199
Good Morning, My Love	200
My Sweet Nina Boo,	201
Love Angel	204
Connected Timelessly through the Basic Need for each other	205
Today and Forever	208
Wedding Prayer	209
Survival Plans 101: Marriage Advice From "Real" Married People	210
This Is Marriage	219
Finances in Marriage	220
Thoughts on Things I Miss…	221
Seeking Validation	222
Right Now	225
The Sad Day	226
Forced Change	227
Standing the Test of Time	228
#TBT Love	233
You Are My Tree	234
Our Love Inside Out	235
SURVIVAL PLANS	237
Takeaways from "Make Love, Make Money, Make It Last"	239
Mom and Dad Nash,	240
The Ends of the Universe	241
Universal Balance…	242
Tale of the Two	243
Through the Fire and the Flood	244
Some Changes	246
The Loss	249
Dreamed	250
Underwater x DC Photography	251
What's Left	252
Heartfelt Prayer	253
The Call	254

Palm of His Hands 255
In Memory of M.M.B 256
Sister Friends 257
My Sister, My Bestie, My Friend 258
Royal Elephant 259
3D Dreams, Daughter, Departure 260
My Soul Is Tired 261
What I Gained From My Loss 262
I Choose to Remember 266
Now I Sit 267
Waiting x DC Photography 268
Second Chances 269
Nightmare into Reality 278
The Phoenix 279
The Dream 280
The Future… Mrs. Nash 281
Love and Loss: Word Search 282

LEARNING AND LEADERSHIP 283

Thoughts on Growth & Good Fruit vs Bad Fruit 284
Simple yet Scientific Thoughts about Life and Energy 287
Mrs. Nash's Leadership Class 289
A Letter for My Daughter Zoe 291
Young Hero 292
I'm Thankful for… 293
SURVIVAL PLANS presents… Storytelling Time:
Education is the Key to Success!!! 294
Song for School 12 Graduates (Paterson, NJ) 297
To: The Graduates of School 12 (Paterson, NJ)
Words of Encouragement 298
LOUD Brown Girls 299
LOUD Brown Girls: Crossword Puzzle 302
Quinceanera. Graphite. 2012 303
Artist Spotlight: BB Keith 304
My… 306

Ocean Jewel 307
What Do You See??? 307
When Will I? 308
Reflection 309
Sometimes you have to look at yourself in the mirror and ask 310
When he rears his ugly head… 311
L I E S 312
Be careful telling them LIES, YOU don't want to end up a … 314
Chronic Complainers 315
The cure for complaining is building gratitude… 316
If nobody ever told you… 318
The Poorest Woman 319
Poor Mentality (quote) 322
Survival Story: Breaking the Cycle 324
Creativity Booster: 326
Change 327
My Reasons to Quit Smoking 328
SURVIVAL PLANS Book Club presents:
Takeaways from "Pimp" by Iceberg Slim 329
When trying to CHANGE beware of the BUM … 330
When trying to get rid of the BUM do more WORK! 331
The Alpha 333
HIS STORY: Curtis Scoon 334
Life is too Short 343
Throughout Time 344
Light at the end of the Tunnel 345
Subways x DC Photography 346
Gazing Up 347
Enterprising Mind 349
WWKD? 2020 351
WHIPPING OUT MY FAITH 352
S U R V I V A L   S T O R Y:
Living MY life with Autism 353
Monumental Joy x DC Photography 356
D R E A M 357

DREAMS "R" 359
From Dreams to Reality 360
For My Sister on Her Upcoming Graduation
And on her Earning her RN (2017) 361
Become F.I.T. 362
Thankful Graduation (thoughts) 363
Grateful. Once was lost. Now found. Planted in faith. 366
She Survived x Doodle and De-Stress 368
SP Spotlight: Taundra Noel, Empowerment Coach 369
Doodle and De-Stress: Grace 376
In The Power of Now 377
Master the Paradox 378
Becoming 380
Elemental Forces 381
I am the Avatar 382
Uncle Iroh x Doodle and De-Stress 383
Maintenance required… 384
Why PLAN? 385
Crowned 386
Victory 387
Learning and Leadership: Word Search 388
Creativity Booster: PLANS Prompt 389
Development of One's Self: Word Search 390

LIVING LEGACIES 391

In the Legacy 392
Congratulations CMD 395
Change at PGCC (Prince George's Community College) is… 396
In the Living Legacy of David L. Nash 397
Doodle and De-Stress x KNJ 409
In the Living Legacy of The Honorable Donna F. Edwards 410
The Legacy Continues… 412
S.P Tips for Working with Elected Officials 413

When I grow up	414
Blaze your own Trail (quote)	416
In the Living Legacy of Gail Smith Howard	417
Reflections of Success	420
In The Living Legacy Nikki Giovanni	432
In the Living Legacy of Tuskegee Airman Major Charles B. Hall	437
The Living Legacy of the Battle and Burgess Family	448
Love Your Family	469
In the Living Legacy of Clinton Battle	470
The Red Door. Painting. 2011.	482
Excerpt from the Journals of Clinton Battle	483
Unfinished Plans…	484
Family Ties	485
The Lord giveth and he taketh away."	486
Living Legacies x Coke	487
In the Living Legacy of Marion Miller Wood	488
In the Living Legacy of Terrance Sterling	492
A Journey of Healing through Forgiveness	495
In the Living Legacy of Kayla Ross Perry	499
Legacies never die	504
Legacies: Word Search	505
"Legacies" Crossword Puzzle Clues	506
Works Cited	507

SURVIVAL P.L.A.N.S

(Pre-PLAN Thoughts)

Survival PLANS (**PLANS** being the acronym for **P**oems, **L**etters, **A**rt and **N**oteworthy **S**ayings) is an anthology and community memoir about life and what it's like to grow, survive, and thrive TODAY.

Better than chicken soup for the soul, *Survival PLANS* is more than a healing anthology. It's a complete literary experience that brings **community, culture** and **creativity together.**

As a collective, we wish to use poetry and arts as a medium to communicate with and support one another through all of life's obstacles.

Survival PLANS is about persevering during the challenging times. It's about having faith- even if it is the size of a mere mustard seed. It's about love even when you have had loss. It's about changing and becoming. It's about US!

Each one teaching one from his or her-story.

Each life lesson creating a lesson PLAN.

Helping to leave a legacy of ...

Survival PLANS

Life and TIMES

"Everyday life surrounds us in a swirling chaos, and it's easy to fall into the grip of our ego's, fears and confusion. Remind yourself each day of your intentions and spiritual purpose."

—Deepak Chopra

Awakening In Rain x DC Photography

From the "New DC" Collection

The First Creation

Awakened

Created of the Earth

In tune with my surroundings

Divinity in the flesh

Bountiful in my bones

Life in my blood

Free to be…

At peace

I'm home

Wake Up x Doodle and De-Stress

The Life and Times Collection XX: HIS-STORY

Proclamation

We, here in this country, where our color holds us captive
We, whose names called out in today's courtrooms
Echo like calls from yesterday's auction blocks

We, who with bowed, all but broken backs
Built the glory and splendor of this nation
On plantations where we were whipped,
Maimed, raped, and lynched

We, who built churches that upheld Slavery Laws
And jails that fail to give us justice,
And keeps parents from children
While making profit and enterprise from their labor

We, who society declares unworthy
Of equality, equity or reparations
We, who strive to educate our youth and ourselves
Banking against the odds of success
On such unleveled playing fields

We, who despite the harrowing pillage of yesterday,
Believe in a God who sits high and looks low
As witnessed by swollen church pews
That reflect hope of undeterred faith-filled folk
Our spirit, like our history, is strong
Lists of challenged injustices and
Wrongs endured, resisted and protested
Document a determination for equality

But emancipation rings hollow
When parity is too long held in wait
And humanity doesn't dictate
Just laws for a land

Despite decades, centuries of
Denials and disillusionment

We return again and again
Holding tight the torch of determination
Our strength and faith resolute
Lifting us past our circumstance

Despite promises not kept, apologies
Not uttered and restitution withheld
Fighting for right beyond might
The parchment proclaimed it so
Yet tests of time glaringly show
Appeasement to be the promised gift

So on fields as unbalanced as staggered
Steps of men drunk with power
So ultimately are unequal lives played out
In today's classrooms, boardrooms
And courtrooms across this country

Til her words be true for all
The ripples and furls of her flag
Only cripple and hurl her masses
Headlong into never-ending nightmares
For false proclamation is worse than none

Such is the dilemma caused by proclamations
Never intended to equate citizens of a nation
For when truths that should be self-evident
Reflect a flawed and twisted democracy
One that resists equality in favor of hypocrisy
When justice and humanity
Are relegated to the realm of myth
This dilemma becomes a danger to the nation
Too long has America remained poised
At this precarious edge. Her adolescence has faded.
She must decide what she wants to be.

© J. Joy "Sistah Joy" Matthews Alford

US BILL OF RIGHTS FOR US CITIZENS

Amendment 1
Promises US citizens the following five freedoms. Freedom of religion, speech, press, assembly and petition

Amendment 2
Promises US citizens the right to have and keep arms (weapons).

Amendment 3
Promises US citizens that the government is prevented from forcing <u>homeowners</u> to allow soldiers to use their homes.

Amendment 4
Promises US citizens that the government is barred from unreasonable search and seizure of an individual and/or their private property

Amendment 5
Promises US citizens several protections for those accused of crimes. Serious charges must be started by a grand jury. US citizens cannot be tried twice for the same offense (double jeopardy) or have property taken away without fair compensation. US citizens have the right against self-incrimination and can't be imprisoned without fair procedures and trials.

Amendment 6
Promises US citizens additional protections when accused of crimes, such as the right to a speedy and public trial, trial by an impartial jury in criminal cases, and to be informed of criminal charges. Witnesses must face the accused, and the accused is allowed his or her own witnesses and to be represented by a lawyer.

Amendment 7
Promises US citizens the right to a jury trial in Federal civil cases.

Amendment 8
Promises US citizens that excessive bail, fines and cruel and unusual punishment will be barred

Amendment 9
Promises US citizens that listing these specific rights in the Constitution does not mean that US citizens do not have other rights that have not been spelled out.

Amendment 10
Promises US citizens that the Federal Government only has those powers delegated in the Constitution. If it isn't listed, it belongs to the states or to the people

Historical Haikus

His Story

His story, not mine

I write mine, in my own time

His lessons I apply

Civil Rights

You can't give me rights

When you can't tell wrong from right

Rights can't be wrong

Black Power

Black power creates

Fear among those who may hate

But that can't stop fate

It is important to remember…

"Every system is perfectly designed to get the results it gets."

-W. Edwards Deming

"I don't know what the intent of integration was, but the outcome can only be described as assimilation into the leftist wing of America. We adopted their values, lifestyles and dogma. In return they've pilfered our economic autonomy. We got f**ked. Literally and figuratively."

My Culture

My culture is black
My black is beautiful
My beauty runs deep
Deeper than the flesh you see
See me not with your eyes
Your eyes they do deceive
Deception tells of lies
Ones that you may believe

I believe with **confidence** in truth
And truth is only factual
artifacts have been taken
Taken from our **ancestors** homes
Home they no longer had one
One people destroyed over time

One time we had our **lineage**
Links to all of our man kind
Now folks don't know where they came from
But we've come way too far to forget some
So we marched and sang we shall overcome
That's what we did in the movement

And when the movement wasn't civil
We decided we would take no more
More became black power
Power then **provoked** a struggle
A struggle from a group of people
People who still hungered for their freedom

Freedom can only be controlled
Controlled if you are a dependent
Dependent on a one-sided system
When the system is not in our favor.
And favor you never will never get
So you just have to above it.

It being hate
Hate only fuels hate
Hate is not the answer
The answer is love
Love starts from within
Within the confines of one's self
With **knowledge** of self you can overcome

Overcoming consists of **persistency**
Persistency means putting on the pressure
pressure leads to leaks
"Leaks busts pipes"

Holes can be found
Like things that are lost
Some of Our past may be gone
But our culture still evolves

My culture is black
My future is bright
I only move forward
Because I cannot move back

SURVIVAL PLANS

Clinton Battle

The Light

Occasion: School 17 (Paterson, NJ), Black History Program in 1997

We walk in the light

Remembering the plight

Of Black Americans by day and by night.

A difficult time, they've had to endure;

This much we know for sure.

Oh, we stand in the light,

What a beautiful sight

To see Black Americans by day and by night.

For they are "One of the Lights of the World"

One of the Lights of the World.

Karen Mayo–Hogan

SIGHT
YOU DONT SEE

my mother as she rakes
the fields

12 hours a day to bring home a
meal of

3 sad potatoes for an evening
soup

she will never
taste,

afraid to ask for
more.

YOU DON'T SEE

my father's face as he
hides

his shame
behind

a bottle with your
name,

muttering underneath
his

borrowed
breath

self-denying
words

of "yes suh, no
suh."

YOU DON'T SEE

my brother searching
the

refuse for something to
sell

from discarded
waste,

seeking scraps to build his
dreams

drowning in the dirty
streets
he
runs.

YOU DON'T SEE

my community living
out

the mirror messages
of

long ago misconstrued
lives

forever telling *big house*
lies

to the ones never freed in their minds.

YOU DON'T SEE

your eager
hands

and devouring
eyes

upon my
thighs,

relishing the
beauty

you say you
despise.

YOU DON'T SEE

I had no
voice

in this horrid
game

where there's no
choice

but to bow beneath
your

demeaning
gaze.

YOU DON'T SEE

your blindness numbs
my heart
and stills my
mind,

while my spirit
survives

underneath your-self-
preserving

putrid
lies.

YOU DON'T SEE

the generational shadow of
death

at your own front
door,

passing down
to

3rd and 4th
generations

of those that hate
me.

YOU DON'T SEE

as you escalate the
hate

to become *great*
again

eventually
vanishing

as the dodo bird you are,
but

I SEE YOU

we all
do,

and that's all that
matters!

P.S. PERKINS

Blinders in the Matrix DC Photography

From the "New DC" Collection

"Our battle is psychological before it's anything. We either don't believe in each other or we're wrought with jealousy and self-hatred…"

But…

"You can't do damage control when you are damaged and controlled"

D. Nash

Enjoy! Brought To YOU by Coke

Zoe C. James Nash

Popular Culture

Popular
Hot, craze, fad
Media, masses, mania
Customer, Consumer, User
Abuser, Misusers, Wrong use of,
Social Class, Social Media, Social Justice
Hurting, Fighting, killing

Destruction, the breakdown of
Values, Respect, Love and Peace
History, days of yore, past
Civilization, cultivation, class
Art, Education, sophistication
Facts, Fashion, couture
Culture

> "In today's society, there is a fine line between entertainment and culture...some things are just entertainment!"
>
> — D. NASH

The Life and Times Collection XVII: Popular Kills

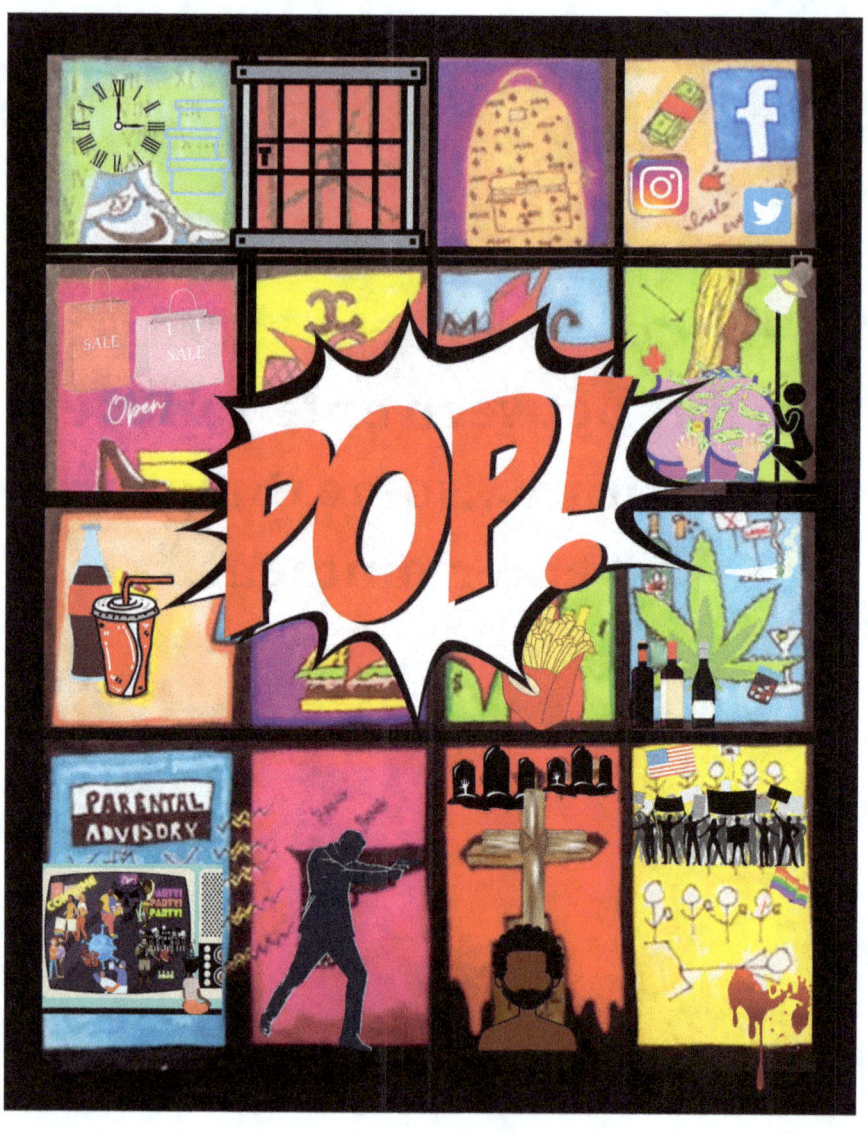

Instagram is rotting my brain
Watching other people's lives
Got me going insane

Images, quick and fast
Selfie paparazzi Snaps a picture.
Flash!

Everyone's waiting for…
Likes!
Cameras!
Action!
Your body the internet's latest attraction

Doing any and everything
Just to get that bag
When I stop to think about it…

It's actually kind of sad.

The Populist Belief System

> "The thoughts, opinions, perceptions, theories and beliefs from the population of people around you."
>
> D. NASH

Editor's Note: Populist beliefs are often influenced by socioeconomic factors including education, income, environment, media and access to these things.

"When it comes to "urban" media, it's gonna be celebrity worship (how much money they got, or TV shows), sex scandals and F**k Trump. If this is the nourishment you give your brain you might as well be braindead."

TRUMPED

LETTERS

CIA FDA NRA FBI EPA GOP AFT ACF NSA TSA FSA IRS FCC NEA DEM DHS FTA FOX CNN MSN ABC CBS BOP ICE FHA FTC FWS DOD DOE DOJ HHS SSA SBA HBO ...whoa!
These acronyms are playing with my mind!
I can't keep'um straight ...
every time we need them they always too late
to handle the weight of a nation
on the brink of **SELFIE** destruction!

So, we demand the **FDA** to monitor our food
while the **EPA** says harmful chemicals and genetic altering
can...
no cannot...
no can, be used...
as the **USDA** turns a blind eye while the fake news hides
farmers dumping milk as babies go hungry!

All the while, the **FCC** bargains net neutrality
 and my speed is slower than ever
because I can't get a signal from behind prison walls
waiting for my day in court
to recognize my continued need for asylum!

But **ICE** won't let me stay
cause the **DOJ** is about JUST-US
while the **DHS** labels me a terrorist
for wearing my brother's hoodie
the only thing left behind
from his too early demise.

As the **CIA** keeps tapping my phone
for information I don't own;
why don't they just LEAVE US ALONE!

CNN reporting children trying to get back home
but **TSA** can't handle the stress
of babies crying for mamas and daddies
exiled God knows where ...
did anybody call the **FBI** to straighten this shit out?

But most ain't got time to care
cause **SSA** cutting grandma's check
and they need another hustle cause
SBA don't really serve
the entrepreneurial dreams of the natives.

So, it's a never-ending nightmare of acronym acrimony,
Passing-the-buck back and forth...
back and forth ...
back and forth...
solving nothing ...
gaining weight like **HHS** that can't figure out
what the hell is going on with health care
in the land of liberty and justice for all!
And the "self-appointed" founding fathers
 are still fighting a war
where the **NRA** is sure to score;
while the **AFT** can't barter
teacher's raise, praise, or a few sick days.

In the meantime, a one-way ticket out of the labor market
 is the pipeline from school to prison,
 even though the **BOP** won't admit that
 prison privatization is a primary tool of population control.

But the happy people keep dancing
and singing
and laughing
cause at least the **NEA** is still supporting dreams!

So, after a tiring day of acronym acid reflux,
avoiding the *Walking Dead*,
I'll just kick back, skip the evening **MSN,**
pop a cold one... "this one's for you",
 and dream of the *Scandal* of *Power*
while building my imaginary *Empire*
that will at least allow me to *Dance with the Stars*
posting it on **FB** while avoiding
the never-ending *Game of Thrones*!

OH! **B T W**...
Anybody got a **J O B**
cause I'm bout' to graduate from this **C C,**
and I need to buy a **C A R**
so I can stop borrowing
from these fake **F W B's**!

P.S. Perkins

"There's no compassion in corporate America."

D. Nash

VIBE: Whitey on the Moon x SCN

Alexa play "Whitey on the Moon" by Gil Scott-Heron

"There's too many people in the world. Not too many for the planet to sustain but too many for the few to maintain total control. Technology has reduced the need for manpower. We have reached a tipping point. Where do we go from here? Mars?"

The Electric Suit

WestCoastAnnie

When I was growing up, my mom use to leave 35 cents on the table for me to make a phone call at a pay phone if I needed to phone home during my outside activities. Back then pay phones where abundant and a vital form of communication. They were on every corner in every restaurant, store, gas station and more. It was a comfort parents felt, knowing that if their kid needed help they could call someone, they could drop a dime and get connected so to speak. Well those days are long gone as you know. You cannot find a pay phone hardly anywhere and if you saw one and tried it, it doesn't not work. You cannot get a dial tone, and in the area where you would insert your money has been blocked off most likely. Even on school campuses you cannot find a payphone that works. Even at a hospital you cannot find a payphone. At the airport, the bus station, the train station, nope. Gone are the days of the little black box with the "chi-ching" sound you would hear when you dropped your money in; "deposit 10 cent please for the next five minutes or your time will expire in 20 seconds" the operator would come on the line and say. Nope ya can't even dial 911 which was free! Today you need a cell phone to call for help, if the people around you wouldn't do so.

Money is tight and so as the story goes with parents my age, many have their offspring living with them until they can find a place of their own to rent. My son lives with me temporarily, and on this day, Saturday, I was up watching TV whilst observing him getting ready to head out the door. And this caused me to realize how times have changed, because first I saw him unplugged his cell phone and put that in his pocket. Then I saw him take his watch off the charger, his watch! And put that on his arm. Then i watched as he unplugged his service unit which is a device that registers product orders which he has accumulated from different stores like CVS, Rite Aid, and the like to replenish their stock order for them, and he put that on his hip on his belt. Then he unplugged the tablet that goes in his car to carry, (he's also an Uber driver) and is provided as a courtesy to patrons to watch streaming shows while riding along to their destinations. Pretty much in all he had about 6 devices that he loaded on his body before he walked out the door. His actions helped me to realize that we are indeed living in a new era, where electronics can define much of your lifestyle. Communication has changed so much, it has become an even bigger business, and unfortunately it has made people depend less on the one on one contact and now has morphed into robotic actions that involve many components for daily living. We no longer rely on talking face to face or writing a letter, now we text, email, Facebook, Snapchat, Twitter and all the rest. There is this lack of personal contact and with that comes a desensitized humanity towards life, losing out on the expression of raw emotions and instead provide a synthesized version of one's self. Why call a friend or family member and speak about how life is going, when you can send an emoji to describe how you feel. Why debate with people you can see when it's easy to banter back and forth on Twitter and Facebook. Who needs to look up from their phone or computer to make eye contact anymore when you can just send a text or an email?

One of the first forms of communication was the telegraph. Back then the excitement of receiving a telegram was an occasion, especially if it came from far away. Or when the telephone came into being, you could call your cousins in Texas and talk directly to everybody one by one in the household if you wanted. In today's world of computers and other electronic devices, a text or email too can be exciting, but void of the basic human instinct to look and listen to the person you are communicating with. Lost are the emotions evoked by face to face, voice to voice conversations, and we are often left with "reply all" form of thought and action. This change in human behavior can be a godsend or be a curse. It has become a stumbling block in how we behave towards one another. We can simply unfriend you when we no longer agree with your comments, or your position on a particular subject. We can block your email address as spam, block your calls if we don't want you to reach us anymore, and block or delete our Snapchat and Facebook accounts so you can't see what posts we uploaded reflecting our daily activities. Yes, we can troll you or support you, not in person but electronically. We can hide behind the electronics and not be seen. Whew! Enough! How much is enough? I ponder this question as I wonder what's next, and am remembering the words of the American singer Sam Cooke, "A Change Is Gonna Come" and indeed it has.

The Life and Times Collection XVII: Creating Belief in Barack

No Justice? No Change.

No justice! No peace!
I hear chanted in the streets…
When is change gon' come?

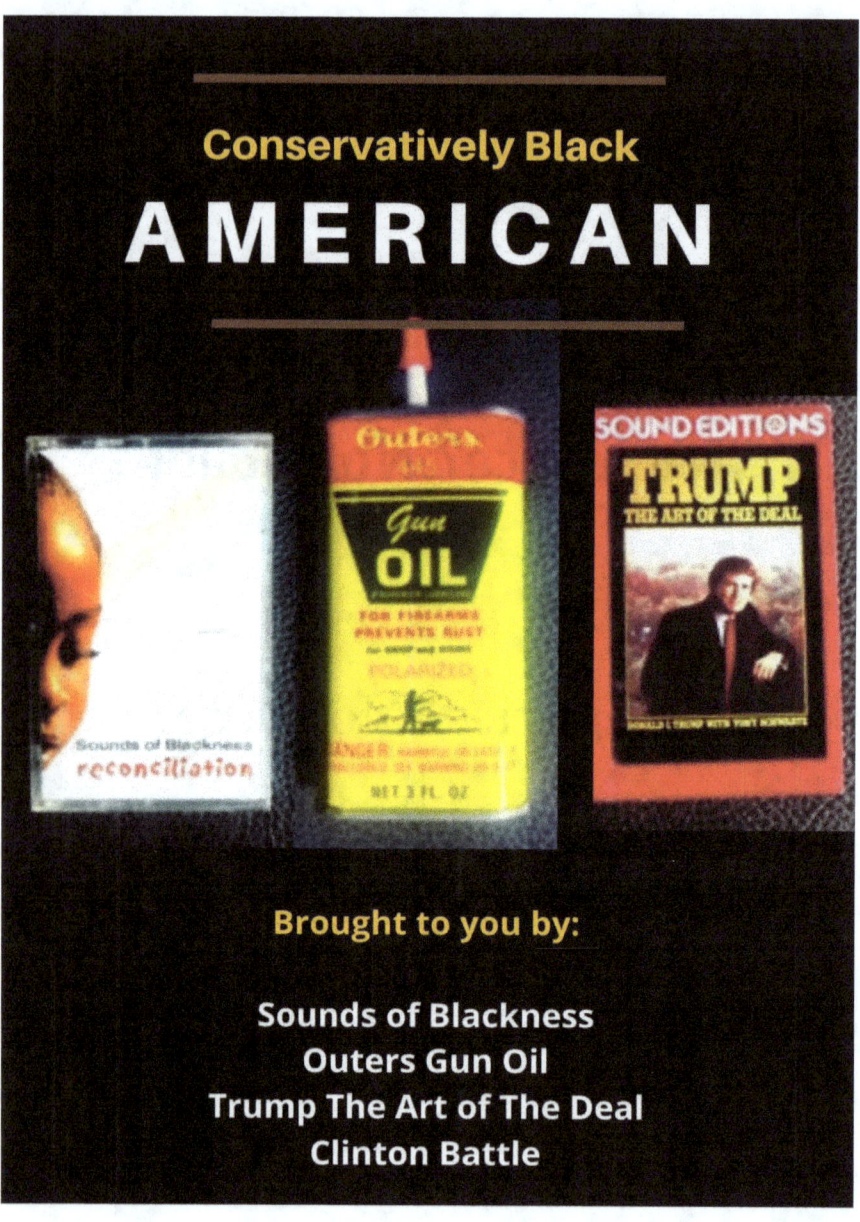

Remembrance x DC Photography

Remembering 9/11

_____
_____
_____
_____
_____
_____
_____

9/11

SURVIVAL PLANS

That Black and Blue

You think you cool in that black and blue
You think you cool with your club and glock too
I hate to tell you that you not
You thought you could get away with the life you took, but now God got
Thought your ego was real high flying in the sky
But guess what? It fell so flat
Flat like that body fell on cold, dark, black pavement
Now you fall on your knees
Trying to pump, pump breath into him in order to get his life back
But it's gone.
How we wish we could hear that motorcycle roar
My sadness is what's roaring in my head like an angry lioness
Warning the enemy that you have messed with the wrong ONE!
Warning that Justice is gonna come.

You think you cool in that black and blue
You think you cool with your club and glock too
Cop you think you real cool in that black and blue
I am here to tell you that it's not true
These tears have been running forming the massive flood to drown you
Submerging you to the point you have no choice but to confess
Confess to the wrong you and your partner have done
Acknowledge that you have taken my brother, my parent's son, my family's cousin, nephew, and to many a friend
You took him and we can't get him back
Don't you know you got to pay for that?
No getting away with this one, like you did before
Cops you gonna reap what you sow.

You think you real cool in that black and blue
You think you real cool with your club and glock too
I pray the scenario of that night keeps replaying in your mind like a broken record

So you feel how my heart has broken, torn out of my chest
An empty hole lies within my soul
A place where my brother's love resides
The great, kind, loving, respectful, hardworking, fun-loving person he was

Will not be overshadowed by the negative you want to portray
I foresee you in a jail cell eating slop off your meal tray.

Man, you think to real cool in that black and blue
You think you real cool with your club and glock too
Those two bullets you shot out the window of your cop car was a coward move
I wish my brother could have done a smooth move to get around you instead of being trapped

He had nowhere to go, but you will feel the same way
Looking at 4 cement walls after your trial has been cracked and solved, GUILTY!
This hatred has to end, with you and your partner ending up in the pen
I put my trust in God to fight this battle for me
To heal my pain and heartache
To regulate my mind and thoughts
I want others to see the God in me, since they definitely didn't see it in you
The ones that are supposed to protect and serve, but instead are committing premeditated crimes
You will not get away with this, God will make sure
His victory will be won, justice we will win.

You thought you were real cool in your black and blue
Thinking you were cool with your club and glock too
Guess what? You Not!
Respect lost, never to be gained back
Get ready for those cuffs to be tight around your wrists
I know you wishing now you could rewind back the time and contemplate risk
Well the both of you took the risk
And have to suffer the consequences

You were trying to be the hero and hit your quota too
But your legacy has definitely ended.
So on the a new dawn,
The legacy of Terrence LeDell Sterling will live on, never to be forgotten.

You thought you were real cool in that black and blue
But that glock you shot got you wearing orange too.
From the angry, frustrated, heart-broken, yet loving, caring, God-fearing, faithful and miracle seeking sister of the best brother in the world.

Chrystal Sterling

Black, White and Blue @ PGCC

Black, White and Blue @ PGCC

10-30-19 B.C.

Photos x DC Photography

BLACK MAN DOWN REMEMBERING *Joseph*

I began writing this **self-examination** article a few, short months ago after journeying through

an extremely emotional experience with a young Black male professional. He had recently experienced

suspension from medical school. He was physically, mentally, and emotionally devasted with more than

three years invested as a top student. He failed one class with a 72 average though 75 was all that was

required. This tragedy ensued during a school year where he suffered a mild heart attack in the spring

and a major bacterial infection during fall finals but finished with stellar grades and an exhausted body.

After suffering the heart attack earlier that year, he was advised by his doctor to adjust his program to

independent study for the rest of the semester to reduce the enormous stress he felt to perform. He

turned the doctor's orders into the appropriate administrative parties, continued his classes spring,

summer, fall without any serious administrative or institutional follow-through. He pulled out As, Bs, and

this low C without any support. To his absolute horror and dismay, the instructor awarding the C grade,

would not relent even after acknowledging the almost insurmountable odds. He left school sick, broken,

and emotionally distraught. He went back "home" to regroup in a city where both his parents were

buried and a surviving grandmother, he was supporting while in school full time and working, remained.

His family had endured the Katrina hurricane disaster, but he survived! He planned to return to the

University later, but he shared with me, "I need to heal." I cried with and for him. His pain was real and

his injury socially and culturally inflicted. He constantly cried the "Black Man Blues" but touted himself

as STRONGER than the rest no matter the difficulty of the test. I prayed for him, wished him well, gave

him home-cooked meals on occasion; but more than these offerings, I lamented the grief I had seen all

too often. I allowed this article to sit dormant for several few weeks enveloped in my own hustle called

living, but the importance of this message kept surfacing repeatedly. As I entered my college classes

occupied by less-hope-filled faces, we often discussed concerns about the non-communicative ways so

many people, especially men, were living and the urban streets filled with the fallout of – **The Black Man**

Down.

>Soon, very soon after experiencing the disappointment of the med-student, I received a phone

call that seared my heart and mind once again, becoming a piece of mental residue I had no choice but

to never forget! It was a call of utter shock, sadness, and the too often sound of hope-LESS resolve. A

student, someone I had come to know and admire, had just died! Another, BLACK MAN DOWN!!! I had

no choice but to revisit the reoccurring pain of this article as I sat at the funeral of a young Black son,

father, brother, cousin, nephew, partner, friend, artist, and college student. He was my student that

semester at a local, urban Historically Black College and University (HBCU). I was his Professor of

Communication. One by one, attendees filed in to pay respects and view the body of this young,

beautiful man. He was an aspiring musician with incredible musical genius. He demonstrated this talent

during his Informative Speech. He made an A. I vaguely remembered having to stop his question and

answer session, stopping the flow of genius because we had run out of time! I wonder if I had more

time...

    Joseph had recently contributed his talent to a performance by a collective of community artists

he was thinking of joining. I was the founder and one of its mentors. I encouraged his joining. He was a

perfect fit. His musical talent was unique and pulsating to those privy to hear and feel his genius. He

WAS a genius waiting to happen! At least I pictured him as such.

    As the pictures of his brief life scrolled by on the screen above the pulpit, I saw he was an

aspiring photographer. I didn't know that. I saw for the first time a picture of his baby boy. I didn't know

he was a young father. I saw his loving, caring, broken family. I did not know them. I saw his still, cold

body absent of his beautiful soul. I knew it.

He died of gun violence. No. He was not in a gang. It was not a drive by. It was not retaliation

for brother against brother disrespect. It wasn't an accidental mishandling of a firearm. This young,

beautiful, passionate, talented, confused, hurt, despaired young man died of an intentional self-inflicted

gunshot - SUICIDE. The mourners mourned. As I sat and watched the flow of tears and experienced the

palatable pain in the chapel, I wondered how many funerals of young Black Males had they individually

and collectively experienced? At the end of the mournful day all I could ask was:

> Where were we?
>
> Where were you?
>
> Where was I?

According to the *Journal of Community Health*, May 17, 2019, there has been a 60% suicide

increase among Black Male Teens between the ages of 13 – 19 during the years 2001-2017. The

number for young girls is even more staggering, 182%, same age range and years. The was little

to no report of increase among teens from ethnicities.

> According to the **Bureau of Labor Statistics, Civilian Labor Force Statistics**, June 2019, White
>
> youth between the ages of 16 – 19 (male and female) have a 11.4% unemployment rate according

to May 2019 numbers. Black youth of the same age range have double the amount of

unemployment 23.5.

According to the *National Vital Statistics Reports* Volume 67, Number 6 July 26, 2018 U.S.

DEPARTMENT OF HEALTH AND HUMAN SERVICES Centers for Disease Control and Prevention

National Center for Health Statistics National Vital Statistics System Deaths: Leading Causes for

2016, "For the population aged 1–44, **homicide and suicide** were major causes of death: Homicide

was the third leading cause of death for age group 10–24 (14.9% of deaths), the fourth leading

cause for age group 1–9 (7.3% of deaths), and the fifth leading cause for age group 25–44 (6.5%

of deaths). Suicide was the second leading cause of death for age group 10–24 (17.3% of deaths)

and the third leading cause for age group 25–44 (10.6% of deaths)."

According to the ***Pew Research Center Report***, February 2018, ***Five Facts About Blacks in the U.S.***,

"Black households have only 10 cents in wealth for every dollar held by white households. In 2016,

the median wealth of non-Hispanic white households was $171,000. That's 10 times the wealth

of black households ($17,100) – a larger gap than in 2007."

"Black people in this country are imprisoned at more than 5 times the rate of whites; one in 10

black children has a parent behind bars, compared with about one in 60 white kids, according to the Stanford Center on Poverty & Inequality."

According to a report by the Prison Policy Initiative, **Mass Incarceration: the Whole Pie 2019**, "It's

no surprise that people of color – who face much greater rates of poverty – are dramatically

overrepresented in the nation's prisons and jails. These racial disparities are particularly stark for

Black Americans, who make up 40% of the incarcerated population despite representing only 13%

of U.S residents. The same is true for women, whose incarceration rates have for decades risen

faster than men's, and who are often behind bars because of financial obstacles such as an

inability to pay bail." The report cites "the onerous conditions of probation" as a major problem

within the corrections system that creates a revolving door for nonviolent crimes.

I contemplated and grieved over these statistics looking out the window at the residences

across the street often referred to as "projects". I spent my formative years in a "project" with my

mother AND father as they made their way up the economic ladder to the so called "eastside"; the

dream side, where the *Joneses* lived. Those projects of my formative years were nothing like the ones I

walk past today where I hear shouts of anger, gun fire, loud music, drug hustling and pimping, children

screaming AS WELL AS the quiet resolve and cultural pride lingering **unsaid** on the lips of elders.

The projects of today often do not have the "Mama Neil or Ms. Thorpe" of yesteryear who were always at

the screen door watching for mom or dad to come home to give a full report of the daily goings on. Nor

the "noisy" neighbor that kept the neighborhood folks abreast concerning young juveniles acting-up and

needing guidance. Nor the visiting preacher inquiring about why the children were not in church or

going to Vacation Bible School...no, I don't see that across this street. Not to say they're not there

quietly, anonymously carrying out their "it takes a village" duties. But many, too many are in

hiding...complicit silence, fear, and "not my business" philosophical rationalizations. Could they have

sounded the alarm for Joseph or his father or his father's father? Could they have opened their kitchen

to a warm cooked meal, taught the young mothers to cook from scratch, allow time for a hot bath, or

offered a tutoring session in family love/responsibility, manners, writing, or math? Could Big Brother

have taken him swimming at age seven when *others* were already competing in swim meets?

> I guess we will never know. He's gone now, this young, hope-lost Black Man down. I wish I had

known him better. I wish I worked in a system that allowed me more quality time with the gifted as well

as the perceived not so gifted. Maybe we could have met at the frequented Spoken Word café for

another life-altering lyrical, poetic moment. Too late...but wait! I still have a class full of Black, Brown,

White, soul-searching others...seeking to be known as they find their way into a world of labels,

demands, social conscriptions, and expectations. I am determined to keep my ears, mind, eyes and heart

open a little wider so the next Black Man to fall, will fall into a safety net entitled - **I SEE YOU!**

P. S. PERKINS

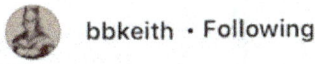 bbkeith • Following

Rest In Peace
Nipsey Hussle
August 15, 1985-March 31, 2019

"There's an obvious complexion caste system throughout the world. Nowhere in this world are the darker ethnic groups or demographics of any population in power. This is true in places like India, SE Asia, Sudan, the Caribbean, Brazil, Cuba and even Mexico. Not coincidental at all."

RICARDO JASON
THE ONE EN EL MEDIO

Ricardo Jason Machado Luces es el hermano del medio, pictured here at the center of our familia...
His ojos steadfast on something unknown...looking at algo que el solamente could see.
Ricardo Jason no era violent, ni ignorant, our memorias tell us stories that either glorify or celebrate his time on this planet...
My memories today focus on how he died rather than how he lived...
I aim to change that by paying honor to his life, the lessons he taught and the people he touched...

La Familia Machado en Horizonte, Caracas 1071, Miranda, Venezuela

MIMITVA

SURVIVAL PLANS

Venezuela is a beautiful country with beautiful people. She has a new generation of people who were raised in the era of Chavez...

Those who hadn't seen a doctor - saw doctors. people who did not have shelter or education, now do.

I saw on the news it told Chavez gave voice to the voiceless... that alone is progress because every human deserves a chance...

MIMITVA
A MEDIA CONSULTANCY

I still have many mixed feelings about Venezuela; one of my brothers... Ricardo Jason was murdered- shot by police in front of the Plaza Central after selling the jewelry he made by hand. He was left to die in that vile violent way.

My brother was a Rastafarian, murdered solely - because of his dreads, his skin and his life style. Jason did not deserve to die the way he did and today decades later I know he is in a better place.

I say Venezuela is for Venezuelans - a sovereign nation with a culture and history that does not need any first world vultures to take, dare we judge, we do not live there we do not know. I pray for God's Grace, for an army of ancestral souls to guide the transition of the Nation where we were born and claim to be proud of our TriniVene Tribe.

Don Pedro & Ricardo Jason en Falcón, Venezuela

Don Pedro y Ricardo Jason en Falcón, Venezuela

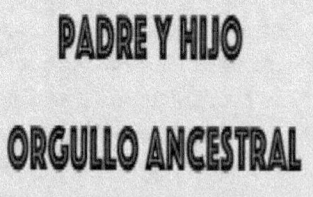

PADRE Y HIJO

ORGULLO ANCESTRAL

I write this

because I had to...

call Your name Brother

Ricardo Jason Machado-Luces.

I call - Your rebellious nature... the righteous spirit... Your cantankerous ways

For the life you lead... was never yours for the making... Was always left for the taking

Of others not in your midst...

Still here " in touch with our blood and kin"

Thoughts of you bring joy now

for our existence, for our family and for your life here on earth ...

Our very real Brother, murdered, executed, gunned down in the street, - the way you left

Your skin, the locs adorning Your head, the ironic words spilled from your tongue

Left an example of unforgettable treasures to define how you lived

Each time our People are murdered,

I hear Josefa's lament

that soul-wrenching sound, now a battle cry for our freedom...

We stand in prayer - for You and all the rest - are now in charge

we call you because as Our Ancestors

Empowered, all knowing, all seeing... You live on...

I wrote this because I had to call your name brother...

Ricardo Jason Machado-Luces

By Mimi Machado-Luces, tu hermana orgullosa

Mimi Machado-Luces

America's Promise: The 2nd Amendment

I Have Feelings Too

GradaLove

Romie's Poem

You tell his stories but don't see him,
let him dance across your line graphs
for the culture, leave his name in your
excel sheet then add him to the masses,
Pie charts and statistics tell the
story of a misfit

But where'd you leave the true consequences
of habits passed down from tribes to Harlem
to bloodlines? Addictive personalities and
alcoholism disease rising in streams- same
water you use to feed him and water his
budding personality

Let it rain bullets in the hood, then
let it rain water in the hood, may it
wash away the blood so that the
children don't see, as if the children
don't see with their spirits

Using dead souls to morph into toy
bodies, should give the children
hobbies paired with their own
imagination but instead, you just
give them blond barbie to play with
Or batman or superman - the hero
Although they relate more to the villain
because you made children out to be
the villain, call them bad as if it is an
adjective of their being, call them
blind dumb and stupid but it's you
who can't see them

Watching data break down communities,
Knowing the facts for the fun of it,
Judging the child's behavior not knowing
he's the son of it, shining bright in life
just to find the sun in it

A smile ain't so easy to come by these days
yet you've found ways to profit off of his pain,
and his joy, see him as nothing but a boy,
but let boy become man, and if you can't put
guns or drugs in his hands, then you make sure
to drop a ball or a microphone, only three categories
fit his trajectory

But there are some things in life that even you
can't fight, and that's love, because good always
wins and his story shall spin, so don't put chains
on my child because you don't even know him.
You haven't danced with his spirit, seen him cry
from absence, tell you he loves you when he
senses pain- you don't even know his name

So, don't tell me what he's destined to be,
because only he can choose his destiny

Gradalove

SURVIVAL PLANS: PRESENTS

ARTIST SPOTLIGHT

Gradalove

GRADALOVE IS A SPOKEN WORD POET, BUSBOYS 11TH HOUR POETRY SLAM CHAMPION, PRODUCER AND VISUAL ARTIST BASED OUT OF WASHINGTON, D.C. HER CREATIONS ARE REFLECTIONS OF HER EXPERIENCES- ALL ASPECTS OF LOVE, SELF- DISCOVERY AND STORYTELLING OBSERVATIONS. IN APRIL 2019, MS. LOVE RELEASED HER FIRST POETRY BOOK, BRAVE NEWSOUL, AND WENT ON A BOOK TOUR WHICH INCLUDED PERFORMING ON WUSA9'S GREAT DAY WASHINGTON DURING NATIONAL POETRY MONTH. SHE HAS BEEN A FEATURED POET THROUGHOUT THE DMV AREA AT BUSBOYS AND POETS, LOVE PAIN & POETRY'S OPENMIC, #WHISKEYGIRLDC EVENTS, AND MORE. GRADALOVE HAS ALSO HOSTED MULTIPLE POETRY EVENTS AT THE PRINCE GEORGE'S AFRICAN AMERICAN MUSEUM AND CULTURE CENTER(PGAAMCC). SHE IS A CO-FOUNDER OF THE FIRST ANNUAL DMV RENAISSANCE AWARDS
CELEBRATING LOCAL POETS.

FOR MORE INFORMATION, VISIT WWW.DMVRENAISSANCEAWARDS.COM. PERFORMANCE VIDEOS CAN BE FOUND ON HER INSTAGRAM PAGE (@_GRADALOVE) AND YOUTUBE CHANNEL!

F.E.M.

Female

Empowerment

Movement

God Must be Woman

The strength of women

Giving birth to all man kind

God must be woman.

Rosa Parks. $20.00 bill. Ink, Graphite. 2019

Her Story

Praise God for Women

Learned what I learned from the best

Women are valued

We Need Strong Men

The strength of women

Should not take away from men

Strong men in demand

Batgirl. Arkham Knight. Ink Pen. 2019

Accessories of Sex-cess

A tube of lip-stick

A pair of laced pan-tee hose

A spritz of per-fume

      Smells soooo sweet to your nose

And don't forget my high heel-ed pumps…

You know the ones I love so much!

The ones I wear to work,

      Happy hour and at brunch

Because as nice as my resume is

It's just not enough…

To get the raise that I deserve,

OH so much!

Black Girl Magic

Rahim Mitchell

"How are you a Socialite,

when you not even sociable?"

D. Nash

#funzitosketches

Georgetown Social x DC Photography

From the "New DC" Collection

I See You

I'm looking at you

I see you for who you are

No judgment I make

Pride and Joy x D.C Photography

From the "New DC" Collection

Pride and Joy

I have pride and joy
No one can ever take it
Can't even fake it

Her

Anzeeno

IMAGINE IF HER NAME HAD YOUR FACE

#SAYHERNAME BY ADMINISTRATION

- Eleanor Bumpurs- October 29, 1984

40th President, Ronald Reagan (R) - 1981- 1989

- Sonji Taylor- December 16, 1993

41st President, George H. W. Bush (R) - 1989- 1993

- Frankie Ann Perkins- March 22, 1997
- Danette Daniels- June 8, 1997
- Tyisha Miller-December 28, 1998
- Margaret L. Mitchell- May 21, 1999
- LaTanya Haggerty- June 4, 1999

42nd President, Bill Clinton (D) - 1993- 2001

- Kendra James-May 5, 2003
- Alberta Spruill- May 16, 2003
- Kathryn Johnston, November 21, 2006
- Tarika Wilson- January 4, 2008

43nd President, George W. Bush (R) - 2001-2009

- Aiyana Stanley-Jones- May 16, 2010
- Shereese Francis- March 15, 2012
- Rekia Boyd- March 21, 2012
- Sharmel Edwards- April 21, 2012
- Shantel Davis- June 14, 2012
- Alesia Thomas- July 22, 2012
- Malissa Williams- November 29, 2012
- Shelly Frey- December 6, 2012
- Kayla Moore- February 12, 2013
- Kyam Livingston- July 24, 2013
- Miriam Carey- October 3, 2013
- Yvette Smith- February 16, 2014
- Gabriella Nevarez- March 2, 2014
- Pearlie Golden- May 7, 2014
- Michelle Cusseaux- August 13, 2014
- Sheneque Proctor- November 1, 2014
- Aura Rosser- November 9, 2014
- Tanisha Anderson-November 13, 2014
- Natasha McKenna-February 8, 2015
- Janisha Fonville- February 18, 2015
- Meagan Hockaday- March 28, 2015
- Mya Hall- March 30, 2015
- Alexia Christian- April 30, 2015
- Sandra Bland- July 13, 2015
- Korryn Gaines- August 1, 2016

44th President, Barack Obama (D) - 2009-2017

- Charleena C. Lyles- June 18, 2017
- Breonna Taylor- March 13, 2020

45th President, Donald Trump (R) - 2017- Present

NOTICE ANYTHING YET???

Source: African American Policy Forum, NY *#SayHerName Report* (2020)

INSERT YOUR RESPONSE HERE:

When your kids watch the news and have access to Social Media…

You begin to find messages on your fridge.

But...

No Lives Matter

All black lives matter

But everyone is dying

So no lives matter

Jason T. Lippman

Reprinted from Hallelujah Anyhow! (2017)

New Age Wharf x DC Photography

From the "New DC" Collection

"Did the water in Flint ever get cleaned up?

Did you ever really care?
We've gone from Black Lives Matter to Flint Water Crisis to Orange Man Bad to Remove Confederate Statues, Me Too to Russia Gate to ADOS to COVID-19 in a 5yr span

I'm not even protesting and I'm exhausted."

Something in the Water x DC Photography

SURVIVAL PLANS

The Water

What's in the water?

Something just don't taste quite right

Too bad I drank it...

DARK SKIES--------

-----------------I'm sad why, dark skies----------depressed why--------dark skies-----unhealthy why------dark skies------not smiling why--------dark skies----Overeating why----dark skies----no joy why----dark skies-----sick why-----dark skies----anxious why----dark skies----crying why----dark skies----no sleep why----dark skies----uninspired why----dark skies----no imagination why----dark skies-----silent why------dark skies----can't concentrate---why----dark skies----mentally ill why----dark skies----no freedom why-----dark skies----no fun why----dark skies----no energy why-----dark skies----no laughter why----dark skies---unlucky in love why-----dark skies----hatred why----dark skies, ungrateful why----dark skies----shame why----dark skies----heartbreak why----dark skies----failure why----dark skies----setbacks why----dark skies----attitudes why----dark skies----hopeless why----dark skies----doubt why----dark skies----excuses why----dark skies---arguing why----dark skies----disappointment why----dark skies----confusion why----dark skies----screams why----dark skies----ridiculous why----dark skies----worthless why----dark skies----challenges why---- dark skies----regrets why----dark skies----no dreams why----dark sky----obstacles why----dark skies----bad thoughts why----dark skies----unemployed why----dark skies----doubts why----dark skies----worries why----dark skies----weak why----demons why----dark skies----confusion why----dark skies----regrets why----dark skies----worthless why----dark skies----unlucky why----dark skies----obstacles why----dark skies----giving up why----dark skies----emotional why----dark skies----no friends why----dark skies----afraid why----dark skies----no loyalty why----dark skies----no faith why----dark skies----illness why----dark skies----healthcare inequality why----dark skies----Covid 19 why---- dark skies----panic why ----dark skies----isolation why----dark skies----social distancing why---dark skies----deaths why----devils why----dark skies----haters why----deadly force by police why----dark skies----disgusted why----dark skies----racism why----dark skies----financial inequality why----dark skies----social inequality why----dark skies----I can't breathe why ----dark skies----Momma, I'm through why----dark skies----no justice why----dark skies----no peace why-dark skies----Murder of George Floyd and Other Blacks why----dark skies ----Black Lives Don't Matter----why dark skies===============UNREST IN AMERICA WHY-----------------------------DARK SKIES----

Karen Mayo-Hogan

B.L.M?

Before/Be For?

I hear, I see

They say,

It is, It will be

I know; I don't know

I feel and I fear

It's here, because

It's now

But will it be, Will we see?

I ache, deep inside

I want to breach,

the divide

But I hide, I bury it

The dirt has been thrown,

From so many places

Before,

Is it more?

Hard to ignore

Tears fall, Hearts bleed

Hope, I hope will succeed

& it's more than,

a Trend

& it will begin,

to end

The hate gate

opening

as Before.

Li'

SELF CENTERED WITH NO NEW GROWTH IN SIGHT

IN A WORLD OF ME, ME, ME!

I AM, MY BROTHER'S KEEPER

AND YOU SHOULD BE TOO!

TRUMP-ISM

BLUE BLOOD-ISM

BLACK-ISM

CHRISTIAN-ISM

JEWISH-ISM

MUSLIM-ISM

WHITE-ISM

BROWN-ISM

BUT HEY! AREN'T WE ALL **HUMAN BEINGS?**

CAN'T WE ALL JUST GET ALONG?......**NOPE, I GUESS NOT** ☹

YOU SEE IT EVERYDAY PEOPLE NOT GETTING ALONG

HATE SPEWED FORTH LIKE VOMIT FROM AN OVERNIGHT DRUNK

AND OUR U.S. PRESIDENT, THAT B.....D

LUST-ISM

RADIO PLAYS IT, VIDEO SHOWS IT, MOVIE THEATERS PROMOTE IT

ABUSE-ISM

MALE AND FEMALE ALIKE! STOP IT! STOP IT NOW!

PEOPLE ARE SCARED

SCARED ABOUT WHAT YOU MIGHT SAY ABOUT THEM

SCARED FOR WHAT YOU MIGHT HAVE ON THEM AS BLACKMAIL

SCARED TO HELP SOMEONE IN TROUBLE BECAUSE THEY

DON'T-WANT-TO-GET-INVOLVED

SCARED TO BE DIFFERENT BECAUSE THEN

COMES THE HATE FOR THOSE WHO DON'T CONFORM TO THE NORM

BUT HEY! AREN'T WE ALL **HUMAN BEINGS?**

CAN'T WE ALL JUST GET ALONG?…..**NOPE, I GUESS NOT** ☹

WestCoastAnnie

2020 Drastically Changed our Lives-------- -Survival 2020-Panicked Out-----A Year to Remember

Volume of Tears: 2020

Karen Hogan-Mayo

Panicked, I do not even know where to begin except to say thank you to all the essential persons including my niece, nurse Sierra Battle and all individuals ---
----

The year had already started out difficult for our family and perhaps other families as well. Our relatively healthy relative who did not really look sick had received news of his pending last days of life. This news may have shattered many but this relative took this information as a blessing. Family was assembled so they could share the news and it was also a time to put affairs in order. Relatives were notified so the pending death of their loved one would not come as a shock when the time comes. This notification also afforded relatives and friends near and far the opportunity to call fly, or drive to visit their loved one knowing their days would soon be no more. In this case, Survival plans included death plans, a time to prepare. Whew, got through this but did not know what was about to happen to turn our lives upside down.

Turned on the television and discovered that China's people were dying at an alarming rate but it seemed our government was downplaying this. In the meantime, my family and others were heartbroken as we heard the news that country after country was being infected. It never dawned on us that this great country we live in, this United States of America acted like this was not of concern to them. My mom always told us to react then act on matters of importance. She would say and I quote "if there's a fire at your neighbor's house and you do nothing to help put out the fire, don't worry because it will get to your house soon enough." -- ----------
-- -- ------------
---------------------- --- --------------
--- ----------------------
-- ----------------------------------

Breaking News-----that fire she referred to now hit our back door and our shores. It's called Coronavirus,-Covid19 pandemic and it seems it cannot be stopped. Hot spots identified include New York, New Jersey, Connecticut and on and on from state to state. Day after Day, hour after hour, minute to minute, media reports, family and friends news, sickness, near death experience reports, hospitalizations with isolations, no communication once you are there, no cure, no ventilators, not enough medical personnel, no knowledge, lack of knowledge on how to take care of the infected people, no vaccine and so forth and so on......OH no this is no longer something you are watching on the news with fears and tears.

Suddenly it has hit home. Three immediate family members are sick, infected with this virus. One of the three goes to the emergency room thinking it is a sinus infection. What happened after that became our horror story. All forms of communication were limited, no physical contact allowed, then all forms of communication cut off because unbeknownst to you your loved one has been isolated. The last message your loved one got to you was they loved you and they feel like they are not going to make it because they feel like they are sinking and will probably die. The loved one is moved to ICU on a ventilator and only GOD can determine if they live or die. The family sprang into action getting down on their knees and in tears cried out to the Lord. They also called on the prayer warriors and took to Social Media to ask for prayers from the whole wide world, Yes, He's alive, you see God cares and answered our prayers. Thank You Lord-------------------------------------- -- -- ------------- -------------- ---

No matter what was going on, even in the midst of sickness and death, families needed to prepare for survival. Food was needed by all and our sick family members also needed groceries. We are in the throws of the pandemic told to self- quarantine, get masks, gloves, protective gear, sanitizing items, water and groceries. Fear everywhere but we began to do grocery shopping for ourselves and others. We also did drive- by delivery .Those deliveries were for sick and shut in, the elders or whoever calls for them. Suddenly we are in the midst of a stockpile episode. What in the world is Happening? We are in the throws of a massive pandemic, sickness and death everywhere, fear of even going out is settling in and a Toilet Paper frenzy has begun to unfold. No toilet paper anywhere, people are hoarding paper. WHY??? My 82 old plus aunt replies that toilet paper is a comfort and luxury. At one time, folks used brown paper bags, newspapers, Montgomery Ward magazine pages and saved

corn storks for bathroom purposes. Wow can you believe that. Now we have another mental stress and duress issue along with the issues of self- quarantine, financial woes, frustration, isolation, social distancing, anxiety. Also inability to get gloves and mask have become a big problem. Then my NJ cousin Denise who brought a sewing machine who is in Florida but not vacationing hears our cries. She purchases a sewing machine and made masks for us. Thank you Lord for giving her the skills and thank cousin Denise for our masks. Problem solved.--- --------------------------------
-- -----------------------
----------- --------------------------------------- -------------------------------------
-----------------------This disease has shattered lives and businesses nationwide and sent the economy into an unimaginable financial and health tailspin. Now still more sickness and deaths. The lethal march of Covid 19 disease has taken over 100,000,00 and counting lives nationwide. Sadly it took our sister friend Marcella Black, may she rest in peace. As if this was not enough there was the senseless death of a black man name George Floyd. More tears, more fears, peace marches, riots, looting by unknowns who just want to take advantage of the situation, and a call for changes again. All of this necessary to get the attention of the nation that once again when white officers take it upon themselves to have vigilante actions they must be held accountable.---
--------------------We continue to pray that God will take away our hurts, fears and tears. People of faith and love know the solution for healing of the nation can be found in the word of God which states" If my people, which are called by my name humble themselves, and pray and seek my face and turn from their wicked ways, then I will hear from heaven and will forgive their sin, and will heal their land. 2nd Chronicles 7:14-KJV.---------------------------------- ------
------- ------------ --------------In the meantime, we will forever have to adapt to a whole new lifestyle. We need to be stronger mentally, trust, stay positive in this scary times, conquer what's next, read, write, go to movies and do whatever it takes to survive during these uncertain times. Wear masks, gloves, socially isolate. People of faith also follow Isaiah 26:20 which states "Go, my people, enter your rooms and shut the doors behind you; hide yourselves for a little while until his wrath has passed by. As we follow the laws of the land we still ask how many more tragedies does it take before we get it? how many more incidences and deaths does it take before the nation acknowledges that we need to love one another? and indeed BLACK LIVES MATTER! To all of this I say HALLELUJAH ANYHOW!

Making 1 Contact

There is nothing but my EYES left to see...
Covered head to toe in my
Medicinal burka...
Is this what she feels like?
Protected? Guarded? Conspicuous?
Only revealing the seeing part of me...
So now I only use my I to connect...
Eyeing others Eyeing me from a distance...6 feet or more... Searching to know,
Are you death approaching my door?
Should I run?
Should I be scared?
As we eye each other
Revealing the dread
of walking into each other's space
Avoiding the connections of face to face.
Listening for a cough ...
Dreading a sneeze ....
"Cover your mouth, won't you please! "
Avoiding human contact that could bring me to my knees. But still I walk silently through the lonely streets seeking contact I can greet, with a wave or a nod Some recognition of my BE-ing...
because the last thing I want to do,
The very last thing I want to do, is return home to isolation Where there is no recognition of who I BE.
So, I wander the neighborhood hoping
Wanting,
Needing,
to make **I** contact.

P. S. Perkins

SISTA ON BOARD

A letter of intent

SHIT! Caught me at a bad time for this shit, I mean, STUFF!

COVID 19 is here and everybody **scattered!**

Back to your homes, back to your cars, your buses, your rails

Back from your schools, your sports games, your workouts

Can't slim down this way!

I'm working from home now and my computer keeps beeping with messages, assignments,

and calendar appointment requests. The refrigerator keeps looking at me, calling my name.

My lunch hour is all day, matter fact, my morning ritual of grabbing a croissant before I hit my desk each day, seems a distant memory, here, now, three plus months later.

SURVIVAL? Gloria Gaynor said it best, "I will survive"

"I'm living just enough, just E-Nough for the city" as Stevie had once sang on a popular song

Marvin Gaye sung it out "What's Going On" - "Picket Lines, with Picket Signs, Don't Punish Me, With Brutality, Come On Talk To Me! So You Can See, Oh What's Going On"

MY PLANS? At least for the rest of the year is to BE STILL AND DONATE. Done! End of story for 2020. If there comes a Covid cure before then, story changes.

I have wanted to say that I am so proud of our young people out there in the struggle. My FIST is Up With U! My protests will need to take place by pen and computer, by phone calls to my congress persons, My

Mayor, My Council Member, My Governor. In Speaking to my fellow man, starting a conversation or continuing a conversation with people of different races. Find some **COMMON GROUND DAMN IT! ... AND REMEMBER, THIS TOO SHALL PASS - JUST GET THERE TO SEE IT THROUGH!**

WestCoastAnnie

Sounding Off

D. Nash

"I wish we had as much passion for building as we do for protesting"

Thoughts On Money

Money is something we all need in the year of our Lord 2020. Money is a devise for trade, food, clothing, shelter, and now medical care. Money is both good and evil. I have traded labor for money since about the age of 8 years old. From picking cotton, cucumbers, pulling corn, picking pine cones, laying bricks, making deals, repairing trucks, t.v.'s, and automobiles, to driving trucks, and providing customer service.

I have never sat down and went into deep thought as of how to make money in large amounts, in which I lose my soul, and I hope I never do. But I realize I should put more time into acquiring money in the right way. How much money does a person need? I cannot answer this question because it gets a little confusing when it comes to wants and needs, and this society has a helping hand in the confusion, by advertising and seeing. This is a means for someone else to acquire money with no regards to what we really need. Advertisements tell you it's time to buy a new car or truck, or wouldn't you look good in these clothes? Or how about that dream house? Try these shoes! Or a cold drink? A vacation? And one of the best is a "diamond is forever." And this is true but it's only a rare rock.

Man have always needed some devise in order that we may live together in a society and use each other to accomplish things we cannot alone. Sometimes and this is more often than not, it takes a collective effort to provide a service or a product in order to make money. But before we explore this let's say again that money is both good and evil. Or to say it better, money can be used and acquired in a manner in which it is good and or evil.

I have been a participant in a society, which have led me to want certain things. It does not have to be the biggest, the most desirable car on the road. I like good cloth, but they do not have to be the latest fashion or most desirable fashion in the world- but clean fitting and complimentary to my body. I like to have a clean decent place to live, and have access to medical care if needed, and to provide the same for family members until they may be able to do it for themselves. Since my only means of acquiring money, so far have been by trading labor for money, I would like to have another means, especially since my better years have been used in this manner. Remember, I started this process at the age of 8 years old and have been at it for around 40 years.

I believe there was life before there was any form of money. So life is more important than any form of money. And there lies my desire to live life free from the slavery of having to trade labor for money. I am in search of a better way. This is very confusing web that we (society) have spun for ourselves and very few find their way out of it. Some do by the will of God, some do by what I believe as selling their souls. We will explore what I believe to be examples later. My question now is, where did it all begin and where will it end?

This question is relevant because I look at society that continues to move in a direction of those that have more and more and those that have less and less. A popular group in my times sang "money, money, money, money, for the love of money, some people got to have it, some people really need it… some people will steal from their father, kill their brother" and almost anything that you can think of- people will do for money. Countries have been destroyed, families ripped apart, humans sold into bondage, and the very planet we live on has been changed to something less than it was meant to be because of the love of money. Jesus said "It is easier for a camel to pass through the eye of a needle, than for a rich man to enter heaven.

Money have also has done some good things, I believe. I am from a family of 13 children, I know it took money to purchase a place for us to live, food, clothing etc… Money built schools which have helped me to write these thoughts. Money has helped build the Church in which I learned of God. Services that I use on a daily basis require money. If I were to guess the amount of money printed in this Country alone, I would have to estimate it was in the hundreds, of billions of dollars each year. As I said earlier, money is a device that allows for trade for goods and services, and by looking at the amount of money printed each year- there is no shortage of it. It's the distribution process that makes the difference, for those hundreds of billions of dollars as they move down the system in this manner.

First, it goes to the Federal Reserve, or the Federal Bank. From there it moves to private banks. These banks lend for a fee to whoever they believe are qualified borrowers-based upon a number of things. Examples are large builders, car dealers, company owners and all is not fair in this system.

For we have a history, in this Country of discrimination against my people of African descent. For this reason, we seem to be lagging further behind than other races, in ability to make money. Those with a special ability to entertain have not been denied. Some of us have abilities that we never learned to develop into a way that we can use to extract from the distribution systems. This seems to be the root of the black people's lack of access to the money distribution system. Keep in mind that I said hundreds of billions of dollars are printed each year… So there has to be a way somehow.

Clinton Battle

The Cost of Living

The cost of living is high today.

More than what people can afford to pay.

Got so many bills that the money's all split,

Hard times have definitely hit,

Got to make the best out of what I can,

Trying to do my best to live off the land,

OH NO!!!!

Done lost my job,

Exalted with other choices;

not to steal or rob,

The cost of living is high today,

More than what people can afford to pay,

With clothes so ragged,

Looking like something that the cat just dragged in,

Shoes so holey from being worn,

Look at my feet, got nothing but corns!

Stomach's so empty,

All you can think of are those with plenty,

Man, times are hard!

Just got to survive,

A man or woman can't do nothing…
and still stay alive.

Darcelle Battle

"...if the world does it to you long enough, you begin to do it to yourself. You become a collaborator, an accomplice of your own murders, because you believe the same things they do.

-James Baldwin, 1971

Media Takeout 2020

Things that Don't Mix...

Drugs

Guns

Probation

Consumers

D. Nash

K.I.N.G.

Robes old and worn from a wearied pride dead limbs, shuffling feet,

burning holes in a pavement going nowhere but past, no longer able to hide

behind the facade of riding high though HIGH he is.

King of a Continent
bought low from unbridled greed on both sides, some knowingly,
some uncaringly.
Sold!
To the highest bidder
removed from all hu-man-ity.

Generations later…

Some escaping the mentacide of genocide

to the fortitude of an unbreakable attitude, while others succumb to populate liquor store corners and rural addresses of corrupted penance while paid pennies for laborious jobs previously denied. So they laugh

and talk loud

about the women they've had

and children they've sired…

(Did he just say 14? He can't be more than 34!) Offspring walking around with

titles lacking entitlement; passing the bottle,

puffing along on stuff too strong to toke

forever broke from

a mind of gift, greatness, genius - gone up in smoke! Why did this happen? Who created this wretched travesty passing itself off as life? How did it move from father to son to son, all sharing the same block on the block

while doing time on the rock?

Insouciantly regarding the world around him, long ago relinquishing his throne

of royalty... Subjects scattered through global channels

of shackled disbursement...

swept away by kingly decrees of worthless worth bearing generations of a

burdened birth

no longer able to retain,

    trying to maintain,

        struggling to re-gain

Knowledge Internalized Necessitating Greatness!
K.I.N.G.!

P.S. Perkins

Tired of being a Nigga!

I'm tired of nigga shit!
Drinking 40s,
Pants sagging,
Cursing like a mother-------,
Pill popping,
Lean sipping,
Slurred speech giving,
Illiterate niggas,
Who don't know their head from their tail,
Don't have a pots to piss in,
Dead beat dad,
Rapping and clapping,
Faking and dating,
Getting locked up for dumb stuff,
Instagram thugging,
Bottle popping in the club'n
Faking a**
Niggas

I'm tired of being a nigga!
Just taking whatever I'm given,
Scrapping for scraps,
Accepting less than my worth,
Because my life is of no value,
To me,
Or anyone else...
Was told I was a nigga so much,
That I believed it myself.
I believed it and I became
The very nigga you named
I claimed

I said I'm tired of being a nigga!
Never on time

Two timing
Hustling and still ain't got shit
Starving
Hanging on the block'n
Hunted by the cops'n
Can't keep no good job
Record having
"Please check Felon"
Getting fired
Never hired
A** nigga!

I'm tired of being a nigga
Air Jordan buying
Waiting in long line'n
For product that don't pay no bills

Tired of being a nigga
But…
I'm a product of my history
A product of my misery

A product of how you treated me

A slave to the wrong mentality
A** nigga!

So what else can I do???

"...It's not the crackhouse, it's credit!"

Survival Can be Like...

Survival Can be like

beating your head against a wall,

Running in place with no breath,

Drinking yourself to death.

Drowning

Survival can be like

Single parents, grandparents, same gendered parents and/or the streets raising kids

paycheck to payless or pay more to

Keeping up with the Jones' (or the Kardashians)

Eating good but can't pay rent

Struggling.

Survival can be like

A hot a$$ mess

Trauma and drama creating

Reality TV at its best

Exploitation

Survival can be like

Policing the community instead of community policing

Everybody has a cause-causing

Confusion.

Survival can be like

Pointing fingers at yourself in the mirror

Anyone can get it

He's packing

The others slinging

Laid out on the block fiendish

Mind your own f***ing business

Backwards thinking.

Everybody just trying to Survive!!!

Creativity Boost:

Write a Poem/Thought/Story or Draw about...

SURVIVAL

Word Associations:

Exist
Instinct
Alive
Resilience
Adapt
Challenges
Carry-On
Remain
Viability
Strength
Endurance
COVID 19

Plans for Survival:

Volume of Tears: 2020

Karen Mayo-Hogan

Ironically this book was written with a Survival Theme. My God, no one could possibly have known that 2020 would become the year that we would ask "Can We Survive"? These last few months had become challenging and it was a difficult time for all of us and the Nation at Large. Minorities were already in the midst of many national crisis as they were already in the throws of Economic, Health and Justice disparities when they were hit with a Worldwide Coronavirus- Covid-19 Pandemic.

Many people had to adapt to this national crisis. Life had been put on pause especially for Minorities who once again were hit the hardest. Yes, the country and most of the World got stopped by Covid-19 and many minorities had to face more hardships. Suddenly, millions of Americans were out of work and left struggling to pay bills and put food on the table. Minorities were concerned if there would be enough money without savings to pay rent and buy food, milk and eggs from weekend to weekend. Some cried out to go to work amid the Health Crisis as they did not qualify for unemployment and were running out of money. Small Mom and Pop businesses were forced to close their businesses, perhaps forever. The nation issued a mandatory quarantine.

This quarantine for non-minorities may have meant moments of reflection and re-connection while for minorities it was a desperate and family crisis. People that lived alone faced endless loneliness while for non-minorities it was peace, rest and good times with family members. Home schooling was no big deal to them either as they spent a couple of hours a day with their children helping with online schooling. Minority parents on the other hand were essential workers who went to work and then spent 2-3 hours a night struggling to assist their ill prepared children with their paper schoolwork. Many had no electronics to assist but parents did the best they could with what they had.

As if this was not bad enough many people came down with the virus. Once again, the ugly truth surfaced as non-people of color viewed the virus as no big deal because they had excellent benefits and were once again receiving the best treatment and life saving techniques. People of color were having near death experiences and spent countless days and nights praying and wondering if their sick loved ones were going to make it without the same care given their white counterparts. Unfortunately, thousands have lost family and friends to this deadly virus. Deaths united many people and it also brought unbearable grief and sorrow. Loved ones left, many from same families without farewells. They died with strangers holding their hands.

For those of us in the faith, we chose to believe that God dispatched his Angels to their bedside and took them on a journey ride to their heavenly home up above, forever with Jesus and others that they love. The other downside to death was the fact that it was weeks before our loved ones could be laid to rest and the number of attendees including staff and officiant was limited to ten. Some left people who passed on left without farewells or services, may they forever rest in peace.

Once again non-minorities believed that this was also no big deal. All I can say is that this Covid- 19 is a new heartbreaking experience and it has affected where and when we can go and this has been a major challenge to all. Faith in God helped us to get through these times, people had to learn to use social media to stay in touch, the human touch had become a nightmare to so many loved ones due to the virus and sickness and deaths that followed when contact was made. It was heartbreaking not to reach out and touch the little ones.

Survival plans included everyone who was told to shelter in place for survival. Older people, sick people and anyone who had to shelter in place and needed assistance became dependent on friends, family and strangers to help. We became grocery shoppers and delivery service people in the midst of the Covid-19. We shopped for and delivered food, water, household supplies, medicine etc. We fearfully drove by the homes fully gloved and masked, dropped off all items with no little to no contact, rang the bell, got back in our cars and prayed to God to keep us all safe and well. We became known as the "drive by, drop-off sisters" as word spread that we were the ones picking up and delivering supplies or whatever was needed without contact.

To be able to do this was a blessing, for people like me, who went stir-crazy at home. I felt like the walls were caving in on me so… I cleaned the house, sorted and threw out old papers, put documents in order, completed church, funeral and wedding folders, wrote poems, prayed, sung, watched television, ran up and downstairs, looked outside, read books, talked on phone, learned about duo from 4 year old. Although life has been on pause it has still presented many challenges. People like me crave **Human Interaction, socialization, fellowship,** the great outdoors, weddings, parties, church, social gatherings and so forth and so on.

Other people like my son, prefer home life, television, computer games, Facebook, virtual parties, duo etc. Mandatory self- isolation and quarantine has created social isolation issues for many people including me. I can only state this phrase for myself "Hated It". In addition to social isolation issues there also arose some mental health challenges. Feeling of panic and anxiety began to surface. I began to question-What in the world is happening to me. All I could do was ask God for help. Mental health challenges also started when texts and telephone called began regarding messages of sickness and deaths of family members and friends. These calls and texts along with the Media's sickness and death reports became a living nightmare. What can be said for thousands sick and thousand dead daily. NJ had the second highest death toll in the nation. God help us all!

Mentally drained, I prayed for all people, all over the world but unconsciously I worried, hence the Devil got a hold on me. I became stressed although I was taught "If you are going to worry, don't pray and if you are going to pray, don't worry." Stress led to anxiety and other physical and mental health issues. I think I began to have anxiety issues and wished I had some of those old folks smelling salts. I also developed stomach problems but that was nothing compared to what I suffered next. Stress started to take a toll on me whew, stress bumps appeared on my face, then cold sores surfaced on my mouth followed by painful canker sores which formed inside my mouth.

You may ask why I am telling you this, it's because I do not want anyone to go through this horrendous self –inflicted stress nightmare. If anyone reading this chooses to ignore physical and mental health issues please add cotton swabs, salt, water rinse and milk of magnesium to dab inside of your mouth (old folks cure) to your list of essentials along with your BIBLE. You may want to pray without ceasing to avoid old folks remedy methods and keep the faith to avoid my Pitfall. This experience has shown that life is fragile so we must not take any day-anything or anyone for granted. We must continue to Love one another, support one another and work together, so we can get through this. We will be stronger because of it and being alive means more now than ever before. We must enjoy each moment and never forget the many essential workers, including my niece Sierra Battle, who served on the frontline of this crisis.

All anyone can say is Thank You, Thank you, Thank you for your courage and sacrifice. You are all TRUE HEROES. THANK YOU Lord for these individuals who we believe are your special angels. We sorrowfully acknowledge all who lost their lives trying to save lives of others. Now, as our nations looks ahead to the rest of 2020 what happens next is and will be another reality check for Minorities. Unfortunately, 2020 has reminded us that we are going through a time when once again, minority perceptions and needs are completely different from others.

Minorities are already still experiencing a different recovery journey. Recovering from this global crisis means that by working together we may be able to look ahead and experience a "new" normal. The only way we'll meet that challenge, as far as I'm concerned is through faith. That idea non-minorities called "normal" was faulty before the pandemic. The pandemic once again, highlighted America's differences in the human dignity of minorities. Minorities rights and their financial, economic, health, social and justice disparities speak for themselves. Proof exists that there is still a lot of work needed to end these disparities.

In this new normal, the nation will have to embark on a new journey. Hopefully, the powers that be, will work toward a much better society with liberty and justice for all. The worst may be yet to come but I have faith in God and expect miracles. I know and you know it will take a Miracle for people of color to become equal in the "NEW NORMAL."

Spirits Lay Broken

We travel throughout this earth,

Separated by our spiritual birth,

Into an unrecognizable place,

Where we hear and see the turmoil of this world,

our hearts saddened by the unbeatable pace,

While we have spirits lay broken,

To that which is unspoken,

Evil verses Good,

Pushes forth when it is for good we all stood.

Sanity verses Sane,

Troubling deterioration of good decisions necessary for bland gain.

Wrong verses Right,

Unable to disarm it without a flight to fight.

Racist verses Races,

Prejudices of people on rise,

killing off our diverse faces.

Wars verses Peace,

Continually bringing about poverty and famine that never seems to cease.

Hate verses Love,

A personal diversion to many dislikes instead of sharing and cherishing that which was given to us from God above.

Sexuality verses sex,

Strayed morals not in line with God's daily text.

Sickness verses Health,

Wanting to eliminate it for the gain of wealth.

We can go on and on, while our spirits lay broken.

To a world that is choking from that which has been chosen,

Only to surrender our spirits once God has spoken,

All should be working to do away with sin and enduring till the end,

Praying for forgiveness,

Only to know through God's love,

Goodness and mercy a chance to begin again.

Darcelle Battle

The Life and Times Collection XX: America is Still Number 1

Triumvirate of the Masses

Idiocy

Ignorance

Internet

D. Nash

D.C. (Haiku)

Was Chocolate City

Now you can't afford to live

Gentrification

Malcolm X Park x DC Photography

From the "New DC" Collection

IMANAPITUP

Imanapitup, Imanapitup, I'm a nap it up, I'm a stop using them chemicals in my hair for a while

You viewed my afro as a sign of radicalism

You viewed my straight (permed) hair as disarming

You viewed my dreads as a sign of cultured expression

You viewed my twists and locks as cute

You viewed my waves as convenient

You viewed my curls as a sign of disarray

You viewed my bantu knots as relief! as I must be going back to Africa

At what point is my hair going to be acceptable to you? As if I gave a damn!

Now your children wear my hairstyles

Now your children dance like me

Now your children talk my kinda slang, ... when I decide to-talk-slang!

They eat where I used to frequent, mmmm.... that potato salad sure has a lot of flavor and those col-lard greens ump! Is that a turkey neck in there?

New growth, yes! The people are changing, growing, evolving; Oh, it's a new day alright, and guess what? You'll find out that we really aren't that different!

WestCoastAnnie

BRINGING COLLARD GREENS TO THE TABLE

P.S. Perkins

The time of feasting had arrived! We all sat down anxious to begin the feast we had starved ourselves the entire day for. Heck, some of us the whole month! It was the holidays and I was invited to the home of Robert and Susan, close associates from work. I think they may have felt sorry for me living on the west coast so far away from my family in N.C.; and then again, it may have just been *chic* to have a member of a different ethnic group at their table. As the only African American on the list of invitees, I had the dubious honor of providing the *soul food* complements to the table. The smells of fresh mash potatoes, cranberry and date dressing, and green beans almondine filled the air, but nothing, nothing could surpass the **scintillating** aromas of **fresh collard greens, candied yams, and macaroni & cheese** as my ethnic contributions to the otherwise "cookbook" feast!

"Oooh, ahhh…," I could hear the sighs of gratitude, the soon-to-be-satisfied gastric gurgles, and the giggles of delight as we passed dish after dish of culinary perfection. It was the holidays, and everyone was "truly thankful for the food they were about to receive." As each dish went down the long procession of watering mouths, too-big-for-your-stomachs eyes, and hallelujah hands, I noticed the polite dishing up of the *cookbook prescriptions* while the generational southern delicacies were reluctantly released from scooping mounds. Once again, the opportunity presented itself to invite others into my world!

(Start with something light, a little appetizer)

"Hey, has anyone seen the latest Samuel L. Jackson movie?

"Yeah! Great action flick!"

"I thought the acting was brilliant."

"Hey, maybe we can go this weekend."

"Yeah, the Shaft's a bad mutha…shut yo mouth!"

We all got a big laugh out of that one. There was a moment of verbal silence overshadowed by the slurping sound of collard green juice and scraping forks against plates.

(Moving onto the 1st course)

"Did any of you get the email I circulated around the office about the Big Sister/Big Brother Program sponsored by Covenant House?"

I noticed the baked macaroni & cheese had a gapping hole in the center and dibs were being placed for the cheese-crusted sides.

"Yeah, I got it before I left on Friday."

"Sounds like a great program."

"We're not that familiar with that uhm… that area of town, but surely there are people in the surrounding communities who will come forward."

I explained that the after-school program served the entire county area and was a mosaic of kids from all over, from a variety of socio-economic levels just wanting to spend some quality time with caring people.

"I'm going there on Saturday morning for an orientation, anyone want to come?"

"Hey, why not. Count us in. We've been looking for an opportunity to get involved with some kids." *(Victory!)*

We continued idle chatter about work related issues and the latest football scores as the *soul* of the feast began to disappear. Yes, this was indeed a feast sharing.

(Time to move to the main course)

"Anyone been keeping up with the voting rights restoration for ex-felons?"

There was a faint sound of throat clearing and last bite swallowing. No takers.

"Someone pass the collard greens please."

I watched the bowl slowly make its way up the line to the requestor and silently wondered if she was gonna slurp the juice? We had filled the bowl three times and now only the *pot licker* remained.

"Humm, isn't wasn't that just done in a couple of states?"

"Yes, only Vermont and Maine have unrestricted voting rights for felons. 14 other states allow voting after incarceration is complete, but most of states require not only completing the sentence, but parole and probation. For many ex-felons, it's a never-ending cycle of **recidivism**! Virginia recently gave thousands of ex-felons the right to vote and Florida is currently battling it out in the courts! It basically comes down to partisan politics as usual these days!"

"Yeah, well I always believed if you don't want the time, don't do the crime." Snicker, snicker. *(Moving on)*

"Sure, you're right but the argument is about punishment that fits the crime. The stats show that the voting laws as the penal system is particularly prejudicial, and disproportionately affects poor people and people of color, dating all the way back to the Black Codes!"

"Heh! I remember something about those in high school!"

"Yeah, well ain't much changed!"

"Man, isn't that always the case."

"We all need to be more informed. Just like I recently read about how the opioid crisis and suicide are disproportionately affecting whites, especially the young!"

"Yeah, I got a young cousin really strung out in West Virginia!"

"So many are disillusioned! We are all going to swim or sink together in these UNITED STATES of AMERICA!"

"Yeah well, I guess it's about being informed; please pass the yams." *(Silence)*

By this time, the candied yams had been reduced to a buttery, syrupy, thick juice, the collards including broth reduced to visible seasonings, and scrapes of the once gloriously cheese-crowned noodles were all that remained of the dishes that had invited **me** along to join the invitation **they** had received to holiday dinner. Don't get me wrong; I was very cordially extended the invitation to *be a part of the crowd*, but sometimes you wonder.

After we finished pumpkin pie (not my contribution), coffee and a cordial, everyone sat back with that satisfied, sleepy-eyed look we all get when "it don't get no better than this!" Folks started stretching and pushing back their chairs. The host even offered, "toothpick anyone?" The air smelled thick with the competitive aromas that had met on the "battlefield" of the dining room table producing the victors of southern tradition. **Our** collard greens, **our** yams, **our** macaroni & cheese had once again shown that the kitchen is mightier than the boardroom!

As we all gathered our wraps, my hosts approached with my cleaned pots in hand.

"You will join us again next year, won't you?"

I looked into her eyes for recognition of a sincere desire to have me come again, and I think I saw a flicker of sincerity. I know I need to stop being so suspect of others! I thought about it for a moment then replied, "Actually, I think I'm goin' home. But, if I'm in town, I wouldn't miss it!" We exchanged hugs that seemed a little tighter than they did when I arrived, and just before the door closed behind me, I could faintly hear a voice cry out,

"And don't forget the collard greens!"

Walking full and quite satisfied back to my car, I smiled and replied, "I won't!"

SURVIVAL PLANS: PRESENTS...

ARTIST SPOTLIGHT

P.S. Perkins

P.S. PERKINS, A GRADUATE OF UNC-CHAPEL HILL'S AND NYU'S SCHOOLS OF COMMUNICATION, IS A NOTED EXPERT IN THE SPECIALIZATION OF HUMAN COMMUNICATION AND COMMUNICATION ARTS. P.S. IS A PUBLISHED AUTHOR OF CREATIVE FICTION, POETRY, PROSE AS WELL AS SCHOLARLY WORKS INVESTIGATING HUMAN COMMUNICATION AND BEHAVIOR. P.S. HAS DEDICATED HER PROFESSIONAL CAREER TO BEHAVIORAL COMMUNICATION HEALTH, INTERPERSONAL COMMUNICATION AND INTERCULTURAL RELATIONS. SHE SPEAKS WIDELY ON TOPICS RELATING TO LINGUISTIC DETERMINISM AND THE IMPACT OF WORDS ON PERSONAL AND PROFESSIONAL DEVELOPMENT. HER SEMINAL BOOK THE ART AND SCIENCE OF COMMUNICATION, WILEY PUBLISHERS, INTRODUCES HER WIDELY ACCLAIMED COMMUNICATION STAIRCASE MODEL AND ITS EFFECTIVENESS ADVANCING POSITIVE CHANGE WITHIN THE PERSONAL, SOCIAL AND PROFESSIONAL COMMUNICATION CLIMATES. RECENT ARTISTIC WRITING CONTRIBUTIONS CAN BE READ IN THE D.C. HILL RAG, REFLECTIONS MAGAZINE – PRINCE GEORGES COMMUNITY COLLEGE 2015 – 2019 EDITIONS AND HALLELUJAH ANYHOW ANTHOLOGY, 2018 AND 2020 ...AS WELL AS OTHER PRINT AND ONLINE PUBLICATIONS. RECENTLY P.S. WROTE, PRODUCED, DIRECTED AND PERFORMED HER ONE-WOMAN SHOW, "FINDING HER: JOURNEYING INTO WOMANHOOD" AT THE DC BLACK THEATER AND ARTS FESTIVAL, 2019. SHE IS A FOUNDING MEMBER OF THE CURRENT UDC-ARTIST COLLECTIVE AND FOUNDING BOARD MEMBER OF BOTH THE SAN DIEGO BLACK STORYTELLERS AND THE D.C. NATIONAL CAPITOL AREA BLACK STORYTELLERS ASSOCIATION. SHE IS A CURRENT CHAIR OF THE WRITERS GROUP POETS ON THE GREENLINE, DMV AND EDITOR OF THE DIGITAL POETRY COLUMN, THE POETIC VOICE CORNER! P.S. IS A PERFORMING ARTIST, POET, MOTIVATIONAL SPEAKER, AND PROFESSOR OF THE POWER OF THE SPOKEN WORD. AND YES, PS ALWAYS HAS ONE MORE THING TO SAY:

MOTTO: BE TRUE TO YOUR WORD, BECAUSE IT WILL ALWAYS BE TRUE TO YOU!...

Malcolm X Park x DC Photography

From the "New DC" Collection

Dear President Trump,

Make America Great
For all of the men and women
Who hail from thee
To employ and serve the best interests of all individuals and every family

Make America Great
With jobs- not oversees
Generous wages and incentives to boost
Our economy and self-sufficiency

Make America Great
With Schools not overpopulated
staff not under paid
Eliminate outrageous student debt
And increase the funding for after school programs, skills and trades

Make America Great
By Reforming the police
and Judicial systems
Get rid of some of these crooked judges
Who only have interests in blacks to prison sentences

Make America Great
By getting back to small businesses
Every enterprising man and woman should have opportunity to get paid
Where the citizens drive profit margins
And get paid in dividends

Make America Great

By jumping off twitter
And not fueling false narratives and hate
I believe you have the power to help Make America Great!

The Life and Times Collection XX: Man on Fire!

Thoughts on Real Leadership...

"We get the leadership we deserve, when we settle for it."

Clinton Battle

U.N.I.T.Y.

Respectfully speaking,
To whom it may concern:

Forget this Birth of A Nation stuff that you keep trying to shove down our throats!

I'm so tired of trauma porn. Periodt. (as the young people say)

I am not a slave!

I need a new agenda!

I need access, education, economics, and....

U. N. I. T. Y.

Community

Families

Love and Respect

It starts with us

Leading ourselves

Protecting one another

Serving hope (not dope)

Teaching the youth

In one cohesive

U.N. I. T

Coming together

Working together

Building together

Voting together

Investing in one another

Keeping it authentic

And it starts with

U. N. I.

ComUnity

Navigating lifes valleys and mountains can be a tightrope balancing act...
My ComUnity is more than those who live in my zip code.
My ComUnity is my neighbors, friends and family who help each other during rough times...
My ComUnity, my tribe is the force that provides the support I need to maintain my balance when life's upsetting events knock me down.

2020
Where is our support and belief in ComUnity?
We say" I don't care about Your health ComUnity" when we choose not to wear a mask to protect others and ourselves from passing the virus

Where is our Support and belief in ComUnity?
We say "i don't care about our elderly ComUnity when we choose not to help them with grocery shopping, cleaning their home or dropping off food.

Where is our support and belief in ComUnity?
We say I don't care about our young boys and girls of color when we choose not to mentor them and choose to accuse them..

Where is our support and belief in ComUnity?
We say I don't care about our ComUnity when we refuse to patronage small businesses and POC owned businesses..

Where is our support and belief in ComUnity?
We say I don't care about our ComUnity's schools, Healthcare, sustainable energy, police and fire departments, finances when we choose " Not to Vote"

I believe in my ComUnity!
I believe in my ComUnity!
U believe in my ComUnity!

See, we are wearing our masks now (even if we do not fully understand all things Covid-19).

See, we are forming small group cooperatives to combat food deserts in our neighborhoods.

See, we are checking in on" Auntie Ruby" and" Cousin John" to see if they have everything they need for the week..

See, we've arranged for shuttle services for those who need transportation to vote ...

See, our fraternities, sororities, and numerous social organizations are enhancing their mentoring programs to impact more young people's lives.

See, we are revitalizing the greenbook digitally and on paper by spreading the news about POC businesses in our ComUnity to revitalize our ComUnity

My ComUnity will thrive! Our ComUnity will thrive because I care,... because you care, because we care

Edana J. Perry

The Revolution

Gil Scott Heron said that the revolution will not be televised

So the revolution cannot be the things I see on, tell-lie-vision, reality TV or on social media

Not to say that it's not happening...but in regards to revolution...
That ain't it.

Gil Scott Heron said that the revolution would not be televised

So I don't think the symbolism of kneeling on National TV or on a man's neck counts

Not to say that it's right ... but in regards to revolution...
This isn't it either

Gil Scott Heron said the revolution would not be televised

So protesting, rioting and looting which is currently televised (for all to see), isn't going revolutionize the thinking (or the actions) of the powers that be- .

Not to say that something good can't come from it.... but in regards to the revolution...This isn't it.

Gil Scott Heron said the revolution will not be televised

But yall didn't truly get the memo
If you did, you wouldn't be checking for minute by minute for posts, or updates on the news and gram

You wouldn't simplify your anger in a hashtag
You wouldn't be trying to speak up and out against every injustice- systemically designed to trigger you to do this...

You wouldn't look to every celebrity or political figure as your great hope or savior knowing you didn't put them in position to save you

Gil Scott Heron said the revolution will not be televised

So stop looking for the change you want to see.

The revolution only starts inside of you and me

And it's not the revolt or fighting back,

That we see on TV

It's not disrespect and destroying our own communities

Gil Scott Heron said the revolution will not be televised

So start in your own back yard
There's 100x more black on black crime

Than police killing you and me

Gil Scott Heron said the revolution will not be televised

The revolution is a change in the black man's state of mind

The revolution requires strong men and resilient supportive women with leadership skills

The revolution has to start in our own families

Protecting and serving our own communities.

Fostering forgiveness amongst the youth

Building each other up

Not tearing one another down

Working to get money together
Then investing in homes, neighborhoods and viable businesses together

That Everybody's gotta eat B mentality

This the revolution you won't see on TV

Gill Scott Heron said the revolution would not be televised
And I'm telling you- it starts inside of our homes and within our communities

To Heal A Wounded World

(With thanks to poet, educator and author, Joseph Ross, for his 2019 essay, "A Wounded World," which inspired this poem)
© January 4, 2020, J. Joy *"Sistah Joy"* Matthews Alford

My tears are not enough
Nor even my prayers

Unlike my pockets
My compassion runs deep
Still, this is insufficient
In the face of realities that
Stifle, strangle and kill

I ask my God
To guide and empower me
To act in soul enriching
Esteem affirming, consequential
Ways that alter the status quo

To ignite in me a righteous will
That indignantly shames injustice,
Is contagious, and by its
Very existence
Challenges bigotry
Maniacal tyranny, self-
Aggrandizement and hate
All of which run rampant
On this planet and
Too often, in this nation

I lift my voice against them
Not softly or with plea
But with rancor and rage
For I too am afflicted
By the influences…
The swill that swirls about me

I too am made jaded
By existing in this
Degraded humanity
Which is our world

Yet I still stand in resistance
Still lift my voice, wave my flag
Still deny and defy
The scourge that oppresses
That would annihilate all
Who are unlike *them*

My strength may seem
Insufficient in the face of
Such huge opposition
But still I come

My voice may seem a whisper to some
But I persist, still sing my
Best song of Love

My words are victorious and yes,
Contagious, for they are words of life

They come from a soul
Connected to a source
Greater than any from dungeon or abyss

They radiate with light and power
Showering down an unstoppable rain
That brings to life all it touches

These are my words
My song of life
I share them freely
Powerfully, with all who seek
Strength to save and set free

They grow even amid these
Days of doom and gloom
Watch my words bloom
Catch hold of their fragrance
As they blossom into bouquets

They have a power all their own
But as amazing as they are
Their power is not fully unleashed
Until they join with yours

It is then that they
Become undefeatable
Shifting paradigms and axes
Awakening and changing
Hearts, minds and conscience
To heal a wounded world

SURVIVAL PLANS

SURVIVAL PLANS: PRESENTS...

ARTIST SPOTLIGHT

Sistah Joy

J. JOY MATTHEWS ALFORD, "SISTAH JOY," IS THE INAUGURAL POET LAUREATE OF PRINCE GEORGE'S COUNTY, MARYLAND. SHE IS THE AUTHOR OF THREE COLLECTIONS OF POEMS, "LORD I'M DANCIN' AS FAST AS I CAN" (2000), "FROM PAIN TO EMPOWERMENT, THE FABRIC OF MY BEING," AND "THIS GARDEN CALLED LIFE." SHE HAS PRODUCED AND HOSTED THE POETRY-BASED CABLE TELEVISION SHOW, SOJOURN WITH WORDS, SINCE ITS INCEPTION IN 2005. SISTAH JOY RECEIVED THE POET LAUREATE SPECIAL AWARD (2002) FOR "HER OUTSTANDING CONTRIBUTIONS TO THE ART OF POETRY" IN HER NATIVE WASHINGTON, DC. SHE IS THE FOUNDER OF THE SOCIALLY-CONSCIOUS POETRY ENSEMBLE, COLLECTIVE VOICES.

VISIT HER WEBSITE HTTPS://WWW.SISTAHJOY.COM FOR MORE INFORMATION AND TO VIEW SAMPLES OF HER POETRY.

Sistah Joy x Reflections Literary & Arts @ PGCC

Today

Thank you for life.
Life Creator
Creator of Life in all things
Things created by all beings
Being a force to be reckoned with
With Me a force to be reckoned
Reconciling all differences
Differences created by indifference
Indifferences to injustice.
Injustices to my people
People crying for their children
Children dying by the hand of the gun
The gun pointed in the wrong direction
Direction, a course in which a person moves
Moves can take you forward
Forward is the way to growth
Growth fuels your mind
Mind body and Soul

Today is the present
Tomorrow is the future
The Future has been written
Written thousands of times
Times are changing
Change with the times
Time is of the essence
Essence is the spirit
Spiritual beings we are
Are you following me thus far?

Far enough to do what needs to be done
Done with all the talking
Talking followed up with no actions
Actions with no repercussions
Repercussions are the consequences, the ones I refer to have no impact
Impact is the influence
Influence is to what you have been exposed
Exposed to drugs, media programming and disease
Disease the sickness that kills off millions with ease
Eased right into glory

Glory be to GOD
GOD have mercy on us
Only you can save our souls

Today.

Life & Times

```
                M F F C A K N T N M
             P T N L N L V N Y I R C A S B I
          N U X E C I T S U J N I I F M B I A S Y
        E N E C Y T I C A P A C V U X O L U O T H D
      O Y C I V I L R I G H T S F U M F C U S Q O J K P N
    Q E O S Z Q Q G K Y I K W R S B V P A O S I H F G K Q N
    V E N X P O W V S A H B N E W U S I Q C V A U P E W M O O B
  Z J M Z J I I L J U U T A T T N W W R I J O B A M A N I E P H V
  Z J M U R E W R G T K P T R M E Z O A G E Z P C E O T Y V E Z E
F V T E E T I R V X Q F A P E V N G L T N Z K R E O A F V O X S Q H
G E E O T B G R C A U X M P M L A E M R E G O B X E G V O T L C L K O F
A M N L A R K J Q H D S I T P V E E S L A G Y U P E Y L I H U E Z S Y J
K H I T E T U W X B Z E I R X I N D M B T N T N K R A E X F D T L I V V Y L
W T N S R C U N R T V Q S C G K I S T E R O A I G K E Z L A O I L F M V T N
C N I N A I F B O I U P B A A A R T V J N J Y E O K T P N W T O E Q N D J G
Z O E S W N D L M L A B A T R T T V H L V U T S F L N U U O A B N N H V O C O S
M N M T V C S N K L U L E W M G N E G D S R U Y N P A E E I F U A C N P C K T Q
F V D P H E U C I S T A B I L I T Y I T P L L Y O E B G M T S O Y E O I E T O X
M I N L Q T A T F E D I N C A R C E R A T I O N I C R N P A K D Y S I Z W N S X
V C E A H L Y L W E A L T H M Q Y F F R X B V R T N B A L L E E T O T T N E R R
U T M I B H N O I T C E L F E R T U O S M A E F A A F H O U T L I L A I L M E U
T I A C X V D Z V N S Y S T E M I E L N Q F R V L D N C Y P R B N U R M W N W B
U O K I C E N A B L E J X U F B N C L O H F X Q I N O J M O I A U T T P U O O O
R N R D L S P S P Z T W Z Y J J U O I J A O V J M U X H E P U N M I S O M R T S
T B X U A Z M N N A Q R B D D D M N B T B R S B I B W C N T M O M O I V A I N O
Q G J S P G G J W T Z U T 5 T M O Q P E D C V 5 A R L T U P S O N N E N V I
T D D S R N C Y Q E G M M M F O M W E L Y Z J S Q P M O P H A C B I R P N W
G P Z I A I T I C P N P F P N C I N C I R P M A S S E S U A E W M M I Z E T
Q B S E N I 5 M O G Q H A R L C A R E X C E Q C Z C B H D R A Q D S R Z
S P M K E I M C E U O E T A U S K E V C C I E Y L Q O Q C S Z A A H G I
E C L K R N J O T P R H C A I O P E N C J M A F Y Y N C E A L V E K
U R L A D V L E N S X 5 I S E E P E H T O I G T Z D B T E U Y R D W
O J W K T K P B T Y G S V H R L U K N C O I H J F R I R E D R X
D A Z B O Z S Q R S M G T O W I O N B N I N F L A T I O N N
Z M W H O I A B I P F I W H T A V U U W P C Y T I N U L
K A X S P M E E B V Y B U N N H D R I J P T C C J G
M N N Q X K D N U Y A I Q A X Y U T L Q R O N U
I G D M U I H T F B T C V R S C W D W G
Q G D E P S E E G W N O I L Y T
W X Y T E F A S E M
```

WORD LIST:

ABUNDANCE	CONTRIBUTE	IMPOVERISHED	SAFETY
ADMINISTRATION	CONTROL	INCARCERATION	SEGREGATION
AFFORD	CONVICTION	INFLATION	SOCIAL MEDIA
AMENDMENT	COVID	INJUSTICE	SOLUTION
ASSIMILATION	DICTATE	INTEGRATION	STABILITY
AUTONOMY	ECONOMICS	JUDICIAL	SUPPLEMENT
AWAKENING	EMPLOYMENT	LOUD	SYSTEM
BELIEVE	ENABLE	MASSES	SYSTEMIC
BIAS	ENVIRONMENT	NAVIGATE	TOLERANCE
BILL OF RIGHTS	ERADICATE	OBAMA	TRIUMPH
BLACK LIVES MATTER	EVOLUTION	PERCEPTIONS	TRIUMVIRATE
BUILD	EXCELLENCE	POPULATION	TRUMP
CAPACITY	FEMINIST	QUALITY	TWIN TOWERS
CHANGE	FINANCIAL	RACISM	UNITY
CIVIL RIGHTS	GUN VIOLENCE	REASONABLE DOUBT	UNITY
CLASSISM	HARVEST	REFLECTION	WEALTH
COMMUNITY	HATE	REVOLUTION	
COMMUNITY	IDEAS	RICHES	

SURVIVAL PLANS

Creativity Booster

Writing Prompt

Directions Part I: Select a piece (poem, artwork, noteworthy saying etc) featured in the "Life & Times" section of Survival PLANS. What feelings, words, thoughts, phrases come to your mind when you view this piece? Why?

Take 5 minutes to jot down your responses below.

Name of the literary piece/art selected: _____

Page Number:_____

Thoughts/Reflections/Emotions:_____

_____
_____
_____
_____
_____

Directions Part II: Now use the words, feelings, notes etc., that you wrote to create a short poem.

_____
_____
_____
_____
_____

Life and Times

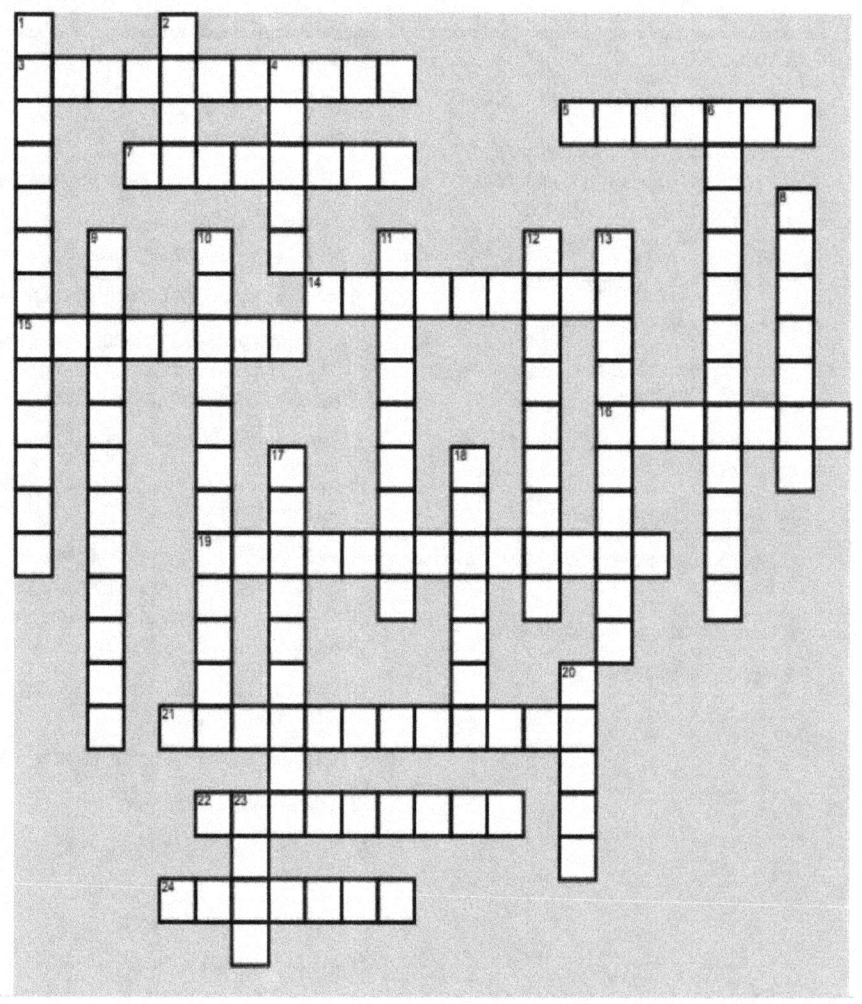

SURVIVAL PLANS

Life and Times - Crossword Puzzle Clues

Across

3 To feed with food or other sustenance

5 A mild to severe respiratory illness/virus characterized by flu-like symptoms. Created a world-wide pandemic in 2019 -2020.

7 Political, social and economic equality on behalf of women's rights and interest

14 People from your line of descent

15 Continuing to exist in spite of accidents, ordeals or difficult circumstances

16 Documents, past events linked to a human experiences

19 Confinement in prison or jail

21 Conforming to a certain lifestyle, consciousness or beliefs

22 Process of altering a law or document

24 Being just, impartial and fair

Down

1 Country located in North America w/ Capital being Washington DC

2 A period during which a person or thing is alive

4 A medium of exchange- used to purchase goods and/or services. Usually in paper or coin form.

6 45th President of the United States of America

8 Customary beliefs, social forms and material traits of racial, religious or social groups- includes music, history, art and style

9 44th President of the United States of America

10 A movement to create equal political, social and equality rights

11 Social Science that is concerned with production, distribution and consumption of goods and services which produce money and wealth

12 People with common interest living together within a larger society

13 The study of mind and how it relates to behavior

17 A socially prominent person

18 To change from good to bad in morals, actions or manners

20 A quality or state of oneness

23 A large quantity, amount or number

Love

and...

Loss

This section is dedicated to my son David Alexander Nash, III born on September 3, 2020 and in the memory of my "Great" Aunt Marion who transitioned on the same day.
Life and death are the epitome of Love and Loss.

Love and Loss

10 years in...

Still feels like yesterday,

With Love and loss, that is.

It's fresh, but not new

Healed skin

Over a closed wound

Fond memories

Of us

The sweetest taboo

MOTHER DEAR

A mother's love doesn't go away

A mother will walk beside you each and everyday

A mother may be unseen, unheard,

but her presence is always near

There is no person more loving than mother dear.

Karen Mayo-Hogan

Mother's Unconditional Love

Unconditional

Before I could love myself

My mother loved me

Prenatal Assignment

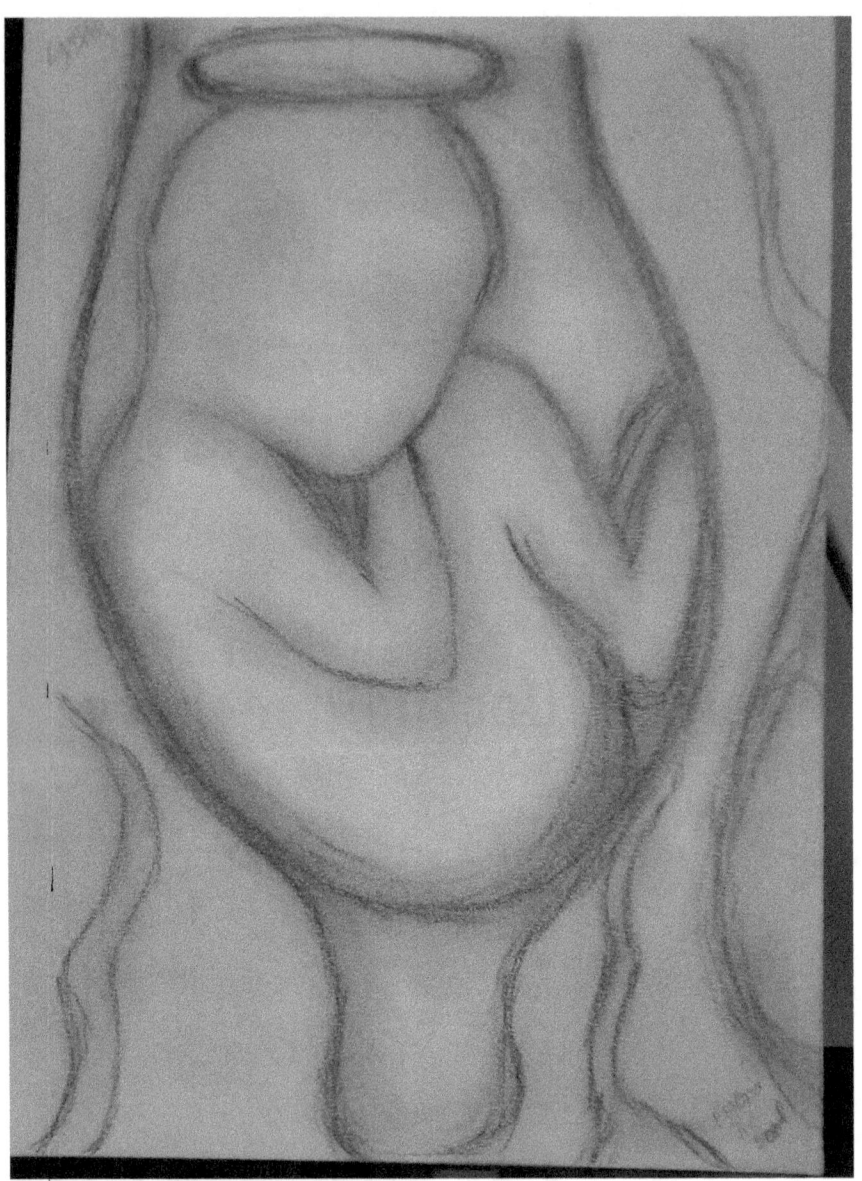

Starchild the Urban Unicorn

Some Days You Just Can't Forget (8/15/05)

Kim Battle

In life there are days that you can never forget. Days that you can't get back and days that change the trajectory of your life. I remember one of those days, as if it were yesterday. It was August 15, 2005 at 9 o'clock AM. I remember that it was a beautiful morning that quickly turned grim and dark. On this day, I received a call that would test my faith and bring me face to face with a living God, my Father God, whom I serve, with all my heart. On August 15, 2005 that faith, my faith was truly tested.

My son was just starting his junior year of high school and decided that he wanted to play football. For years, I was against it but my husband was like baby "let him grow up." However, I was hesitant because my son stayed so sickly as a young child, suffering from allergies and asthma attacks that put him in the hospital for weeks at a time... so again, it was hard for me to consent to him playing football- but I did have to "let him grow up," so I agreed.

The telephone rang and my when my husband answered, I heard his tone and I knew something was wrong. He told me that we had to get to the hospital because my son had been hurt on the field. I was thinking that maybe he broke his leg or an arm but never in million years did I think my 16 would be fighting for his life after having a heat stroke. The ride to the hospital was the longest 15 minutes of my life, I just wanted to get to my child.

Once we entered the hospital a doctor walked up to me and said "you might want to get your pastor on the phone, your son will not make it through the night." My heart stop beating and I checked out mentally for a few seconds/minutes. Once I gathered myself, I immediately asked that that doctor be removed from my son's case. He had given up on my child from the start and I felt as if he would not do everything in his medical powers to make sure my son survived. My faith overrode my fear at this point, so I didn't want anyone near my son that felt as though he was going to die. As I walked in the room, I saw my son laying on a bed of ice with IV's in both arms, in his neck and in his foot. Utility fans were blowing directly on him and he was just lying there like he was sleep. As I went to approach him he let out a scream like someone was doing grave harm to him and I broke down. He began to vomit up something that looked coffee sludge and his body went into seizures. As I stood there my feet wouldn't move I couldn't speak, cry, blink or even think. I was watching my baby but it was an out of body experience.

The new doctor on the case informed me that his brain was in overdrive, his organs were shutting down, but he would do everything in his power to save him. The doctor also informed me that his body core temperature had gotten up to 106 and this was why his body was shutting down. So, the sensitivity in his brain was very much heightened because it was trying to repair itself. As my baby remained in a coma, I laid on that bed of ice with him and prayed a prayer like never before. I didn't bargain with the Lord, I just thanked Him for the 16 years of a wonderful blessing, I thanked Him for allowing me to be the vessel that bought forth this wonderful human being… and in that very moment a peace came over me and I just laid with son in my arms and sang to him. "You don't know what He's done for me, He gave me the victory" and that was all I sang for hours just those lyrics and nothing else. I told everyone to leave the room and for the next five hours it was just God and I in that room watching over my baby. I was silent and I was able to hear from Him (God). As He spoke to me it gave me a spirit of calm through the worst storm of my life. At that very moment I can clearly remember my relationship with Christ became so real. I've always prayed and trusted the Lord but at this moment it went to another level of trust and peace. Some of my memories are blurred (even now 14 years later) and I can only remember things in spurts. But what is clear is that when I couldn't even hold my own head up, God was there.

I was present in the physical form but mentally I was not there. God covered me so that I was able to stand for my son. People spoke of how strong I was and I laughed because I had to let them know it was by the grace of the Lord that I stood because I had checked out and didn't even realize it. Day four my son opened his eyes and said that he was standing in a white room and he heard music but it was dark in the hole that lead to the party. He said his cousin asked him to go to the party and he told him no he couldn't go because I wouldn't know where he was. He said once he told him "no," he woke up.

My son had some organ damage but for the most part he recovered. He is now 29 and the proud father of 2 beautiful girls. All I can say is My God, My God. Thank you, Jesus! for your unwavering love, grace and mercy.

I know you are probably wondering where my husband was during all of this. He sat in the car at the first hospital and sobbed like a baby because of his guilt (I found this out later, like months later). Once he was moved to the next hospital my husband would show his face to see if I wanted to eat and see how our son was coming along but then he would find a reason to leave. At the time, I couldn't even process the fact that he was leaving me alone to deal with our son, I just knew that I couldn't leave my child's side, what others did wasn't even a thought to me. Once my son came home, I noticed my husband was very distant as if he was uneasy in his own skin. I didn't know it at the time but God was dealing with him in a way that I could have never imagined.

Months later he broke down and told me he felt guilty because he was the reason why it happened because he wanted him to play and I didn't. He told me how much he prayed to God and he went on to tell me that he knew God would answer his prayers but he still felt that guilt. I told him that if I made him feel like he was responsible I apologize for that. I also apologized for not allowing him into my space while we were both going through it. He was riddled with guilt and I was so engrossed in being a mother in pain, that I forgot that my husband was also dealing with his pain as a father as well. I know that when you are going through it is easy to close yourself off but when you are married shutting down it could possibly break the bond if it is not addressed, sooner than later. We were able to talk and pray it through. We've grown even closer after that. I also saw a shift in the way my husband handled us (our family) he had become a man that allowed God to lead him so that he could protect, provide and lead us. The old people use to always say if it doesn't kill you it only makes you stronger, that it has done both spiritually and emotionally.

Mommy

The essence of my existence,
Providing unconditional love in my life,
A wonderful mother,
You loved me at first sight,
You have shaped and molded me into the person I am to be,
How could I ask the Lord for a mother better than she?

A support system stronger then my own,
Your strength has shielded me,
And welcomed me home.

How blessed I am to have your love so true,
How blessed I am to have a mother like you,
I can never repay you for all that you do,
So, I'm forever in debt,
In debt to you,

Mommy.
The essence of my existence,
The achiever of all my achievements,
I may say less-
But these words, I forever mean them

There are not enough words to describe those precious hands,
The hands that cradled me,
Hands that guided through,

So, I wrote this poem,

Especially for you!

#GIRLDAD

Inspired by McKinley Frances Gray
Dedicated to Kobe & Gianna Bryant
By Mark F. Gray

They make you feel happy. They make you feel sad.
But there's no better love than to be a Girl Dad!

There are moments so special that time can't replace because they're embedded in your soul; in an everlasting space.

The joys are many and the heartache is too.
But there's nothing better than hearing those 11 letters and four words when she says: "Dad, I Love You".

There's a warmth that you feel deep in your heart that gives you strength to keep charging when you're apart.

It's a connection so real and a bond that's not fake;
something intangible and true that nothing can break.

You live through their joy and hurt when they're in pain;
hoping to give them confidence and courage to try once again.

Daughters make you look at yourself through a whole different light. Daughters are the best teachers of what's wrong and what's right.

They can call you out with their tears and a whimper. They are the only ones on the planet who can make you put the clamps on a bad day's temper.

As she grows and matures into a bright young lady;
the smile which brightens your day is a reminder that she's still just your baby.

You learn to love your mother and for those times together you'll always be glad;
but forever is the blessing of being a #girldad!

-24/8

Love Haikus

Love Drug

Love is like a drug

Getting high off dopamine

Rushes in to crash

Love Hurts

Love can hurt like hell

Haven't you been hurt before?

I know, we all have

Love Leaves

When love and kindness

Is not enough to keep you

It's time to move on

Love Grows

Love grows with time

You have to develop it

Nurturing its grace

Love Poem

I love it when you hold me in your arms so nice and firm

Then suddenly release me so it's my turn,

To hold you and kiss you, all the rest of the day.

The feeling is so good,

I'm glad you came my way,

With smiles, hugs, and kisses just for me.

These are actions that made me as happy as I can be.

I thank God for letting me find someone like you,

Yes I do, I do, I truly do.

Karen Mayo Hogan
(Written in 1970s)

Lust Rush Crush

Dear You,

Your love has me on a high
I'm a dopamine fiend
And you…
you got what I need

I'm addicted to you
Those sweet somethings that you do
Makes it hard for me to keep my cool

My body rises
I'm in heat with desires
Soul on fire
I got the hots for you

Time is not of the essence
So I'd waste away
Just to be close to you

I imagine us married
At the alter…
we say our "I do's"
We'll build us a family
Have a kid
Maybe one or two

We would be so happy
Imagine me…
The Mrs. To you

Please tell me
You feel this way too
For if you didn't…
I don't know what I might do

Become a fatal attraction
Follow and cyber stalk
Pop up where you are

Yes…
I would go the extra mile for you

Your love is everything
So I would hang on
With nothing to lose
Your love could make me act a fool

I'd blow up your phone
Call from blocked numbers
Just to hear your breath
Hang up
And dial again

So don't leave me hanging
Play with my heart
Or leave me with regret

I would hate for you to see
My crazy side

Sincerely your,
Lust Rush Crush

Lusting Go

Sex
Use to be the best
Now it's not enough to make it last.

I reminisce about rocket ships
Love overflowing
Sheets filled
With us

I digress to passionate nights
Kitchen countertops
Hotel Rooftops
My body lusts

I think of your touch
Sweet wet kisses
Nipples rising
Toe curling
Tenderness

The heat of your body
My body
I inhale…
Loves got such a sweet
Smelling musk

But all of that good lovin
Midnight stroking
And morning wood

Is simply not enough
To keep us connected

Especially when you're giving it to someone else.

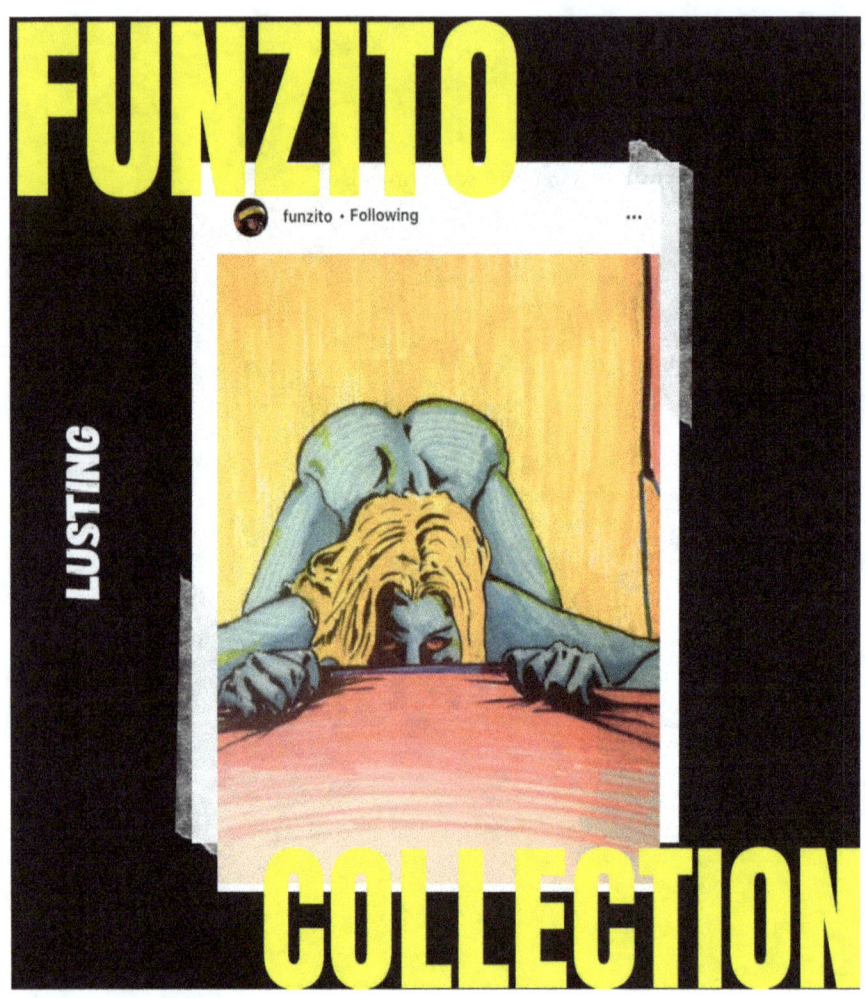

#funzitosketches

At some point every man is…

Young, dumb and full of cum!!!

D. Nash

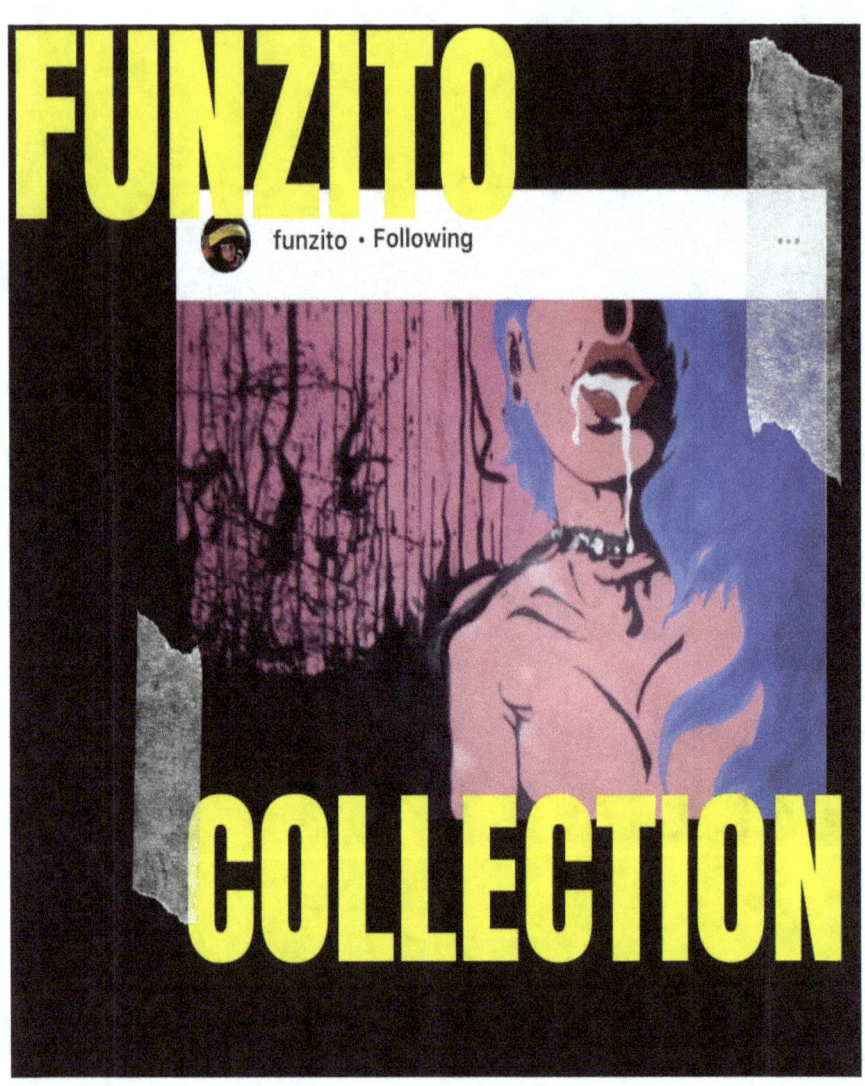

Even with Love...

I see how people can use your insecurities against you...

To control you

To manipulate you

To use you

I know, that's why it's so hard for me to open up and let you in.

I learned that people can hurt you...

Even if they do love you.

These words,
like a favorite shirt
used every week
washed every Sunday
until the prints became
unrecognizable
its colors, faded
aged like raisins,
its sweetness, all dry and gone
you used them, until

it was never the same, until
it meant nothing

  -The words "I love you"
  and "you're beautiful"

-Efflorescent_Child

Lesson from a Train Wreck

Seen this train wreck coming a mile away
Yet and still
It may have seemed completely surreal
Arriving home with your tail between your legs
After yet another domestic display

He said like a hundred times he just wanted to be "friends"
But…
You wanted more
You showed him more
You gave him more
More than he deserves…
IN LIFE!

Lord forgive me,
who am I to judge.

From the sidelines
I watched you
You, picked this guy up from the mud
Clothed, fed and sheltered him when he needed it most.
Provided his basic needs
Satisfied his wants

You became his calm in the storm
And he became your great black hope
Your King
With fantasies of future
Marriage, kids and a home that you two would build…
On a lot so quaint,

with turf so green
Made on a paved quick sand

But from a mile away
I could hear this train running off the track
It was screeching and roaring
And holding you back

I'm not sure if it was the shot nine times
The walking from Bowie to Baltimore
The wife and kids situation
or the PTSD that gave me unease

As a sister...
I offered my support
As an advisor...
I cautioned and offered advice
I wish my words could have stopped you from making the same mistake twice.

But they couldn't
Do more than fall on a flat plane
And
Glide right down the side of your right arm
To
Roll the dice that you held so tightly
Blowing on
Calling out lucky number seven
With the last nickel and dime in your pocket

Hoping for that JACKPOT
Waiting to hear that CHA-CHING
Taking a chance on what could be
For something that never was

And as painfully clear as it was to me
You had to go through this
So that you could see

See that overcoming, growing
and learning
from your own mistakes
Uncovers your true value
and Innermost beauty

See the lesson in a train wreck
Pray And Move forward

You got this!

Reminder

Accidents happen So, proceed with caution and faith.

A Leap of Faith

Today I couldn't see the light…
See this was the last fight …
Heartbroken and ready to die…
The person I loved was only a lie…
I saw the cliffs in the corner of my eyes…

Found peace in the sweet reset…
From the pieces I called life.

I jumped right off with a middle finger to the sky…
Saying f**k that guy!
And in that moment…
I wanted to cry…
But looked at my past and said f**k it…
Goodbye.

And all to my surprise…
I remembered I could fly…
I had wings
And I soared so high…
Right into my new life…
Among the stars in the sky.

Remember who you are…
And the power you possess…
Know your worth…
Expect it…
And break your own heart if you have to leave.

Nothing is more important than being free…
I Love you all…

We are one…

This is our story…
But it is not done…
Flying free now so we already won.

Starchild the Urban Unicorn

Reaching

Why you reaching out to me?
Especially after all this time...
You trying to tell me Facebook suggested you to be-a-friend of mine?

Nah... I'm not buying it.
I been on your mind...
Just admit it... that's why.

You been lurking trying to be friends...
With my friends-
Trying to catch my eye.

How many girls you kick this to?
Maybe two? Or three?
You reaching
Still running these tired college games at the age of thirty-three

How you going be cool with me?
We not cool-
Ain't been cool since like 03'

You reaching-
Knowing I got a man...
Cause you watching me on the gram.

It's funny how the ones who didn't want you before

When they see you doing more...

Always come back around

Stop reaching!

Cause I am always going to be out of your reach!

Exist

What happens at the end of a love affair?

The shattered dreams that you once shared.

Do you retreat and admit your defeat?

Or do you swoon into your cocoon to hide away,

Feeling sorry that you could not stay?

Then emerge into a beautiful butterfly;

Ready to flutter out into the sky?

Or is it gloom and doom for you, can't go on;

Can't never navigate out of this storm!

Do you go on living or merely exist?

Do you accept the Blessing that's coming your way;

Or do you resist?

Well, the first thing you should do before you cease,

Is open your mouth, inhale and just breathe.

Margo Mayo

Simple Truths about Love

You are Love…

Everything you see is simply vibrating with the force of that Love…

Open your mind and heart so you can feel it as well as see it…

So you can embrace it as well as share it…

Do more things that allow you to feel it deep within your soul…

Be patient…

Be consistent…

And trust the timing of your life…

You are eternally Loved…

Love yourself…

And reflect to the world how you want to receive that Love back in your life…

Starchild the Urban Unicorn

Beauty

What is beauty? The birth of a new day? What is beauty? The way a woman hips sway? What is beauty? The bountiful essences of a soul, that past hurt broken, but present peace made whole…

An epiphany, clearing the cloud of confusion, which divided you from me, debunking the illusion, the I is better than we…

Oooowee, the ever so slight fragrance of past tense fear, being over run with the cleansing scent of common sense, right now, right here…

The breeze of future ventures flowing through each strand of your hair, the wings of a million butterflies, lifting you above the fountain of tears…

I do swear, to tell the truth, cutting you loose, to let go, of so and so, Billy Bad Bozzo…

The one with two faces, the familiar and the one you were surprised to find out you didn't know…

So! I take a stand and come against, that which would have you straddling the fence…

One foot out, the other in, I got ten toes in, proclaiming the end of the questions…

My quest, is to be able to make a confession, to the generations soon to come, that I didn't run, when it was time for the healing to be done…

I just spoke of the beauty of the one, that provided a fresh wind to my lungs, made the grass seem greener, the birds tweets sound like music, gave even more brightness to the sun…

I stand in the gap, interceding for the heart that was so guarded, while processing the reality of what just started…

Yes, that's right, the sight of the moon light, in your cool calm demeanor, got me acting a fool tonight, running through the streets, asking any and every one, "Have you seen her?" "Have you seen beauty?"

No, No, Not the lips dripping with seduction, No, No, Not the booty, that freezes every man in time, causing his discipline to malfunction. No, the beauty I speak of, functions more like a flock of doves, delighting the sky, in the brink of tomorrows sunrise…

The beauty that is like the whispering tone, of I love yous, signaling me to come home…

The moon of intense sensation, tantalizing my very core, mi amor, oh, mi amor…

Four score and seven years ago, could not declare or fathom what I would have had to endure…

The years of lost dreams, seemingly out of my reach until now, at some point, somehow, heaven had to have had a breach, and allowed beauty to be unleashed, into my life…

Generations I beseeched, beauty to come into my life…

Beauty…

Oh beauty, What are you? Beauty, who are you? If you are reading this, Beauty, the Beauty I speak of, is You!!!

Troy Lockett

Rare Rose x DC Photography

From the "New DC" Collection

Good Morning, My Love

Waking up to you is everything
Everything I dreamed of
Everything I prayed for
Everything I deserve

You are my sunshine
You rise in the east
Your warmth penetrates my flesh
I roll over and lay on your chest

I feel love
I feel safe
I feel protected
I feel respected

Feeding off your energy
Finding myself vulnerable

Suspended in your air
Surrendering to your love

I fall asleep in a sunset
And wake up,
Where the sun always shines
Good Morning,
My love

My Sweet Nina Boo,

As I sit at my desk, I find myself thinking about you and missing you as usual. I understand all too well the strife that you have going on within yourself, but I want you to know that I am here for you, now and always. I know it's hard to let someone in 100% and I get that. But just know this… I love, respect, cherish and adore you. I wouldn't do anything to hurt you. I need you at my side. You are the first thing I think about when I wake up and the last thing I think about before I go to sleep.

Please understand that these are not mere words that I say (or should I say write). You are my sun, moon, stars, my world, my universe and I would do anything for you. When I see you, I see my future. I see where I want to be and who I want to be with. No matter how bad of a day I'm having, I know that seeing or talking to you will make it better. I'm not ashamed to say that I need you.

People always say that you don't need anyone but, I beg to differ. If people didn't need each other God would have programmed us not to feel alone or the feel the need for companionship. The world is a cold place and for the most part, people don't give a fuck. They'll use you just to get what they want from you and then toss you to the side like garbage. The only thing that I want to do is make sure that you never feel like that.

You should never feel alone or feel like you can't come to me. I'm here to help and support you. I know this may sound like a fairy tale or some Hollywood b.s. but this is real and it's all for you Sabrina Battle- no one else period. Like I told you earlier, the love that I have for you is unmeasurable and incomprehensible- it goes far beyond human logic. All I have for you is undying love and that's all I go off of… nothing less.

The only thing that I want from you is for you to let me all the way in so that I can show and treat you the way that you need and deserve to be treated. And that is with the upmost respect. You're a beautiful flower who only deserves the best.

If the people from your past were too lame, stupid, wack etc. to realize then shame on them. I won't ever give up on you, you have nothing to fear from me. The whole reason we took our relationship to another level is because we knew we had each other's backs. We want something real and in order to do that we have to let go of the past and put our faith in one another. I'm all in, no faking.

It shouldn't be hard for you to understand. You are a beautiful woman, you're funny, kind and sweet behind that wall of yours. I know there's much more- and I want to see it and feel it because I know its real and rare.

Please do not keep things from me, it makes me feel like you don't want to confide in me or trust me. I won't ever judge you- never have and won't ever do. You're my other half I don't care if you've been bruised or broken. I just want to heal you with my unconditional love- that's for you and only you.

I've been hut too. I've been fucked over, played all that b.s. but I love you too much to ever let that lame ass bitch from my past affect you. You're my Queen and they were nothing. Period. Point blank. That's why it's easy to move forward and say fuck them all. Once I met a real woman who was so genuine, the others eradicated from my brain. Now the only love I know is the one that we share.

I want to grow old with you, marry you (or should I say ask you to be my wife). I will cherish you until the end of my days. I want you to bear a child for me, to carry my seed- to create and start a new life together. I want to show you what it means to be a real man, a provider and a protector. I would never allow you to work two jobs or give birth without my financial support. I'll work my fingers to the bone before I allow that to happen.

Nina,

Please, please, please understand what I am telling you because its real and uncanny. It may be only one in a billion chance of it happening but it did and it happened for us. You have to open your receptors so that you get what I am sending to you- pure unconditional love, the stuff dreams are made of. I know that you're a sweet, loving girl that's why I want to be with you despite what you have been through and the circumstances. I just want to be there for you, to love you.

I know we have had a few disagreements but it's only human. My love and respect for you is of the upmost so it will never get out of hand. I told you since day one (February 12, 2010), that I was not going to yap your head off with what I would do for you- instead, I will show and prove to you that I deserve all of your unconditional love. I will make it a priority to make sure that you know you can count on me for anything, no matter what.

With all of that being said, Nina just remember this one thing. I love you with all of my heart and more than anyone else. You are my best friend, lover and so much more that words cannot explain.

Read this anytime that we have a disagreement or if you need a reminder about how I feel.

Love Angel

Rahim Mitchell

Connected Timelessly through the Basic Need for each other

I feel like you can control my body movements

You're the snake charmer, and I the snake

My body rises and falls to you… as you rise and fall

I breathe in your essence and it's intoxicating

You my friend are the moon,

And I the sun…

The man of my dreams…

I have been waiting for you…

You are the ONE

You absorb a certain amount of my fear with your embraces

I'm wrapped up in the warmth of your arms and it becomes my shelter

A basic need.

You roam my intimate thoughts… like a nomad

Arousing all my senses

You are no intruder yet your invasive

You're tuned in to my station

I'm defenseless or submissive to the radioactive interference

I'm waving a white flag

Surrendering to an endearing moment

A moment that I hope transcends to be a lifetime

Timeless.

Now we move as a unit

I flow into you like the sea to the ocean

Wanted advances become the "norm"

And you are my calm in the storm

I'm your rib and you my backbone

We are Connected.

This is more than attraction

When soul mates meet, this is the reaction

We are Connected Timelessly through the Basic Need for each other

Alexa, play Sade "Kiss of Life"

v

SURVIVAL PLANS

Today and Forever

Today we are all gathered here together,

In and at our best, justly in despite of the weather,

To share our vows, making our commitment before God,

And before every other.

Never to forsaken nor to smother,

While we are evolving from these earthly bounds of leather,

We'll hope to come to an awakening in the fields of heather,

Once to be said to one another, unrehearsed, and not even written in a letter,

Let the love and truth of our hearts make life much better,

We know with the possibilities of just living life there will

be no exact time setter.

So we pray, that if worst should ever come to worst,

It may not bring about our sudden burst,

Less we are said to depart this fertile earth,

Into a paradise of our now fore seen rebirth,

Where our ties are never again to sever,

Thus dwelling with our Lord and Savior, forever and ever.

Darcelle Battle

Wedding Prayer

Blessed by God, he heard us pray

That he'll stand beside us as we perform our vows each and every day.

He'll be with us through tough times when we are sad,

He'll hold our hands through good times and bad.

He is our Savior and our Best Friend.

No wedding or any wedding day would be special if we did not know him.

Karen Mayo-Hogan

Survival Plans 101: Marriage Advice From "Real" Married People

(Collectively Over 200 years of Marriage Experience)

"Remember this is your lifetime partner. Honesty and truth are a necessity. LOVE is a must. The plans developed are for your lifetime together."

Merrill and Keith Alston

"Show love, speak love and share love."

Leslie Carr-Miller

"Try to really focus on listening to your spouse vs. hearing the words that just come out of her mouth. For example, if she is speaking to you, men tend to say "I hear you" which is really a strategy to stop talking. Merriam-Webster defines hearing as the "process, function, or power of perceiving sound; specifically: the special sense by which noises and tones are received as stimuli." Listening, on the other hand, means "to pay attention to sound; to hear something with thoughtful attention; and to give real consideration- and in my own word "focus." If you can do this, you will create a strong foundation of respect for each other's opinion because you would have really listened to their point of view."

Edwin "Greg" Miller

"Do not have <u>expectations</u> or expect perfection. Both will lead to disappointment. Do things because you want to, not because you believe you have to."

Karen Burks

"Choose your battles and let go of the small things. No human being is perfect, so why hold your spouse to an unachievable standard? If you dispute every little issue or criticize that which displeases you hour-by-hour or day-to-day, you will exhaust yourself and your marriage will suffer."

Beth Cruz

"If you truly want God's results and God's blessings in and upon your marriage, do life in God's way—PERIOD. Put pride aside and read his Word together and independently. Don't allow an unholy and sin-sick society to pervert the <u>sanctity</u> of God's creation. What GOD has joined together, let no ONE/THNG put it <u>asunder</u>. You can't be married by yourself or do marriage by yourself. Marriage is a commitment where a husband and his wife forsake ALL others. Each party in the marriage (husband and wife), must leave singlehood and singlemindedness and bound together as ONE FLESH."

Alicia Jackson Warren

"Don't seek perfection in your partner or in yourself. The journey of marriage will take you on many adventures along the way. Remember why you fell in love and never stop being friends. Sometimes it's the friendship that will be the only thing that sustains you through the tough times. Most importantly, never stop dating. It matters!"

Crystal Smith

"Don't forget that you are still an individual and it's ok to do things separately sometimes."

Jazmeen "Jaz" Ritz

"Keep in mind that you don't own one another. She doesn't BELONG to you and vice versa. Get that out of your head. The sooner you do and just work on mutual respect rather than <u>carnal</u> ownership the better off you will be. When you have that basic respect, that says "I love you, regardless of whether I can control you or not" everything else kind of falls into place."

MENHEFEN

"Communicate and Compromise! And try not to go to bed upset!"

Camille Tyson

"Getting married is not about giving up on who you are and leaving that person behind, its about sharing all of yourself with your partner. Remember that the two of you are stronger together. Listen carefully, love often, and date each other forever."

Dominique Jones

"Don't forget who you were before the marriage because that's what made you fall in love with each other."

Keyonna Andrews

"Marriage is constant! Marriage is effort! Marriage is work! And it takes time, effort and work to earn the rewards of Marriage!"

SCN

"As a married woman, it is important to hold fast to your wedding vows: for better, for worse, for richer, for poorer, in sickness and in health, to love and to cherish, till death do us part.

Has marriage been easy? HELL NO! Love encompasses your feelings for one another and the ability to forgive (you may not forget). Love is compassion and compromise. For love, you are more willing to compromise. It's hard work. Some days are better than others. At the end of the day, you must be able to answer a simple question: do I want to live the rest of my days on this earth with this person (no matter the challenges)? If yes, then go enhance your relationship; if no, do not waste one another's time. Move on.

…And

One more thing: KEEP YOUR BUSINESS TO YOURSELF!!!! If y'all start arguing or if something happens, don't go tell the world. And that includes your best friends! Work on your ish in house!"

Alecia Sillah

"The one thing that I would say is to always find ways to keep the trust in your marriage. Ways to keep trust is keeping no secrets, no hidden friends, no second phone- unless it's for work. Let your spouse know who you're with when leaving out. This helps to stop the insecurities.

Once the trust is broken there is no communication, respect, or emotional connection… all of that goes out the window when trust is broken and it is so hard to rebuild trust. Some relationships don't come back once the trust is gone. Remember to be **mindful** of how you speak to your mate, speak love into them don't make them feel as if you're talking down to them, encourage them with your words and actions. Build them up, don't knock them down."

Kim Battle

"Marriage like any relationship has its peaks and valleys. Not everyday will be sunshine and flowers. But when there is sunshine, bask in it! When dark days come (and they will), choose your words wisely but don't neglect your feelings. Respect **opposing** perspectives but don't feel obligated to abandon your own. Understand that with respect, respect (and did I say respect), those dark days can be short lived. Marriage is about compromise. Work together daily to find common ground and when new challenges arise, remember to seek your partner to solve them. Marriage is not a one wo(man) band, but a trio. Yes, I said trio. God is the lead singer. Now you two get to singing in the background!"

Cassandra Creek

"Women and men think differently. Remember, his way of doing things is not superior or inferior to yours. It's just different from yours. Value him & give him credit for his contributions, even when you wanted something different than what was offered. Fix your face and be gracious. Then, he will be more open to your suggestions and feedback later. Also, appreciate the little things, the routine things, the things that require effort but get lost in the rest of what's going on. You may ask "Why should I appreciate him for doing what he's supposed to do anyway?" Because you are sowing seeds of love today that will grow into a harvest of helpfulness and strategic thoughtfulness from him later."

Crystal Williams

"A few of things that I have learned in the (short) six years that I have been married is that for one, you have to communicate. It may sound cliché but it's the truth. Communication should be a foundation for your marriage in addition to your religious beliefs. Another thing that is important is your ability to compromise. This is the stage that I am in now… I can admit, I can be a very selfish person when it comes to certain things. This is something that I have to work on. I recommend that you start compromising before you go *to the altar. Lastly, your ability to listen is a big factor. Listening to what your spouse is saying, feeling, how things affect them is important and you have to work on improving these things."*

Veronica Bert-Jackson

"Be careful with what you say because angry, hurtful words once spoken, cannot be taken back and will not be forgotten."

Jeanette Riggins

Here are my thoughts on a healthy marriage... Accept and embrace the imperfections and the differences of your spouse to complement yours. This will enable you to grow together into a perfect union, which is more powerful than the two separate individuals. Remember "TWO ARE BETTER THAN ONE."

Edana J. Perry

"You must always put in your best effort. Emotionally, intimately and intellectually. Choose to love each other when it's hard to like each other. Forgive easy and learn from one another. New experiences help to keep the heart happy. Always set goals that better your lives together."

"It is also important to understand your mate. What they like and dislike about you (and vice versa). It's important to understand how your mate views the world... do you have a similar point of view?

I think that having a good understanding of these things and of each other will help you to communicate and grow together."

Anthony & Tiffany Battle

"Everyone can't be the boss in or of the marriage. You have to play on the strengths and attributes that you have and bring to the marriage.

Make sure that you make quality time to spend with each other.

But… some individual time and time to self-reflect is important too."

Anita "Mom" Nash

"Take heed to who people are when they show you who they are. Work as a team with your spouse. Work as a unit. Be fair to each other and no matter what, you have to have each other's backs."

Nicole Jones

Remember that...

Anything worth having takes hard work...

marriage is no different.

This Is Marriage

So… I'm not cool ???

Yeah, I'm just going to fly WWAAYY OFF the handle?

Like I did the last time, right?

So you just going to put me on the need to know...

Basis.

The grounds for arguing,

The underlying foundation for your idea.

Implicated, you got me pegged.

A decimal in a box.

Period.

Can occasionally skunk the groove

But come on now!!

You don't know me better than that!

Sometimes it just comes down to that.

Sometimes it's not all about the facts-

There are no RULES of ENGAGEMENT at home

WE ARE MARRIED!!!!!

Finances in Marriage

It gets CHALLENGING when YOU and I talk about money...

We EXPERIENCE a COMMUNICATION break

The funny thing is...

We want the SAME thing

To work together as a TEAM to accomplish goals

We KEEP TALKING about it.

However, temperatures will continue to rise until we find a SOLUTION

IMMEDIATE ACTION Is required TODAY

We should act NOW

Because…

I LOVE YOU,

I NEED YOU

And I PLAN to spend my life

With YOU

Thoughts on Things I Miss...

Let me begin by saying that I appreciate you and all that you do to keep our family going.

However, with all do respect, there are some things that I miss and feel as though I am missing.

I miss you listening to me, without a quick response.

I miss you writing me.

I miss you rubbing my feet.

I miss you buying me little gifts on my birthday, Valentine's day, Christmas, on our anniversaries and just because.

I miss you kissing my lips (with tongue).

I miss passionate sex.

I miss you making me feel special.

So, now that you know…

What are you going to do about it???

Seeking Validation

Sometimes, I don't feel validated as your wife.

As if everything that I am and have accomplished is because I have you.

Not to say that you haven't been my number one supporter, protector and help mate,

But it feels as if there's nothing that I have added or done for you to make you the man whom I see as great.

Maybe I have....
Maybe I have not....

I couldn't tell you
Because you don't tell me

Maybe I too was always an "x factor"
(In the making anyway...)
Not just you

When we met, I was becoming
Became more than what many expected
Possibly more than even you expected

But I can't tell you that
Share my feelings so openly
Knowing that the defense mechanism will go off
Sounding like an alarm
And firing back the depressing stats

You remind me that...

No black men want to get married
Half of the married ones don't do shit
Or give a shit
The rest aint shit

Most of them don't have a pot to piss

Don't want to be around
Nor help out with the kids

I know, I know…
There is only one you!
And only you could love and do the things you do.
It's because of you that I achieve

And yes, while some of this may be true
You didn't just come in to my life by happenstance

I prayed to the highest of the high for a man like you
Who would truly love and support my wants, needs, dreams and values too

You came into my life and provided that
You shared your knowledge
And I took it and applied it
Taking advantage of every opportunity to manifest

Since day one, I too have been holding you down
I'm loyal, hardworking and financially sound

Today,
I am reminded (maybe not by you)
That he who finds a wife has found a good thing too.

I have been a good thing.

Proverbs 18:22 (NKJV)

> *He who* **finds a wife finds a good** *thing,*
> **And obtains favor from the L**ord**.**

Happy wife, happy life.

Everything is good,
When you have a happy wife,
What they say is true!

Right Now

My husband's hands are full
Right now

My hands are full
Right now

OUR hands are full
Right now

Lord,
Lift this heavy load.
I'm not sure how much longer
Our hands can hold

Permanent changes are unfolding
Emotions are on high
Causing feelings of uncertainty.
To dwell and arise

This is why I pray
Right now
For us
Today

The Sad Day

Today was a sad day.
And the clouds could tell you so.
The ground was drenched in tears.
For reasons you have yet to know.

My friend's love was leaving her.
Said he was walking out the door.
For their vows never meant a thing.
So he would stay with her no more.

She solemnly rode the metro to her new place, in which she found. Not
knowing what to expect on the second time around.
Suddenly her life had changed and she couldn't say if for better or for worst.
Her head hung low from her hearts pain
Outside, you could hear the rain.

Today was a sad day.
And the clouds could tell you so.
The ground was drenched in tears
For reasons that we all now know.

Wanting to comfort my friend,
I told her what is written below...

Rain clouds don't last forever,
The sun will shine again,
Pick your head up my friend, Remain open,
That's how the change begins.

Forced Change

It wasn't what I wanted.

How did we end up here?

The relationship has died,

Yet I am left with the seeds that you have planted here.

Pressing on for little ones who are depending on me.

Smiling at the world because teas; no one wants to see.

As the tears dry and the smile becomes real.

Forced Change has become growth.

And I am happy to be planted here.

Angela D. McPherson

Standing the Test of Time

By: Anita Battle-Williams

Haggai 2:9 "The glory of this present house will be greater than the glory of the former house, says the Lord Almighty. And in this place I will grant peace, declares the Lord Almighty."

As a little girl and teenager I was always somewhat alone. I never had many friends and I always kept to myself. My biggest dream was to graduate from high school, complete college, have a career, marry, have children, take vacations once a year, and live happily ever after. Sounds like a good plan right? Well God will definitely give you your hearts desires, but often times, there will be challenges that will also test your faith.

In October 1990, I met the man of my dreams and did not know it. He knew after two weeks he wanted to marry me as he proclaimed it to my face. I laughed at him and overtime we became friends. A year later, I knew I was falling in love with him, I asked him about his future. More specifically, "What are you planning to do with your life? I am looking for someone who could push and motivate me, not someone I had to drag along." His response was, "I am planning to go into the military?" I said, "OK". At this time, Tony is his name, was a senior in high school and I was a junior in college.

As Tony graduated high school, the day approached for him to leave. I was nervous as I was the one who would take him to the MEPS center in Raleigh, NC where we would sit for an hour crying and wishing each other well. I told him that I would write him every day and that we would see how we would respond to each other upon his return. I told him if he did not come back crazy that we would have a chance to be together.

So before he left, we sat in the car and listened to "End of the Road" by Boys II Men.

The day before bootcamp, I was entangled in a fight with two of Tony's sisters. They entered my place of employment, came behind the counter, grabbed me in my face and began to punch and scratch. I really cannot remember what happened next, but I know I mustered up some strength and threw them both off of me to the point they both went running out of the specialty shop where I worked. The customers who were present asked if I wanted them to call the police and I told them no. It will work itself out.

The next day, I hopped in my rental car and drove to Beaufort, SC to witness Tony, now a US Marine graduate from bootcamp. When he saw me, he asked what happened and I told him. He was very apologetic and I told him not to worry because if and when we marry, I will be marrying him, not his family. So after approximately three months, Tony asked my parents for my hand in marriage, he purchased the ring, and then proposed on Christmas Eve and I happily accepted. Four months later after trying to plan a wedding, we both decided to go to the justice of the peace and begin our lives together.

The first year was great, but the next six years that followed were rocky. You name it, we went through it. From dealing with hanging out with the boys, drinking, pornography, and feeling alone and abandoned as we both disrespected each other in our role of husband and wife. During these years, we having three children did not make it any easier. The buildup had gotten so bad that we separated for a year and a half. I was left alone, a mother of three young daughters all under the age of three. I cried and often found myself going into a depressed state as I cried because of the mess that was created. During this time I tried endlessly to try to fix Tony as he was supposed to be a part of my childhood dreams. But each time I reached out, I could see the further he would run. Then I had a cousin say to me, "Why are you chasing that man? Don't you know that a man is supposed to chase the woman. In the Bible it tells us that a man who finds a woman finds a good thing and obtains favor from the Lord." After hearing this, I stopped chasing my husband and began moving on to start a new life. Deep in my heart, I wanted my family back but also realized that it takes two. So I went to Tony, as it was a weekend for his visitation with his daughters, and told him that I was done chasing him and I was moving on. He will be receiving papers from my lawyer. I also informed him that he would eventually be seeing his daughters with another man in their life if he did not want to be the full time father.

I began seeking the Lord in all of this and began understanding that Jesus loves me more than any man could ever love me. I began to gain strength and know that I am loved. My strength and desire started to come back. My confidence level soared and within two months I was hired on at a local kids clothing store as an assistant retail manager. It gave me hours where I worked a second shift Monday-Sunday with varying days off, but it was a great opportunity as a fresh start. I attended church as my hours allowed and spent time with the girls in my off time. My oldest would look for her daddy, but her twin sisters did not know any better. Then after one long evening at work, I received a several phone calls from Tony and after not answering them, a voice mail was left. When I answered the voice mail, Tony was pleading for his family and wanted a second chance to work on our marriage. I cried because had answered my prayers! God became real to me. I called him back and we began working on our marriage as more challenges began to follow.

After about a week of trying to pull our relationship back together, one of our infant twins were diagnosed with shaken baby syndrome at the local daycare I had them in and all of our daughters were taken away from us. At the time I was staying with my mother and father and we were all suspects as the doctor's reports showed that there had been prior trauma to my daughter. She was in the hospital for three days before Tony went into the hospital, laid hands on her and she woke the next day. The doctor's said a miracle had taken place. But they did warn us that she will have some disabilities that will need to be addressed. Upon releasing her from the hospital, my other-in-law had stepped up and agreed to watch her granddaughters.

In the meantime, I had taken a lie detector test and passed with flying colors, but I was still not allowed to have my children. I had to be supervised when I was with them. So again, I am thankful to my mother-in-law as she became my supervisor so I could take care of my children in her home. During this ordeal, Tony and I became closer, but also knowing we needed to work on us and to try to keep our separation under cover due to other accusations that could be made. We hired legal consultation and after ninety days, our children were returned back to us and we received permanent change of station (PCS) orders to California where we would begin all over with our family. My parents were not happy about my decision to leave for the fear of Tony not living up to his part in the relationship. But I had to look at my mother and tell her that I am trusting God and I have to go to save my family.

I wish I could say that everything was perfect when we arrived to California and settled in, but it was not. For seven years we had to learn to trust and work together to raise our girls. It took dedication from both of us and eventually Jesus settled strongly in both of our hearts to where we began to repair, recover, and flourish. But again, it took both of us wanting Jesus in our hearts.

So since this time, trusting in Jesus Christ has been and still is the center of our marriage, family, and our home. He is the one who has strengthened us and has repaired everything we lost and in the beginning and he has exceeded in meeting my childhood dream. I have not only a bachelor's degree, but two master degrees and four education credentials that I did not have to pay for; my dream career; an amazing man of God; various ways to vacation throughout the year; children who are following the Lord Jesus, a son-in-love who loves his family, and a beautiful granddaughter. I have two beautiful daughters in the US Navy and the daughter who was diagnosed with Shaken Baby syndrome recovered 100% and never had any issues. So Jesus is good and if you have not received Him as your Lord and Savior with an open heart, I encourage to do so by reading the following:

John 3:16 "For God so loved the world that He gave His one and only Son, that whoever believes in Him shall not perish have eternal life."

#TBT Love

YOU ARE MY TREE

I have often wondered what you are to me?

You are my tree

Your strength, to me is like that of an Oak tree

You are my tree

Just as oak trees provide years of longevity and posterity for us to enjoy, so you have been the constant support in my life for over 35 years.

You are my shade, when life's scorching summer heat tries to burn away my ideas and aspirations

Your presence in my life protects me with cool breezy layers of encouragement

You are my protection, when life's rain showers try to wash away my plans and purpose

Your presence in my life is a shelter with leaves of warmth, tenderness and passion

You are my tree

You have been planted by the rivers of water, you bring forth fruit in its season, your leaf does not wither and whatever you do prospers.

Psalm 1:3 New King James Version (NKJV)

[3] He shall be like a tree
Planted by the [a]rivers of water,
that brings forth its fruit in its season,
whose leaf also shall not wither;
and whatever he does shall prosper.

Edana J. Perry

Our Love Inside Out

Our love inside out

Our commitment endures

Our faith fuels our union

Mountains and valleys

Pressure produces strength

Our love like fine wine

My Love overflows

Oceans can't contain it

Philia Agape

Edana J. Perry

Love it when one of the kids say…

"Mommy, you and Daddy are relationship goals"

Ariyah C. Nash
Age 15

SURVIVAL PLANS

Book Club presents:
Takeaways from "Make Love, Make Money, Make It Last"

1. Each partner's perspective is valued. It's putting the perspectives together that helps you to see the bigger picture.

2. Friendship first is one of the keys to a healthy and happy marriage. Friendship develops naturally but like all relationships, it takes work and time to develop and maintain. (So don't just jump in the sack with someone before you get to know them!)

3. God should be an equal (or greater) partner and stakeholder in your marriage. God 34%, you 33% and spouse 33% each. When at a stalemate, take your challenges to the Lord in prayer. Together, ask God for clarity when you are unsure about how to move.

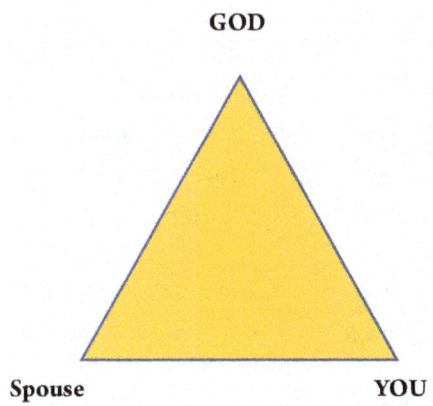

4. Mediate, pray and read scriptures together daily to develop your relationship with GOD and each other.

5. Love is an emotion but marriage is a decision and commitment.

6. Compromising (often) helps keep the decision and commitment together.

7. Do not ask people who are not married or unhappily married for advice- In other words, get you a happily married mentor!

8. It may sound cliché but COMMUNICATE- Talk about the good, the bad and the ugly- and Listen to the good, bad and the ugly.

9. Don't let the things that bother you build up- because it will spill out (eventually) and more than likely turn into something bigger.

10. Decide to have a drama free home- where peace is nurtured-and crazy not an option.

11. Choose your battles wisely. The question was proposed "Do you want to be right all the time? Or happy?" - Know when to let things go.- know when to use your emergency only VETO power.

12. Marriage is multi-dimensional encompassing love, friendship, values and more. Sex is an important ingredient but NOT the main dish. Men need sex and respect while women need intimacy and security. Friendship and communication is the gateway to true intimacy, fulfilled needs and a loving sex life.

13. You must be on the same page and work together when it comes to finances. Finances can make and break some marriages.

14. Bonus- whether you marry the right person or the wrong person it's up to you- Zig Zigglar

Mom and Dad Nash,

Making Love, Making Money, Making It Last (40 years and Counting)- even when times get rough!

SURVIVAL PLANS

The Ends of the Universe

If it's possible, I'd like to travel to
the ends of the universe.
I'd like to see things, live in a new life.
Die and live a new one.
Remember everything, forget nothing.
Give me a sign it's possible.
Even our eyes that see the farthest don't see
anything at all.
I'd like to know if I would see nothing too.
I'd love to know what lies ahead.
Thereafter, let's talk.
I'd like to know why this plane of existence is built this way.
I will speak any language the universe wants me to speak.
Can my mind handle it?
The mind adapts when it's overwhelmed, for sure.
There's no other way.
Maybe it will deteriorate gracefully and become
better the next time the next time around.
Is that all?
Stars, planets, black holes, galaxies,
Supernovae, clusters, rebirth, death?
Is there anything else we haven't thought of?
Is there something more than human experiences that which are universal?
I'd like to know too.

Efflorescent_Child

Universal Balance...

Tale of the Two

Alpha and Omega

Raava and Vaatu
Light and Dark
Gift and Curse

Right and Wrong
Ignorant and Educated
Young and Old

Mistakes and Milestones
Hiring and Firing

Riches and Poor

Breakups and Makeups
Marriage and Divorce
Life and Death
Love and Loss

The Tale of the Two

Through the Fire and the Flood

My life's story, I shall not speak
until I've reached my highest peak
struggles' blows, I dare not show
through the dirt, I tread on slow
held firm by love, my temper's meek
on passages narrow, yet sleek
still, on I go, though death may crow
my battered blood within will flow
though trampled on by moments weak
left a smidge drifting down the creek
when stricken so by vertigo
my soul still lingers down below
while, behind the havoc that life does reek
lay an undesirable, unforgotten streak
press on a flow past the crimson foe
I surpass under stars aglow
pass my cries at a level of shriek
to be absorbed as a little squeak
unjust misfortunes; I'll undergo
as my immaturity, I do outgrow
my foolish ways are an antique
I've found polished ones for the critique
I did bestow a seed to sow
for a chance to see it grow
In a wondrous world mystique
Where unheard comments are oblique
Yet on I'll go, with faith I'll tow
All the way til the finale of my show

Shantayah Murray

Abidemi Hunpon

Abidemi Hunpon was a 2019 candidate for the Hallelujah Anyhow! Scholarship at Prince George's Community College (Largo, MD)

SOME CHANGES

Some changes I have control over

I can change my hair color from brunette to blond,

I can change my nail color from pink to peach,

I can change from living in a house to living in an apartment

Some changes I declare I have no control over

When the sun sets,

When the moon glows,

When a flower blooms,

Your time to be born,

Your time to die,

I can't change the fact that you are not here. I don't like it.

That change came too quick....That change.. That change.. That change...

Some changes I can control

Some changes I can't control... Fact.

Edana J. Perry

Sierra Battle
October 11, 2015 at 12:56 AM

Rest.. Grandma.. Rest.. rest in peace my love.. you have gone home to be with jesus above.. and although we weep here on earth in your absence.. we are so blessed to had enjoyed so much of your presence.. i will cherish every moment we shared together.. from the laughs the cries to our very last goodbyes.. and with every memory i keep.. i vow to also teach.. so one day whn i have children they will know u even though you will never meet.... ill buy them hess trucks for christmas and make them candied yams. Ill tell them how You made them for me everytime i was in town. How they were the best hands down and all around. And ill laugh and smile if they have a thing for pepsi.. ill tell thm they inherited that one staight from their great grandma Colen.. ill tell thm how u had cases stackd up and cold ones guaranteed.. ill be sure to tell them every fond memory.. i promise.. n youll see.. tht one day every little one of me will have a little bit of you for the world to see.. and that is called genetics.. 😅 incase you were wondering.. and i hope that makes you smile.. spent a couple hours writing before i came up with that line.. but all jokes aside.. one day.. theyll know all about their great grandma Colen.. and although its goodbye for now.. one day we will see each other again.. and although i feel like i cant wait.. The Good Lord knows that i will.... so until then.. ill just say rest..rest Grandma.. rest and know that youll never be forgotten by all who loved you.. and all who will learn of u..

Something I wrote for my Grandma the day after she passed but couldn't get myself together enough to utter these words at her funeral... i guess it's better late than never...

Grandma,

I had a hard time coping with your departure.

Wish that I could pick up the phone and just call you.

973-595-9025…

I dial in my head.

Pick up a scratch off and a Pepsi on my way in.

Watch the Price is Right with eggs, bacon and buttered toast in the morning.

Stay up late and talk all night.

The last time I saw you just didn't seem right

You couldn't remember my name… sake

Now nothing will ever be the same again.

The Loss

We had been married so many years,

The pain of losing you caused a flood of tears.

Faith in our Heavenly Father up above

Helped to cope with the loss of the one I loved.

Comfort is knowing God will take care of me while you're away.

Rest in Peace, farewell my Love.

God will reunite us someday.

Karen Mayo Hogan

Dreamed

I dreamed that I fell into deep water
I learned to breathe and adapt
I lived and existed under the water
I ate the colorful dough that was provided to
me by my daughter
I woke up with the notion

that I had actually survived a drowning.

Darcelle Battle

Underwater x DC Photography

From the "New DC" Collection

What's Left

My life has ruptured

Hard to adjust without you

Hole in my heart

Soulful Melodies

Lyrics from your heart and soul

Tru blu expressions

Cities, Countries seen

Reflections of a full life

Rich memories to relive

Edana J. Perry

Heartfelt Prayer

Precious Lord up above,

Please help him cope with the loss of those he loved.

Help ease his immeasurable sorrow and pain,

His life without them will never be the same.

God, grant him serene inner peace,

This will help his heartfelt tears cease.

God knows death of loved ones is so hard to bear,

But He has them in His Loving Care.

Today there's so much unspeakable sorrow,

But God has promised a brighter tomorrow.

That's when you'll be able to embrace,

The memories of your loved ones smiling face.

Remember the love you feel for them will never part;

It's embedded deeply within your heart.

This is my heartfelt prayer and may God continue to keep you and your family in His Care.

Karen Mayo-Hogan

The Call

He was not asleep when he heard the Master's call.

His spirit rose slowly and he stood, oh so tall.

His heart was filled with cheer

As he saw God standing near,

Telling him he was not alone.

He said come in my child, you are home.

He hurried as he could not wait,

To enter into those beautiful pearly white gates.

Then God looked at him and saw a tear,

And he knew why it was there.

They could hear loving family members cry.

Why wasn't he given the chance to say he loves us all, farewell, goodbye.

God told him he'd be with his family in this time of sorrow.

He promised that a brighter day for them is coming tomorrow.

And shorter will be the days that grief embrace;

Replaced by a sense of peace and grace.

Yes, God has placed a wealth of sweet memories so he'll never depart,

A million loving memories of him will forever dwell, deep in your hearts.

Karen Mayo Hogan

Palm of His Hands

God holds my life in the palm of His Hands,

Already he has decided when I will enter the Promised Land.

For me, I have no fears.

I've already lived beyond the promised years.

But I don't want to see my children cry,

I really, really don't want to die.

Yet, I know my time here is no more,

So I'm ready to enter Heaven's Door.

I know for you all, it may be a sad day

When the Lord's Angel comes my way

To take me on a Chariot Ride

To that Heavenly Home where I will Eternally reside.

But please don't spend much time weeping,

Cause I'm no longer sleeping.

Truth be told,

Jesus and I are walking those Streets of Gold.

Now I just ask that all live right so someday you can see,

King Jesus and other loved ones standing beside me.

And one day when your own journey begins,

Jesus will let me open Heaven's Gate, so we can all meet again.

In the meantime, to remind you I will always be in your midst,

That passing warm breeze you I feel

Karen Mayo-Hogan

IN LOVING MEMORY OF A MOTHER, GRANDMOTHER, SISTER-FRIEND, AUNTIE

Marcella Mickle Black
May 30, 1958- April 26, 2020

"Sister Friends" 4-Life and Beyond

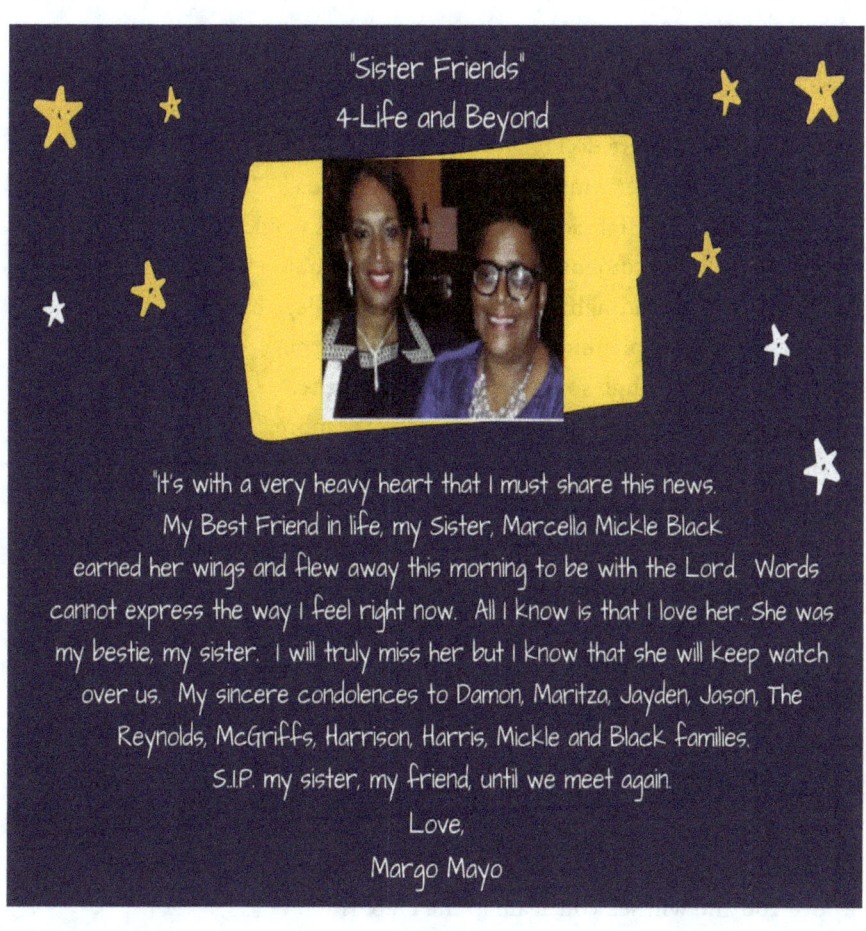

"It's with a very heavy heart that I must share this news. My Best Friend in life, my Sister, Marcella Mickle Black earned her wings and flew away this morning to be with the Lord. Words cannot express the way I feel right now. All I know is that I love her. She was my bestie, my sister. I will truly miss her but I know that she will keep watch over us. My sincere condolences to Damon, Maritza, Jayden, Jason, The Reynolds, McGriffs, Harrison, Harris, Mickle and Black families.

S.I.P. my sister, my friend, until we meet again.

Love,

Margo Mayo

My Sister, My Bestie, My Friend

What can I say? Where do I begin?
For as long as I can remember we have been friends.
We met just before High School so that each of us would know
That we always had someone where in times of trouble, we could go.
We stomped right through High School, took College by storm.
We burst into Life's planning like locusts that swarm.
Oh, we've been through some things, that's for sure.
And that's how we knew we'd be friends forever more.
We laughed through the good times and cried through the bad.
Marcella, you were the best friend that I had.
You were my Sister, my Bestie, my Friend and
We'd remain that way until the end.
That's why it's hard for me to understand;
This turn in our lives that was not planned.
But God stepped in, He had a Plan of His Own.
He looked in His Book, saw your name, and called you Home.
And off you flew, no time for Good-bye.
You saw your Mansion in the sky.
So as I sit here, I imagine that I hear your laughter.
I Love You and will see you again in the Here After.

Covid 19-20? Or Forever

Margo Mayo

3D
Dreams, Daughter, Departure

My dreams of picking up a mocha frappe and pumpkin bread for you... ... Lingering

My dreams of the two of us spending hours in the make-up store without condemnation... Fading

My dreams of getting up early, letting you sleep and then swinging by and picking you up so we can have a Girls Day Out... evaporating

My dreams of hearing your say, "Ma" or "Mother"... ... Hopeful

Dreams having you by my side preparing your "spicy" macaroni and cheese for the holidays... ... Lingering

Dreams of hearing you sing around the house ... ... Lingering

Dreams of spending all my money so you can furnish your first apartment... ... still hopeful but not reality

Dreams of me, you and your sister going on our mother/daughter vacation somewhere with a lot of sun, sand and adventure... Fleeting

Dreams of showing how proud of you I am at who you continue to evolve to be... Fading

Dreams of seeing you again, because I will see you again in Glory!.... Just deferred

3D_ Dreams, Daughter, Departure are lingering, fading, evaporating, hopeful, fleeting but more importantly just <u>deferred!</u>

Edana J. Perry

My Soul Is Tired

My soul is tired, this I know;

And I told the Angels so.

They can come to give me a Chariot ride

To that Glorious, Wonderful, Heavenly Side.

Sorry dear ones, I know you did not want me to go.

But there is something you should know.

I'm here now with loved ones about to meet

King Jesus, guess what, I have a front row seat.

Dear loved ones as you weep, keep your heads held high,

So that Jesus can wipe away the tears that you cry.

And as your tears begin to fade,

Think of the loving memories that we made.

Also remember my intrusion in everyone's life was out of love and affection,

Just wanted to make sure your life's decision was guided with God's direction.

Continue to follow God, love one another, so that we may

All be together again someday.

Karen Mayo-Hogan

What I Gained From My Loss

Written by Jason Whiting

"Robinett, Jason, come here. I have something to share with you kids." During a day of my preadolescence for which the exact date I may not recall but the events of the day remain true to memory, my mother called my sister and I to the living room of the roughly 700 square foot two-bedroom apartment in which the three of us lived. On that day, my mother revealed to us that she had previously been diagnosed with cancer, and that she was recently informed of a diagnosis of the same plague in a severer form. At the time, I had a superficial understanding of what the illness was, what it meant, how it affected my mother, and how it would change my life. What I did know was hair loss is a notable effect of the disease, so my mother's full head of hair added to the flood of curiosity and inquisition that followed the revelation. The revelation became real to me a few moments later when my mother swiftly removed what I recognized as her full head of hair and what my older sister understood to be a synthetic hair piece. What my mother had revealed to us that day was shocking to us both, but the immediate worry and anxiety quickly dissipated due to our mother's assurance that her prevailing strength and faith in God would make everything ok.

My sister began religiously tracking our mother's newly established hair growth journey. I grew to appreciate the short, textured, curly hair that was beginning to resemble my own. I also grew to enjoy the morning walks my mother and I began to take to school on weekdays that replaced the car rides I was once accustomed to. One of my favorite additions to our transitioning lifestyle was the weekly deliveries of numerous hefty bags containing a variety fresh produce, whole foods, and most importantly, sweet snacks and kid-friendly fruit juice pouches. As time progressed, time spent with mom grew less and less. Habitual chemo-therapy treatments and hospitalization not only retracted our physical presence together, they withdrew our conscious connection. On visits, she often laid in a vegetative state induced by opiates. The casual conversation and motherly affection I was used to disappeared. Our time together came to an end on April 2nd of 2014.

Abruptly, I distanced myself from my mother's death. I withdrew from familial conversations centered on her passing. I was hesitant to attend the celebration of life ceremony my family and our home church collaborated on to commemorate her life. The day after she passed, I returned to school dressed in a demeanor of normality. It was not an intention of mine to make the news of her passing available to any close friends, teachers, or counselors. My dissociation from the tragedy eased my departure from middle school into high school, allowing the transition to be one thought of with optimism and hopes of high achievement. The ending of my freshman year was marked with the first grade point average of my academic career with a weight of less than 3.0. It was during this period that patterns of tardiness and subpar performance occasionally arose. These patterns became normal throughout high school, but worsened nearing the end of every school year— typically around April. My academic performance paled in comparison to social performance. Making friends and establishing diverse social connections was not necessarily challenging given my quirky and goofy yet friendly and sociable persona, but soon normal patterns of interpersonal presence drastically declined. In the final quarter ending my senior year, absence was at all time high and interaction with life outside of my bedroom was at an all time low. During my isolation my closest connection was to my bed, where I laid for weeks overcome with sadness, grief, and apathy. For weeks, I covered up in depression.

"Jason, your counselor called. She said they're going to work with you and have counselor there that just wants to talk to you. You just have to push yourself to go to school on Tuesday. Being behind on schoolwork and having countless absences, I accepted the possibility of me graduating high school was slim to none. Somehow, I managed to detach from the comfort of my bedsheets and the anxiety of what students and faculty would think of my resurrection and return to school. After spending some time working on classwork in a study area that I that I was granted the comfort of having to myself, a gentle-faced woman with a serene aroma introduced herself to me as a social worker. During the encounter, I tearfully found the courage to open up about what I had been going through. And for once, I acknowledged that my mother had passed away.

About a month later, I proudly walked across the stage of Towson University and received my high school diploma accompanied by the cheers of family, friends, and faculty. After returning to my troop, I pushed my way through time constraints and earned the highest rank of Eagle. Most importantly, I regained the sense of joy, optimism, and ambition that was lost and gained the courage to share personal experiences of loss, pain, and hardship that I distanced myself from. The courage and strength I gained helped me to overcome a crippling addiction to pornography, forced me to replace a tendency of procrastination with efforts of productivity and personal development, and renewed my passion for academic achievement and non-profit service. These changes led to a variety of personal achievements including earning a 4.0 GPA in my first semester of college, becoming more actively involved with volunteership, and developing an aptitude to learn more about business and finance by reading and networking.

This year has elucidated the importance of acknowledging loss, and the necessity of experiencing the grief normal to losing a loved one. Although my mother i no longer wi me, I know she would be proud of who I've become

Jason Whiting (Son)

SURVIVAL PLANS

I Choose to Remember

Remembering hurts sometimes, remembering helps sometimes.

Your favorite sayings, keep you alive! I choose to remember.

Your favorite foods, I eat, keep you alive! I choose to enjoy!

Your favorite songs; trap, R&B, or gospel, i listen to, keep you alive! I choose to listen!

Your favorite wardrobe pieces I smell, I wear or just stare, keep you alive! I choose to embrace!

Your photos, I look at and place close to my heart, keep you alive!

Even with the bittersweet, I still choose to remember.

Remembering redirects the energy from the pain to focus on precious memories.

Memories, moments and mayhem all wrapped in love.

I choose to remember, I choose to enjoy, I choose to listen, I choose to embrace, I choose to view.

I choose to remember and keep you alive forever!

Thankful for the twenty six!

Edana J. Perry

Now I Sit

I sit and look out the window at the stillness of the day pondering the reality of your absence... I daydream about yesterday and yesteryear. My perspective is beginning to be molded by what I gained as well as by what I loss...

Yes, I miss you immensely but I am thankful for your birth... I gained thankfulness

Yes, I miss those future opportunities that we could share but I am thankful for the memories that we made.... I gained appreciation

Yes, I miss the intertwining of your life with mine but I am thankful for you being in my life... I gained a robust sense of who I am.

Yes, now I sit and ponder your absence. I am thankful for being able to love you and you loved me back... I gained thoughtfulness.

My pain is great because my love for you is larger than the Sun.

Now I sit and I am thankful and appreciative that your spirit came thru mine... that your time on earth I was apart of...that, I loved you and you loved me

You are forever engrained in my life.... your influence and personality will live on forever...

Edana J. Perry

Waiting x DC Photography

From the "New DC" Collection

Second Chances

Alan Kahn

This essay will be very different from essays that I have previously submitted to this journal. My previous essays dealt with issues and concerns in the Human Services field on either a global scale or the Human Services, A.A.S. program at the College. This essay is different from those, as it recounts a transitional period in my life- and therefore is very personal and cathartic in nature.

My wife was diagnosed with cancer in 2008… During that time, she endured a horrible 6 weeks of suffering, until she died in Hospice on April 23, 2008. Once she died, I continued to work and live in our home. It was not long before my life fell apart. I was depressed and could barely get up in the morning. I was often late to work and subsequently, I ended up getting terminated. Eventually, I stopped paying my bills and the bank began foreclosure procedures on our home. I had hit rock bottom and was at the lowest point in my life.

One day (during this time), I went to "hang out" with a friend of mine, but when I was ready to leave, he begged me to spend the night because he knew that mentally and physically, I was in no shape to drive home. However, I left… As the story would go, I ended up driving "erratically" and was pulled over by the police. From there, things progressed quickly but, I can recall the officer asking me to "get out of the car." In that moment, (as I was getting out), something "happened" to me (I am still not sure what), but I came out of the car swinging. I hit the cop in the jaw and he went down like a "ton of bricks"… Then the next thing that I recall is that his partner struck me over the head with his baton hard, so hard that I still get headaches from it to this day. As I attempted to get up, the officer struck me with his baton again, this time hitting me in the back until lost my breath.

When I woke up, I was in a jail cell. I was completely disordered and mad as hell! I refused to say anything, so the police had no choice but to keep me locked up for about a week. What happened next is still a "bit blurry" and complicated, but let me say that when I appeared in court, there was my son (seeing his Dad in an orange jump suit w/ a psychotic look on his face)." I also noticed that my son and my lawyer (a friend of mine), spoke with the judge for a while before the procedures began. When the judge came back into the court room, he said to me that he "was releasing me into my son's custody," and he also expressed his sympathy about the recent loss of my beloved wife. He stated that the only reason he was releasing me was because of my military service to our country… but my release was conditional. I had to leave the county and State of Georgia ASAP. I was released from jail that day and on a plane to LA the next morning.

So, I up and move to Los Angeles (LA) toward the end of 2008 to live with my son. Although I was grateful to be out of jail, I felt that my life was over. I thought "the sooner I die, the better life would be." So during the early days living in LA, I stayed in my son's home, I did not venture out or socialize with anyone. In fact, for almost 2 months I basically stayed in my room… but as time passed, I slowly began to feel a little better… Then one day, my son took me to the Veteran's (VA) Hospital in LA, where I spoke to a psychotherapist. She was very kind and supportive of me- which eventually helped me to recover. She recommended that I attend therapy, so each day my son would drop me off at the VA and return to pick me up later that day. This became our routine until one day, I told him that "I will catch the bus home by myself."

From that day forward, I slowly began to get up early and catch the bus to the VA for group therapy, recreational activities and of course the food! The VA in LA had a robust program of helping homeless veterans- and technically, I was homeless since I no longer had a home to call my own. At the VA, I received support and funds while I worked hard to get back on my feet. Then one afternoon during a visit with the staff psychiatrists, (who looked at my military and medical records) I was advised that the best thing for me to do was to file for disability. I learned that if I get diagnosed as 100% disabled, I could live in VA Housing (the old soldiers home) and enjoy the beauty of leaving near the beach in LA (the VA was a mile from Santa Monica Beach). So I filed for disability and waited patiently.

Within that 6 months, I had finally began to venture out to explore LA and its surroundings, while waiting for my disability paperwork to be approved. One day, as I was traveling around (walking), I came upon a "soup kitchen" and I stopped and talked with the folks there. I even sat down and had a bite to eat with them. The director came up to me and stated that I had a "knack" for talking to these folks. I said "well I am just like them!" He looked at me with a "puzzled" expression on his face and then asked me if I "would you like to volunteer at the kitchen?" I told him that I would need to think about it but agreed to stop by the next day with my answer.

Once home, I told my son about it… but before I could finish he stated "you are going back there tomorrow and will take that volunteer job!" So it was confirmed. The next day, I went back to the soup kitchen and embarked on what would soon become my road to recovery and a way to tap into my true calling – helping others. By the end of my first year in LA, I was working at not only the Soup Kitchen but the homeless shelter and a family counseling center, all as a volunteer.

My time at the family counseling center gave me the opportunity to connect with the director who eventually stated and re-affirmed that I "have some essential skills for working with people". I told him about my background, credentials and then she asked me to bring in my resume, professional and academic credentials. It took me awhile to gather all of my diplomas, transcripts and professional licenses but I finally I did. When I brought them in to her (the director), she was impressed and asked me if I "would like a paying job." At first I was scared, I was convinced that I would never work a "real job" again, nor did I want to… "my plan" was to collect disability from the VA and live in the "Old Soldiers Home," retire and walk the streets of beautiful LA.

But that night, as I recapped my day with my son over dinner, he told me (before I could even finish my words/thoughts) – "you are taking that job!" Therefore, the next day I went to the director of the Family Counseling Center and told the director, "yes" I am interested in getting this job. At this point, everything went fast. Within the week, I was working (part-time) at the Los Angeles Veterans Hospital- and I was convinced, that I was dreaming! I never thought in a million years that I would ever work again… never mind working at the very VA Hospital that gave me so much help and support.

On my first day of work, I was scared to death… and my boss was a "youngish" psychiatrist with long blond hair. She came over to welcome me and said that she has read over my resume and was very impressed. She also stated that I would be working on the "in-patient ward" with homeless "Vets", who were dealing with drug, alcohol addiction and/or PTSD. She said to me, "are you ready to get to work?" I said "yes Mam!" So for the next year, I worked on Ward C of the Veterans Hospital in LA, a mile from Santa Monica beach.

My first assignment was to make sure that all of the veterans who were admitted to the ward were bathed and fed. I went from sitting in my son's home watching TV eating & sleeping to grabbing angry and "filthy" Veterans and getting them bathed and fed. Some of these individuals had been living on the streets since Vietnam… I kept on thinking "what have I gotten myself into??" However, as days, weeks and months passed, I realized that the VA runs very much like the military, which means that you give the new guy the crappiest job and see how he handles it! I did this thankless job for 3 months before my Boss (the psychiatrist), told me to start a Group Therapy program with the group of Veterans applying for benefits on the ward… Again, I was really scared as I have not done this kind of work for a least 6 months before my wife had passed.

As I approached this group of Veterans, I felt happy and sad all at the same time. I realized if it wasn't for my son's help, those Veterans could be me. I felt a small surge of some kind of power inside that me grabbed each Vet and hugged them! What I was feeling was the "calling" that first propelled me into the helping profession. Needless to say, I got into my work and developed a well-ran Veterans group psychotherapy program that benefited all of us! A few months passed and already, I was back to counseling and running Vet groups. It was here that I realized that despite my inner pain, the emptiness of loss and abandonment that I was "really" working again!!! I was a "helper" doing my life's work and living in my life's calling. Within a year, my boss called me over and asked me if I would be interested in a full time job? Again, I was scared at first but I realized that I was working to overcome my fears by helping these Vets. This could also mean more money… But the caveat was that the job was in Washington DC… As my Director disclosed this information, I felt a cold chill run through my body. Stuck, my boss said "think about it for a few days" but "no longer than a week." She stated that they need a good person there ASAP.

That night I talked to my son about the opportunity, as I had in the past… This time he was skeptical. He knew what shambles I was in when I arrived in LA and he was afraid that if I lived on my own, I would end up living on the street, be back in jail again or worse…. Fortunately, he called his brother, who was living in NYC at the time and they both decided that it would be good for me to take the job. The plan was that I would work during the week and spend the weekends in NYC with my oldest son…, so within a week I was on a plane headed for Washington, D.C.

When I finally arrived in D.C. and went to my room, (my son found me a room in a boarding house in the Petworth area of D.C.) which is in walking distance to the VA Hospital where I would be working. We all agreed to make my life as simply as possible- no car, no home or apartment, just a nice clean room where the only thing that I had to do was pay my rent once a month. My oldest son ended up paid my rent for almost half a year before I was able to do so for myself. The full time job at the VA gave me something that I did not expect, a decent salary (well at least to me), which my sons took from me every month except for a small living allowance for me. The DC VA is nothing like the VA in LA, the VA DC was fast paced, loud and I had very little time to get "adjusted" to life here. I was immediately given 40 cases and I was told that I had to "follow up" with all of these Veterans by yesterday. So for the next year and a half, I lived on my own, working in our nation's capital and doing something I never would have imagined 2 years ago ... I had a life again.

As agreed upon, I got on a bus every weekend and traveled to NYC to stay with my older son. One other very "important" aspect of my story is the fact that I ended up rebuilding a relationship with my older son, who I had a strained relationship with since his mother and I had divorced. So with my traveling to NYC to stay with him, I seen it as an opportunity to repair that damaged relationship with my son/sons. These (relationships) are still a challenge (and opportunity) that I work on regularly. But one thing that I have learned is that no matter what the circumstances are, a divorce is a traumatic event for children of any age. So (back to the story) there I was in NYC staying with this grown man who for the last 10 years had a terrible relationship with me. What a dilemma? I thought to myself (as I still do to this day) can I do this? Can I improve a relationship with my son who "feels" I abandoned him, his brother and mother almost 20 years ago? I often asked myself "Can I overcome all the mistakes and errors that I made when they were growing up?" I prayed to God every day to give me guidance to do this monumental task.

I had been able to return to a meaningful and productive job doing what I love "helping others" Could I do this again? With my sons? I was guided by two fundamental ideas in this quest: **1) He is my son and I am his father; 2) Unconditional Love,** as simply as I can put it, unconditional love for meant no matter how my son treated me, I responded with the love of a parent and promised myself that nothing he could say will ever push me away from him, trust me he tried!! He was angry, condescending and hateful of me. Well, to condense this story a bit 10 years later, my son and I still have "issues" that need to be resolved between us, but he has become my best friend and I rely on him in so many ways. We talk daily (text) and spend most of my free time at his home.

There is also one other and more important development that occurred in my time at the DC Veterans Hospital… I applied for a very unusual job, a coordinator position for the Human Services program at Prince George's Community College. After a few interviews, the Dean at the time (John Rosicky) offered me the job! So I not only did I come back from either being dead from suicide or 100 % on VA Disability, but here I was on the verge of running a Human services Program at a college! So my job has turned into a career that has entrusted me with helping young people become "Helpers" just like me.

I have a wonderful and meaningful career (teaching at Prince George's Community College) and a really great relationship with my son's especially my older son! This is where the story gets complicated, currently I am very happy, and I have a great job and a great relationship with my sons. I work hard during the school year at the college and when the summer comes, I spend my entire time with my sons who live and work in LA. I hike, eat great food (my younger son is a chef) spend quality time with my sons talking about world issues, social justice topic's and of course our relationship. I find it hard to imagine that 10 years ago, I was depressed, devastated, traumatized and suicidal. I truly believed that I would never work again. My life was destined to living in

VA housing, being labeled as a "disabled Veteran" and my happiness was going to dinner at the VA mess hall.

Then one day while hiking around Mt Hollywood, I noticed something I never noticed before? It seems like all the folks, that I watched on top of Mount Hollywood, were actually couples and families. I thought for a moment, could I ever be in a relationship again? I thought about it all week and as I hiked through the summer, I saw couples everywhere! Again the thought ran across my mind – can I ever be in a relationship again? Could I ever find someone like my wife? Who is as thoughtful, kind, giving and most important my best friend? Also someone who was great at taking of me, while I took care of other less fortunate in society. Then the rational part of my mind spoke up (Not much of a rational mind) "Listen, you got a great job and career, more importantly you have a great relationship with your sons, and you are 68 years old,- a relationship- forget about it!! Come on 2 out of 3 isn't bad!"

In conclusion, I guess what I want everyone to take away from this memoir is how important finding meaning and purpose in your life is when you go through a traumatic catastrophe! Also, I want you to remember and cherish how important family and friends are in your recovery! I firmly believe that without the love and support of my son's, I would be dead or homeless! Also despite my ambivalence about the VA, it served me well and helped me to get back to a meaningful life by offering medical, psychological, and employment assistance. I believe that I am a very fortunate individual who has so much to be grateful for in my life. I try to apply what I learned from this "ordeal" to my being a counselor/educator. What do I mean?? Students come into my class with all sorts of baggage and even traumatic issues (not unlike myself) ... I try to offer the same patience, and kindness that was shown to me. I try to show them empathy, understanding and even love! As Carl Rogers stated over 50 years ago that "teaching is like counseling" it is about facilitating a positive, healthy and growing environment. My son's and the VA created that for me, so my goal now is to create it for the students.

I have no doubt, like me, all my students are very resilient. I will do this work until the day that I die. As for me, I am currently still searching for a special woman in my life, I am not sure what I am looking for in a relationship, should she be a New Yorker? Should she be younger than me, my age, should she be Jewish?? I know time is not on my side, my long-term goals are not to attractive" So here I am, near the end of my life but also at the beginning? Could I ever find a partner again? Who knows? However, 3 out of 3 would be ain't bad- in fact it's good.

Nightmare into Reality

    Some say, my life is a nightmare
Horror in their eyes and heart in the despair
    But what if I told you, life isn't fair
But hope for your future that she is dressed and prepared

    Yes, she knows how to please you and meet your every need
She is as beautiful as a light. Through your tunnel of life. It is her that you see

    We all have possibilities made in the fantasy of our mind
But life is not so, it is an experience through time
    When we sleep alone, and things seem out of line
A woman called future will whisper in our ear and ease our mind

So, think not of your tomorrow as a chance to miss
But live your present as a gift. So tomorrow will add to your filling of bliss

    All things come together as we live in the now
Just remember, the nightmare is the reality of meeting your future with a smile

Kevin Harrison

Starchild the Urban Unicorn

The Dream

Before I married,
I dreamt I died

I stood veiled in Ivory
Amid the greenest pasture
It was the size of a large football field
And I was alone

The sun shined like a beacon
So bright.
I shielded my face with my elbow
As it reflected off salt stained eyes

I heard the trumpets sound
 harmonizing with the other instruments
A small jazz funeral processional
Approaching
Everyone dressed in black

Instruments beautifully wailing

I'll fly away

As I realized what was happening
I was no more … …

I think I flew away

March
2013

The Future...

Mrs. Nash.

Love and Loss

```
              F Z V M H J                     R C E T D N
            K S J H U G S E                 F E K S T R K V
          C J O U R N E Y C A             O K Y S S N A I I A
        P T S U O I C E R P J L         R P I L H E Q O M M S K
      W G H A N D S O M E I G P       G C L S I O R P T S L L S
    C N N P E A C E V X H L T G N   I P Z O S M L T C R F S U B B
    G V I S N O D E T C E N N O C V H I C S I A Y S O U E I E O A
    Z V L U C E L I N E A G E L E S H H S S N F M W M H L I B L S
    I E A U N W F I F H V M F N E E Y S L S G C A L M D B K L H F
    N A E B E C A I H Z E W E X L L V N Q S H I T I U M A S M W J
    S O H G P L O R L P N S Y P X R D O M E O T R N N T R S G T R
    Z D I R V S A N M N S G N C I J N I L L P S I K I Y E S S S K
      M N G V S U N D E R S T A N D I N G E E E M H C Q N E X P
      R G E I Y H W K I N D N E S S N A H C P M O Z A C L R G X
      V T C I L L T T Y T R B E V O L P E I S O N W T K U A D C
        I L Q R E E G N H I L J I W R M H R J D Y O I C V C L
        H N O E F R N E E T O T X X Z O R P V W K R O E C E D
        S E V E T T O M M C N P N E C B R X L D Z N L W R
        I U N E M S A L A L H A D E H S I N I M I D E E J
          E N V M G E R C K L T L D B P N F H T H J H C
          Z E Y A T B P S R I W Z A Q F F S Q N T E
            I E T K K F W F E F O Q E M U N A E R
            Q A D C I K E O N H L R Z L S E G A M
              B E S X N Z R C B E U G P N O C I
              Z R D F G E E N K C F X T V Q
                T U O A V C L E A B U S E
                  P L G E P E T A L E R
                    S R U N I O N
                    W A N T S
                      G B B
                        G
```

WORD LIST:

ABUSE	FULFILLMENT	KISSING	PRICELESS
ATTRACTION	GOD	LESSON	RELATE
BESTFRIENDS	GROWTH	LIFE	RELIGION
CARE	HANDSOME	LINEAGE	SEXY
CARESS	HEALING	LINK	SOULMATE
COMMUNICATION	HEAVEN	LONELY	STRESS
COMPANIONSHIP	HELP	LOSS	TOGETHER
CONNECTED	HOLY MATRIMONY	LOVE	UNCONDITIONAL
DIFFERENCES	HOPE	LOVEMAKING	UNDERSTANDING
DIMINISHED	HUGS	LURE	UNION
DOMESTIC	HURT	LUST	VULNERABLE
ENERGY	JEWEL	NEEDS	WANTS
FAMILY	JOURNEY	PATIENCE	WARM
FOREVER	KINDNESS	PEACE	
FORGIVENESS	KISS	PRECIOUS	

Learning

and

Leadership

"Adversity and challenges are life's way of creating strength. Adversity creates challenge, and challenge creates change, and change is absolutely necessary for growth. If there is no change and challenge, there can be no growth and development."

—Willie Jolley

Thoughts on Growth
& Good Fruit vs Bad Fruit

I have always believed that new growth was a fruitful good thing,

But as I have grown in time, insight and wisdom I have come to realize that all fruit doesn't reap the sweet rewards.

If you plant your garden in good, fertile soil and water it with love, it often reflects that. It grows upward and towards the sun.

Strong rooted, these plants have the ability to blossom and bloom into beautiful flowers, developing resilience, even when weathering the storms of life.

But...

If you neglect your garden, plant it in an unsustainable environment, shade the sunlight and harvest it in negativity... chances are that the same seed can wither. It can bear fruit that is sour and seeps in bitterness.

I've been around long enough to know and see with my very own eyes how two of the very same seeds can have two very different life trajectories.

That same seed and garden, with unlimited potential to be beautiful and radiant, can become weeded, shrouded by adversity and littered with thorns. Twisted and winding in a fight to survive.

When it comes to people... that seed can be the same.

I have found that our environments, situations, relationships, decisions, choices and trauma can have the same impact on one's ability to produce good fruit.

It can even be passed down in the DNA like your hair, eyes and skin color.... and as you marinate on that... I can attest to the fact that;

I have witnessed, with my own eyes examples of this.

I have known a brother who murdered his own brother- birthed from the same mother, due to a seed of jealousy.

I have seen two sisters from the same home, with the same parents take two different pathways- one fruit bearing and the other path barren.

I have had cousins and friends who have had crack addicted parents and unstable home environments who either rose up or fell down.

Family members and even family friends who chose to sling dope and or sell guns- having been reformed or incarcerated now.

Children raised in Christian homes, who turn to a life of sin-despite their upbringing.

And Sons and daughters who harness self-hatred for the ones who love, have provided and protected them… Misdirected anger and confusion- leading to poor decision making and isolation.

That's right, having been on this earth for well over three decades I have seen quite a bit.

And I have yet to say that I have seen it all!

But what I have seen has taught me that we are very much like a seed. In the right conditions- with the faith of a mustard seed, we can either be supportive, resilient and bloom, bearing the sweet fruits of life- love, happiness, money, success in the careers of our choice.

Or we can enable poor behaviors, allow our adverse conditions, lack of, environments and misunderstandings to dictate our actions and swallow up our lives.

Each day we all have a choice to choose!
A decision to make!
A cross to bear!
And a fight to fight!

Pick your fruit!

Or…

Your poison!

Harness and spread love and light,

Or..

Suppress it in negativity and darkness…

Because that seed can be YOUR child,
That seed can be YOUR student,
That seed can be the people YOU work with,
That seed can be the people you live amongst,
That seedcan be those you break bread with,

That seed can be your family members,

Or

THAT SEED CAN BE YOU!

Simple yet Scientific
Thoughts about Life and Energy

Energy is so real
Energy can be positive and negative.
...it can also be neutral.

Energy balance can be achieved!

Energy is power,
Power is electric!

Electricity equals Energy!!!

Energy that is produced by Man is manpower
Manpower, is a valuable resource
Money is also a valuable resource

Having money and manpower is an invaluable asset- made from valuable resources.

Value is determined by what that thing can do for you.

Invaluable assets are resources which money cannot buy or measure worth
Some invaluable resources include love, positive relationships, knowledge, freedom and free will.

Free will is also a form of power!
Free will can lead to freedom!
Freedom is power!

Power is not free

Power must be handled responsibly.

So now, let's recap...
Energy is electric
Electricity produces power

Power created by man is manpower

Manpower is an invaluable asset

Freedom is power

Great power and freedom comes with great responsibility or a greater cost.

Now, let's move on…

Power must be directed

Power is energy
Energy emits signals
Signals are messages
Messages travel as directed through receptors

Receptors are the persons, places or things on the receiving end!

Please read again!

LEADERSHIP CLASS

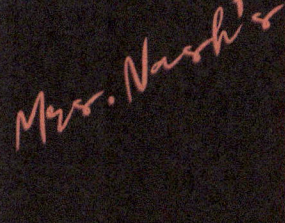

Mrs. Nash's

1) Leadership is a verb, it requires action

2) Leadership requires integrity

3) Leadership requires good listening and communication skills

4) Leadership requires teaching and mentoring

5) Leadership requires problem solving and decisive decision making

6) Leadership requires a pleasing personality

A Letter for My Daughter Zoe

Zoe,

I love you very much.
The way that I show my love is by helping, teaching and preparing you to be the best version of yourself.

Sometimes I have to be firm.
Sometimes I have to be more soft.
But know that I want you to be GREAT!
Because I see greatness in YOU!

Right now, it is more important than ever that you learn about good and bad decision making- They say that by twelve years old, you should understand the difference between right and wrong.

I want you to understand the difference as well as, begin to understand how your decisions can lead to different outcomes that may impact your life. Every action, decision and choice that you make can lead you down a path.

I have found that good, pure hearted actions and choices often lead to good outcomes, more friendships, and more opportunities.

I have found that poor decision making often leads to consequences… When you make a bad decision (which you will, we all do) take responsibility for your actions by owning up to your mistakes. Then work hard to learn from them.

Remember, I'm not asking you to be perfect. I'm not expecting you to be perfect. I myself, am not perfect! But I do strive to be the best person that I can be each day. I pray to God and my Lord and Savior, Jesus Christ that you will do the same.

I love you - and I got your back!

Mommy

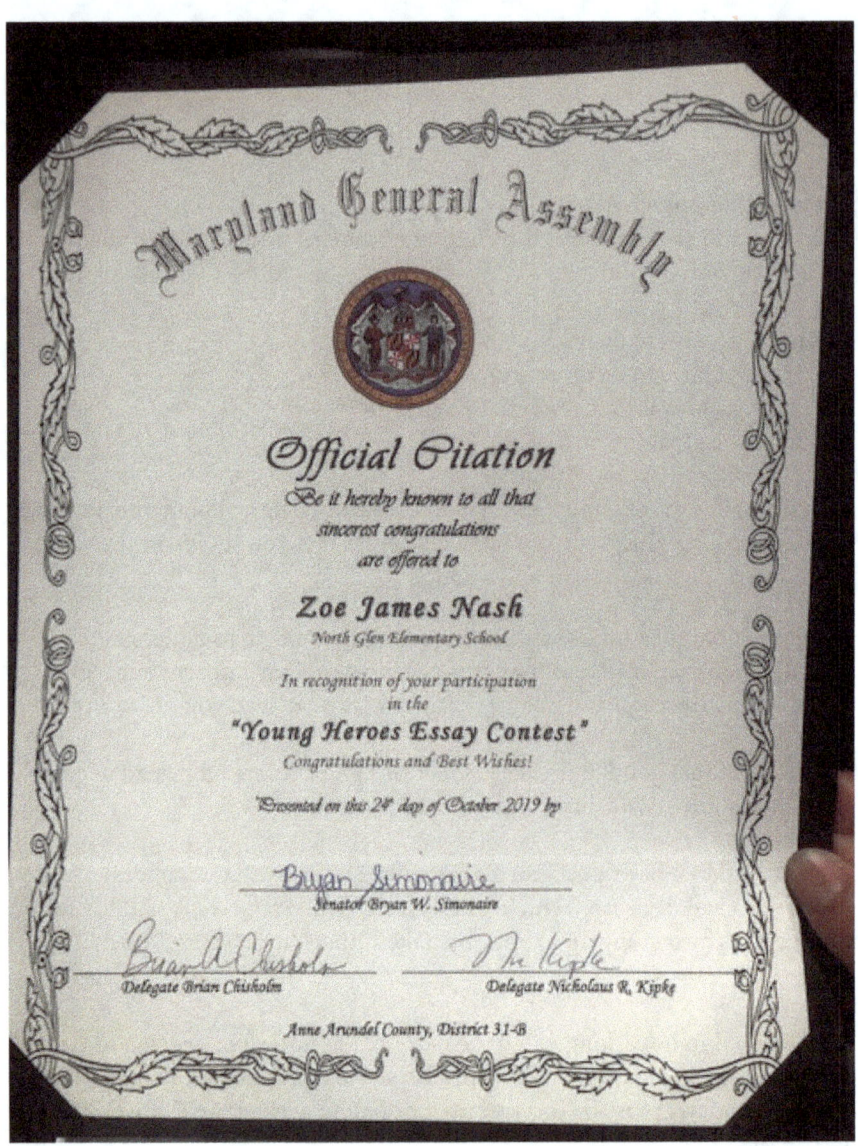

I'm Thankful for...

Dana's helpfulness

Ariyah's positivity

Mom-Mom's wisdom

Mommy's leadership

Daddy's sense of humor

Auntie SiSi's good spirit

Lexi's playfulness

Zoe James-Nash

SURVIVAL PLANS presents...Storytelling Time: Education is the Key to Success!!!

During my 6th grade year of elementary school, our music teacher, Ms. Martin gave our class an assignment to write a song. We could do this assignment alone or with a team but you had to create the song from start to finish. Once the song was written she would record us and we would listen to each recording during class.

I was excited to get started- being that I loved to write. I went home that weekend and listened to every instrumental tape and cd that I owned in my 90's stereo system. Eventually, I landed on this Donnell Jones instrumental that was on one of his singles (can't remember which one because it was not one of the popular songs).

I began to write a song entitled "Education is the Key to Success"

Education is the key to success
If you want to make that money then you better past the test.

Education is going to get you there,
You can be the man or pay the fare.
I want you to go this way don't turn around
or wear a frown Education is the ahh key

Education is the key to success
If you want to make that money then you better past the test

So here I am,
And here I go
Education is on my mind
So you better think twice
And take this advice, yea..

There was also a rap that I wrote to finish the song off- but I have since forgotten the words to it.

Anyways, I returned to school on Monday excited to share with my three girlfriends (Tamika, Jessica and LaTonya) the song I had written for us to perform. And just like that we had us a little song and a group. We practiced over the next music class and would record in the music room one day during the week.

We came to see Ms. Martin before lunch when she had time to record us. After we finished recording, she commented that we should sing the song for our upcoming 6th grade graduation! We were so excited and said YESSSSS!!!

Was I going to be a singer one day? Or maybe a song writer? A girl version of Robert Townsend in the Five Heart Beats??? I smiled, wondered and imagined.

At lunch my girls and I planned our graduation outfits and looks as we prepared for the big day.

Within a few weeks that day came. Before the 6th grade class marched on to the bleachers to begin the ceremony, I made sure that my friends knew their parts. In fact, I was so busy rehearsing them that I didn't prepare myself.

Finally, the big moment had arrived- I could feel my heart jump to my throat as Ms. Martin announced to the guests and visitors that she had a special treat- 4 graduates singing an original song entitle "Education is the Key to Success."

We stepped down and forward, with our white dresses, stockings, shoes w/curls and "pumper-do's" in our hair and began to sing.

Everything was going good until it was time for me to sing my part- instead, I started singing Tamika's part… I realized right away and I blundered "wait can we start over- I sang the wrong part." I could hear my brother snicker in the auditorium and see people's families recording the whole thing. I was mortified but Ms. Martin signaled for us to continue and we went on.

Throughout the rest of the ceremony, I had to fight back tears. I couldn't even sing the Mariah Carey version of hero that was selected for the class. I just moved my mouth a bit.

I learned that day that I would never be a singer, a song writer or a girl version of Robert Townsend in the Five Heart Beats.

Decades later I can laugh about this and tell my husband and children the story. Although I packed away my instant singing dreams- the one thing that I still believe to be true is that Education is the key to success.

Song for School 12 Graduates (Paterson, NJ)

Now's the time for success;

We will pass life's test.

We are School 12 strivers;

We're made out of School 12 tough fiber.

Say hello to our future,

Which will be sunny and bright,

We are School 12 survivors who strive with all of our might.

We hope you'll continue to support us,

Cause we're a worthwhile group.

Wherever we go, we'll make our mark;

School 12 students are very smart.

CHORUS; Yes School 12 students are survivors,

School 12 students are strivers,

Wherever they go, they'll make their mark

Cause they are very, very smart.

Karen Mayo-Hogan

To: The Graduates of School 12 (Paterson, NJ) Words of Encouragement

It's that time of year when I say farewell to our smart, survivor and striver students. I do this with a sense of pride for I recognize these young people have overcome the first obstacle on their road to success by graduating from grammar school. It's my hope that our students will continue on to success by furthering their education and remember that I am supporting you all the way.

School No. 12 graduates have a high self- esteem, which will help each and every one of you overcome obstacles that may lie before you. Remember to never let anyone break your spirit. Remember also that life is tough but school 12 graduates will make it because they believe in themselves as much as I believe in them. As smart, survivors and strivers, I am confident our students will be actively working towards their goals of being successful in all of their future endeavors whatever they may be.

Love all of you.

Karen Mayo Hogan (1990s)

Alexa, play Eastside High School Song (Lean on Me)

LOUD Brown Girls

LOUD Brown Girls,

LOUD does not mean you create too much noise
LOUD can be silent when you have the right poise

Brown Girls,

Haven't you heard **ACTION** speaks louder than words???
Advocacy, leadership, education and excellence is thy sword.

Slaying current issues like dragons
With **MY** voice and some poise

My **LOUD** is thunderous
And it pierces ears like Claire's stores

My **LOUD** speaks truth, fills rooms and opens doors
My **LOUD** brings people together

Because I understand that **CommUNITY** should be at our core

My **LOUD** moves on the Righteous path
Because I know that little good can come from the bad

But I know that bad times brings the biggest problems
Ones that require **LOUDEST** Solutions.

LOUD Brown Girls,
YOU are the line of demarcation.

The link between today and tomorrow
Revolutionized solutions walking upright, proud and loud and Brown-

LOUD brown girls realize that opportunities are limitless
Open your eyes wide to see how Possibilities are endless

And...

Just be you!

Ariyah,

I am very proud of you, **LOUD** brown girl. Continue to explore opportunities, and pursue excellence because you never know what might click! Be yourself - and be proud to be you- know matter what challenges may come please remember that we love you and are here to support you!

Love,

Step "Mommy" Nina

L.O.U.D. Brown Girls

Across

2. To carry one's self with elegance, self assurance and self control
6. guide and direct peers to common goal
7. Not a lie
9. Quality of being extremely good or outstanding
10. To be united or come together
13. To do something
14. A situation that requires a solution to resolve
15. A loud sound that can cause a disturbance
16. Loud and roaring

Down

1. A thing that could happen at any time
3. Circumstances that make it possible to do something
4. To do what is morally right
5. A line of boundary or the limit
8. To go against a system or social order
11. feeling satisfied with self or achievements
12. Persons living in the same place or sharing a common characteristic
13. To publicly stand behind an issue

bbkeith • Following

Quinceanera. Graphite. 2012

SURVIVAL PLANS: PRESENTS...

ARTIST SPOTLIGHT

BB Keith

BARRY BARNETT KEITH IS A NATIVE OF ALEXANDRIA, VA AND A PRODUCT OF ALEXANDRIA CITY PUBLIC SCHOOLS. HE BEGAN DRAWING MARVEL AND DC COMICS SUPERHEROES AT A VERY EARLY AGE FOR FRIENDS IN GRADE SCHOOL AND AFTER SCHOOL. KEITH WAS ALSO AN AVID READER AT A VERY EARLYAGE BECAUSE OF A SET OF ENCYCLOPEDIAS HIS PARENTS BOUGHT FOR THEIR HOME. BY THE TIME KEITH WAS IN FIRST GRADE, HE WAS READING ON AN EIGHTH GRADE LEVEL, AND HIS PRINCIPAL REQUESTED KEITH READ TO HIM IN HIS OFFICE EVERY FRIDAY AFTERNOON. AFTER GRADUATING FROM T.C. WILLIAMS IN 1978, KEITH WENT ON TO THE UNIVERSITY OF DELAWARE ART SCHOOL WHERE HE MAJORED IN PAINTING, DRAWING AND ENGLISH.

UPON GRADUATING, KEITH ALSO TOOK UP WRITING NOVELS. HIS FIRST NOVEL WAS PUBLISHED IN 2000, ENTITLED THE WAITER, ABOUT A PROFESSIONAL WAITER IN THE RESTAURANT BUSINESS WHO CARES FOR A WOMAN HE LOVES WHO SUFFERS FROM DEPRESSION. KEITH HAS SINCE WRITTEN FOUR OTHER NOVELS (THE CYCLE- 2002, THE APOCALYPSE-2004, THE SILENCE- 2009 AND ARAVENE- 2012).

SURVIVAL PLANS: PRESENTS...

ARTIST SPOTLIGHT

BB Keith

OVER THE YEARS KEITH DEVELOPED HIS SKILLS ENOUGH TO BE ABLE TO PAINT IN THE ENVIRONMENT OR PLEIN AIR. KEITH DEVELOPED HIS OWN DRAWING STYLE THROUGH THE YEARS BY PRODUCING PORTRAITS FOR LOCAL PATRONS BUT LANDSCAPE PAINTING BECAME HIS LOVE. KEITH'S GOAL IN LANDSCAPE PAINTING IS SIMPLY TO TRANSLATE WHAT HE SEES AND HAVE THE PAINTINGINDICATIVE OF THE MEDIUM OF PAINTING, RATHER THAN PAINT A PHOTOGRAPHIC PICTURE WITH BRUSHES. KEITH REGARDS THE ACT OF PAINTING DRAWING AND CREATING ART IN GENERAL AS ACTS OF GRATITUDE FOR THE OPPORTUNITY TO LIVE. "I WANT TO BE AS PROLIFIC AS POSSIBLE AS A PAINTER AND AS A TEACHER SIMPLY TO SHOW GRATITUDE, NOTHING ELSE."

KEITH HAS TAUGHT THE ARTS IN THE PRINCE GEORGES COUNTY MARYLAND PUBLIC SCHOOL SYSTEM FOR FIFTEEN YEARS- TWELVE YEARS AT SUITLAND HIGH SCHOOL AND THREE IN ELEMENTARY SCHOOL. HE IS PRESENTLY THE LEAD ART TEACHER AT MATTAPONI ELEMENTARY SCHOOL IN UPPER MARLBORO, MD AND ROSE VALLEY ELEMENTARYSCHOOL IN FORT WASHINGTON, MD.

My...

My wisdom is from my experience.

My passion is from my pain.

My confidence helps to hide my insecurities.

My weaknesses helps to make me strong.

My calm hides my storm.

My innocence is not ignorance.

My strength is not an illusion

My past does not define me.

And our bond will not be broken.

Ariyah C. Nash

Age 16

Ocean Jewel

What Do You See???

Dana Anita Nash

Age 5

*** She drew a girl, Mommy saw a dinosaur. ***

When Will I?

When will I be confident,

In who God has made me to be?

When will I trust that circumstances,

Are here to make me stronger?

When will I believe that true friends,

And family are one in the same?

When will I understand that this,

Is a chapter of many in my life?

When will I see that my feelings,

Won't be the same tomorrow?

When will I find my purpose,

Is not to satisfy myself?

When will I realize that I can do all things,

And that I have the power to sink or steer my own life?

-**Chanler Crawford**

Chanler Crawford was a 2019 Hallelujah Anyhow! Scholarship contestant and former member of the Reflections Literary and Arts Magazine leadership team, Prince George's Community College (Largo, MD)

Reflection

Rahim Mitchell

Sometimes you have to look at yourself in the mirror and ask...

Have you ever checked your personal energy at the door?

Or have you just been masterfully disguising it?

D. Nash

When he rears his ugly head...

LIES

Your memories are distorted around what someone else says and the story that you're telling yourself... neither experienced nor grounded in truth.

LIES
Develop over time,
Contagious
It's a chronic disorder
Designed to cloud your judgement
While working hard to cover the truth

LIES
Begin to creep into your beliefs
Drown out sound...and logical Thinking
Playing broken records on repeat

LIES
Over time disturbs
otherwise peaceful waters
Stirring up waves of E-motions
Creating hazardous fire storms

LIES
Finds space where they feel there is a there is a void
Patches walls with silly putty
And scotches up holes in kitchen floors

LIES
Can't admit when they are wrong
May cover your butts now
But can't buy you comfort or peace
On the long haul

LIES

Take you on a trip to denial
Sunbathing in carport beaches
Escaping to luxury motels

LIES

Have you taking less than what your worth
Shopping ONLY in second hand stores
Moving in with and taking care of a grade A jerk

LIES

Will keep you from facing and fixing what's really wrong
Developing relationships with under quality people
Putting faith in man
Trying to back it with The WORD.

LIES

No matter how big or small
Eventually make you a LIAR!

Be careful telling them LIES, YOU don't want to end up a...

Living

In

Alternative

Reality

D. Nash

Chronic Complainers

I'm irked by chronic complainers
It's like they chew with their mouths full
I'm reminded of an old saying-if you don't like it, don't eat it...
I never hear hungry people complain

It's annoying that every time you speak,
Your glass is always half empty
I'm beginning to think your glass will never be full
You've poked so many holes in the glass
Now all the water falls through 😤 🧶 ■ ♀ ☐

Sometimes I wish I could go on and on
about all the complaining that you do!

But if I did,

I fear...
I would end up a chronic complainer

Just like you!

The cure for complaining is building gratitude...

Morning and Evening
GRATITUDE
Log

The cure for chronic complaining is undoubtedly forcing yourself into a constant state of gratitude. Gratitude helps YOU to appreciate the "little" things that are happening in your life every day. Being grateful even when times are tough, will help YOU to improve your mood, relationships with others, reduce stress while increasing your faith.

Use the notebook paper below to log at least one thing that you are grateful for each day and/or evening for 30 days. Begin your day with an affirmation of gratitude and by reviewing your gratitude log. In 30 days not only will you feel better but you will also see that you have so much more to be grateful for than you thought.

_____
_____
_____
_____
_____
_____
_____
_____
_____
_____
_____
_____
_____
_____
_____
_____
_____
_____
_____
_____
_____
_____

GRATITUDE AFFIRMATION

Each day I have something to be grateful for. I am learning to appreciate the small things each day. Lord, fill my spirit with gratitude today- as I continue to
be thankful for *(read from your list here)*.
Amen

If nobody ever told you...

You eat the words that you speak.

You attract the company that you keep.

The Poorest Woman

I know a woman with the poorest mentality
Ain't never been broke
But is the poorest person I know

Her complaints about her financial destitute
Are like nails on a chalk board
A broken record
And the song that never ends

Every conversation
Begins with and ends with
what she don't have
Giving to her, seems like never enough
Been repeating the same thing for so long
That she too believes herself

She doesn't have enough
So she holds on to everything that she has!
Daily thrift shopping sprees
Hosting lavish tubberware pity parties
With attendees who may leave with
food, shelter and/or cash dividends

They emphasize and sympathize
And see your point of view
But after a little while
The party dies and they realize the rest was all untrue

There are two types of party goers
That seem to come through

The one who truly pities you
And
The one that sees your riches
Shine through

So they throw themselves a party
And invite you to come through
You fit right in
And socialize
That's when their own sob story comes true

And instead of you looking at everything you said "you didn't have"
You go right into your wallet
Offering to give a helping hand

Just to return home and play the song that never ends.

I don't have!!!!

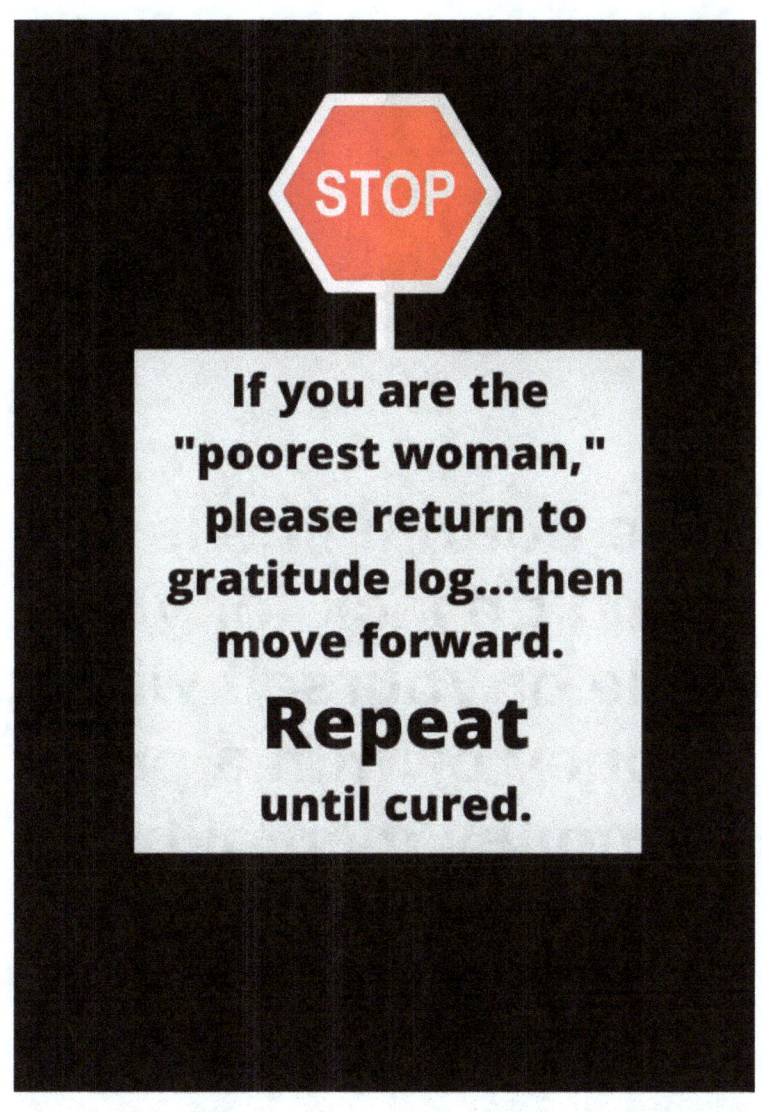

"The bottom line is you can't do jack for your people or yourself without money or with a poor money mentality.

It's a ton of bricks
When reality hits…

I blew it,
Atomically!

Both figuratively and literally.

Almost outer body
Acted out of character

They (being he or she),

who control my emotions

control me.

Pinocchio
Who is really pulling the strings

Have to look at myself
To see my won reflection

This is my own

Self reflection

 OMG

I need to change

SURVIVAL STORY

BREAKING THE CYCLE: PASSAIC, NJ MAN CHANGES HIS LIFE WHILE GUIDING LOCAL YOUTH

SURVIVOR PROFILE

Name: Rahim Hassan "Coach" Mitchell

Hometown: Passaic, NJ

Occupation: Entrepreneur (CapWear), Athletic Coach, Community Mentor

His-Story:
Coming of age in the 90's, Coach Mitchell looked up to the hustlers (drug dealers) and overall allure of the streets. By the age of 18, he caught his first drug charges (1998)- which would be the precursor to other charges/indictments and prison time in 2002, 2003 and 2008 respectively. This time quickly added up to nearly 10 years of his life being spent in the prison system.

Turning Points:
While serving time, Coach Mitchell realized that he was missing out on precious time with his family and his young sons. He realized if he did not find another legit way to survive that he would continue on the path he was on. He also recognized that this would increase the likelihood of his sons getting caught up in the streets... a cycle that he did not want to "pass down."

SURVIVAL STORY (CONT)

Upon being released for the last time, Coach Mitchell committed to making a change. This took self-discipline and understanding the consequences of his own actions. It was during this crucial time that he came to see that his "friends" would be quick to offer him drugs, alcohol and a good time- but no one could offer a job, help with a resume or anything productive enough to help him get ahead, feed his family or put a roof over his head.

He focused on spending more time with his sons taking them to football practice- which motivated him to get involved with youth athletics. During this time, he went back to school at Passaic County College in search of skills to develop him in business and leadership.

Today, Coach Mitchell is a graduate of Passaic County College (Paterson, NJ) and holds a degree in Sports Management. He coaches and serves as an Athletic Director for the youth football team the Passaic Cavaliers. He has spent his last few years hosting and facilitating trainings, mentorship programs and fundraising for the youth in his community. In addition he is a entrepreneur, having founded CapWear, which designs and provides sporting apparel.

Coach Mitchell enjoys spending time with family and nurturing his artistic and entrepreneurial talents. Some of his artwork and uniform designs are featured in this publication.

Future PLANS

Coach Mitchell's future goals include opening his own youth athletic training facility for local youth as a way to keep them off the streets and help them achieve their dreams.

Survival Takeaways:
Take accountability for your actions!
Develop Self-Discipline!
Learn new skills and trades!
Remember that hard times don't last- but you can't get time back!
Get active, Be creative!
Invest in the community, invest in youth!
Stay Solid and stay out the way!

SURVIVAL PLANS

Creativity Booster:

Write a Poem/Thought/Story or Draw about...

CHANGE

Word Associations:

New

Uncomfortable

Growth

Different

Season

Adapt

Transition

Switch

Adjustment

Development

Learn

Change

Out with the old

In with the new

Change is hard

And so is breaking in

These new red bottom shoes

My Reasons to Quit Smoking

1) Fear of GOD.

2) To maintain my health.

3) To maintain my appearance.

4) To cut down on my expenses.

5) To protect my environment.

6) To clear my mind

7) Gift my family All of the above.

Clinton Battle

SURVIVAL PLANS
Book Club presents:
Takeaways from "Pimp" by Iceberg Slim

You have to stand guard at the gate of your mind.

At some point in life someone you care for will cross you. But sometimes you can't let them know how bad you feel. Proceed with caution

Payback is a b***h- and you don't always have to do it yourself.

Fear is a tactic to enforce submission.

Shiny and clean trinkets, cars, cash and clothes (material things) attract those who like shiny, cars, clothes, cash and materials things.

Ain't no love in the streets

Everybody makes mistakes, even your parents.

The street life (drugs, alcohol, hanging, staying up all night) will wear you down. It's draining to youth, appearance, mental health, health.

Women tend to blow out in the streets before men. "Cop and blow"

Sometimes you need someone to "pull your coat"- You know, check you, hip you, school you- let you know when you wrong

You gotta stay on top of your money!
A fast girl will play a square dude. A fast man can turn a square girl fast.

If you are intelligent, you can always find a way to do what you want to do.

So, succeed at something!

Never give up on your dreams- but note that plans can and do change.

Be flexible.

When trying to CHANGE beware of the BUM...

Being

Un

Motivated

When trying to get rid of the BUM do more WORK!

Willing

Opportunities to

Reinforce

Knowledge

Grandpa James use to say...

" *Nothing is holding the black man back but the black man himself.* "

The Alpha

While writing his second screenplay, Curtis Scoon was named a suspect in a high profile crime. Curtis was then forced to re-direct his goals of writing spec scripts, and give his full attention to a real life drama: his own life. It quickly became clear to Scoon that he would need to find media outlets to tell his side of the story. This effort to clear his name would be Scoon's introduction to the world of media and entertainment.

In 2003, Curtis got his first opportunity, by writing a "sidebar" entitled "Framed and Defamed" for Playboy magazine after pitching it to the executive editor at the time, Chris Napolitano. Soon after, Scoon crafted a book concept that would tie the subject of the Queens gangsters of the '80s to the world of pop culture and his work in Playboy was instrumental in making that a reality. He is the sole contributor. That book idea became "Queens Reigns Supreme: Fat Cat, 50 Cents, and The Rise of the Hip Hop Hustler." The book became not only a must read for lovers of hip hop, but received a starred review in Publishers' Weekly and was yet another stepping stone for Curtis Scoon.

The success of Queens Reigns Supreme pushed the story of Lorenzo "Fat Cat" Nichols into the media spot light, thus causing it to be featured on the debut season of BET's "American Gangster" Series. Scoon was offered a consultant position on the show. After proving his worth in gold, Curtis was offered a co-producers position in 2007 on the Kenneth "Supreme" McGriff episode of the American Gangster series. Scoon's uncanny ability to penetrate the urban underworld yielded yet another score: an exclusive jail-house interview of Fat Cat in 2006, for KING Magazine. It was the only interview given by Fat Cat in over 20 years of incarceration.

HIS STORY CONTINUES

In that same year, there was a feature article written about Scoon in Groove magazine. The magazine is based in France, which gave him international exposure. Having consistently proved himself Curtis was given the opportunity as a producer in 2008 on the "Shower Posse" episode of the series American Gangster. Given his track record his selection was a natural progression. Curtis was the only producer in the world that was granted an interview with the infamous Vivian Blake, former leader of the "Shower Posse."

In addition, Mr. Scoon has been featured on news outlets across the nation and notably interviewed by The Breakfast Club; Mario Lopez and Jason Whitlock.

In 2018, he released 'Black White & Blue," a controversial documentary about race, police, and politics. Today, he continues to pursue his ambitions of producing feature films and documentaries that tell the true stories of our communities- from our communities.

You can get access to more information about Curtis Scoon, his work in the community, cultural commentary and politics by following him on instagram and Twitter @ScoonTV .

HIS STORY CONTINUES

"Throwback Thursday. In 1986, I entered Hampton University as a 22 year old freshman out on appeal bail in NYC. Although I only attended for one year, I made relationships there that changed my life. I won my appeal and I hit the social network jackpot that's paying off to this day. You never know how things are going to play out. That's the scary part but that's also what makes life so special. Life will test your FAITH!"

-C.Scoon

Beginning with exclusive Baltimore riot footage, 'Black White & Blue' tells the story of police brutality, race, and racial politics in America. Incorporating diverse perspectives from an assorted group of: authors, attorneys, historians, socially active pop icons, politicians and clergy, a more complete image of the trials and tribulations of African Americans emerges.

Available on Amazon

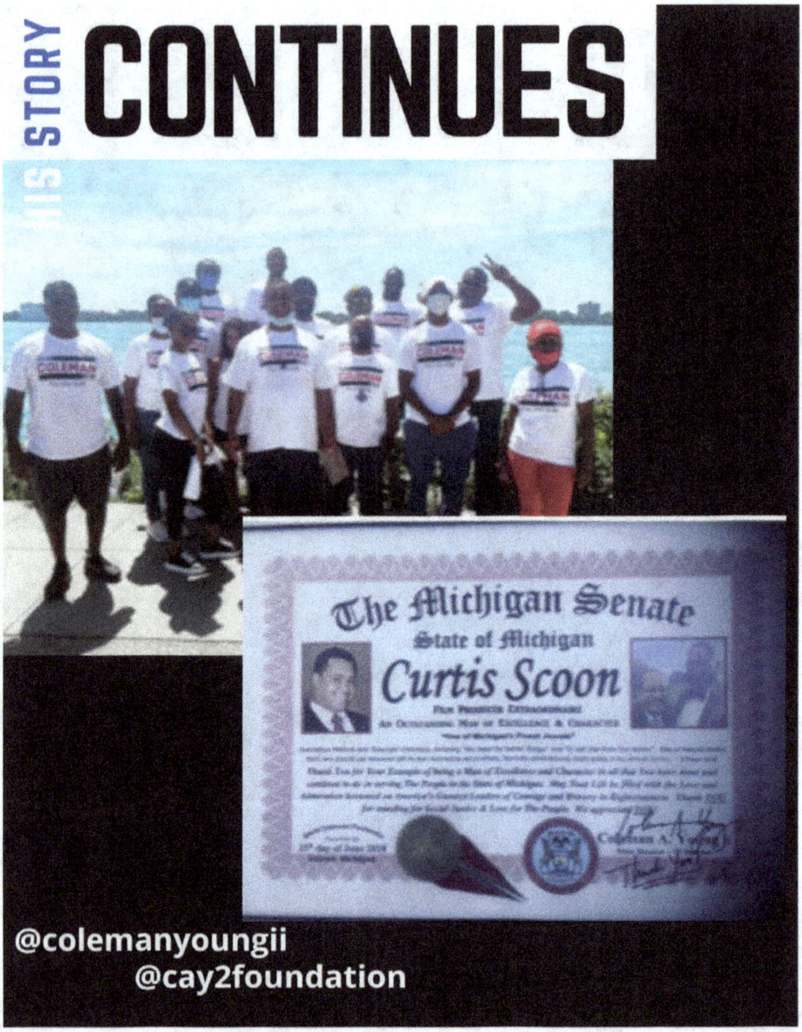

HIS STORY CONTINUES

@colemanyoungii
@cay2foundation

Me: "Alexa play Gil Scott Heron- We Almost Lost Detroit"

SURVIVAL PLANS

HIS STORY CONTINUES

"I had an interesting day at the White House yesterday. I play for position not paper. Position gets you paper. The reverse isn't always the case. It's called POWER politics not partisan politics. Playing from the neck up is how I live."

-C. Scoon

SURVIVAL PLANS

HIS STORY — TAKEAWAY *Notes*

1) Play from the neck up

2) Don't play for paper, play for position

3) Invest in your own economic empowerment- businesses, properties, political interest, community, projects, and the stories etc...

4) Keep the Faith

Life is too Short

That's why I have no time for petty

Constant reminders to self

Need to keep my mind set on plenty

No time for the "lack of" mentality

That's what keeps people trapped in a poor man-tality

Your words become thoughts

Turning alphabet soup into YOUR reality

So be careful because you find what you seek

You eat the words that you speak

And you attract the company that you keep

Live long enough and you will see!

Throughout Time

Time waits for no one, not even me.

Unfortunately, procrastination leads to consequences that only you alone will see.

Well the years of being complacent, when in reality you are burdened with agony and anxiety.

Demanding circumstances anchored to work, personal relationships and finances lead to automatic negative thoughts and dogmatic views of friends, foes, and family.

Childhood, adolescent, adulthood and motherhood…voicelessness, numbness and accustomed to the life I unknowingly created, hiding the pain with a smile that is phony.

Always helpful, always kind, always taken for granted, yet no one cares until I no longer provide the amenity.

Fake friends, detrimental relationships and intoxicants only increased my inner toxicity.

Blurred vision, unable to determine the true **intentions** of many

Desperate to find the beauty embedded in life's **milestones**, filling the silence with senseless hysterics to mask the pain associated with each eventuality.

Whether pleasurable or wretched, I am thankful for each event and its outcome for it has revealed God's grace and mercy.

Everything that happens, happens when God sees fit.

For the only person that knows the purpose is he.

Latoya Latasha Jones

Light at the end of the Tunnel

Oh God!!!
Where is thy face?
This burden is weighing me down
I cried all night seeking your face
I walk, I run, I search
Looking for a direction for my life

Oh God!!!
Ease my affairs, Oh, God
I finished high school several years ago
I raised a family, yet I got no fulfillment
I did various odd jobs to make a living
Then, I thought education I must obtain

Oh God!!!
I started college nursing a six week's baby
I burnt the night candle to study
I worked hard in the day to support my family
The path is rough and bumpy
There is light at the end of the tunnel.

-**Adeola Adeniya**

Adeola Adeniya is a 2019 Hallelujah Anyhow! Scholarship contestant, Prince George's Community College (Largo, MD)

Subways x DC Photography

From the "New DC" Collection

Gazing Up

First, my eyes look up…

Past so many fears, stresses and doubts

Limitations, negative voices

Bad choices I made during dark times

When I peered downward into churning, meaningless dark pools

I was mesmerized by swirling despair that pulled me deeper and lower

And showed me another me I never wanted to see

So empty and sinking lower, then lower

But then a shaft of light above

A whispered thought "Hey! Hey! Look up"

I cried "I don't know how"

"It's too hard!"

"I don't have the strength"

The whisper replied "Then use mine"

I slowly raised my head and my eyes opened to light

My pupils adjusted to newfound sight

I see you world. I finally see me

So this is who I was created to be?

I finally get it! I realize the value

My worth is set and can never be changed

My eyes look up

It's strange!

Now I see new goals, purpose, peace

My eyes look up

To see another me

Another version

New and complete

She's sober-minded with batteries included by her creator

To jettison her, propel her up into the greater

Stratospheric places of purpose, self-love

But first, first, my eyes look up

Crystal Williams

SURVIVAL PLANS

WWKD? 2020

Alexa, play Kanye West "Follow God"

WHIPPING OUT MY FAITH

In times of trouble

In times of turmoil

If timing just can't seem to be right

There is a light

if you whip out your faith,

always keep it in your back pocket

always keep it in your purse

Everything is going to be alright

If you just step out on faith

Your path is already lit

The new growth in U

Shines bright in the creator's eyes

Just as you have found out

Coming through the storm

You have grown in your belief

Your mind no longer worn

Step out on faith

Your path is already lit

The new growth in U

Shines bright in the creator's eyes

WestCoastAnnie

SURVIVAL STORY:
Living My life with Autism

Inspiring   Survivor   Aspiring   Dreamer   Creating   Reality

My name is DeVante Capers. I'm an individual with great potential and a good heart, filled with many gifts and talents that will one day change the world! I plan on making a difference in the communities that I am apart of within the District of Columbia, Maryland and Virginia (DMV) areas.

I was six years old when I found out that I was diagnosed with a disability known as autism. This diagnosis would change my life. During this time, it was hard for my mom and for me to adjust. My mother (who is my biggest supporter) even had to fight against the school system, so that I could attend a special school that would nurture and educate me as a person.

But before that, during my elementary and middle school years, I didn't have any friends. I was teased so I played by myself during recess, talked to myself and was often called "retarded" by my peers. Because of this, I made excuses for not going school, I was extremely depressed and emotional. Not only did I have to go through this stress, but my family was also impacted by these events. No family or individual should experience or go through those types of struggles. The struggles that I had to overcome.

Eventually, I found my stride. By sixteen, I was enrolled in a school that supported me with peers who understood me. I began to flourish as I took an interest in dancing. By the age of nineteen, I started taking dance classes at the Joy of Motion Dance Center in Washington D.C. My dance of choice is hip hop, other styles from breaking, popping, locking, house and krump. Other activities that I took interest in and enjoy include journal writing about my everyday life, creating artwork of all types (drawings, paintings, collages and more). My love for the arts and talent helped me to win medals and trophies in the Special Olympics, receive an "Honor of Accomplishment" from former Maryland Governor Martin O' Malley and graduate from Kennedy Krieger High School in Baltimore, MD. I received a "Letter of Recommendation" from President Barack Obama and filmed a documentary on "My Dance Life TV" which you can see on YouTube. I also joined the hip hop dance company, Kaution Dance Kru and participated in that for three years.

Most recently, I was awarded the "Culture Shock DC, Community Award" at Howard University for all of the inspiring and hard work that I contributed to the dance community. I am also enrolled at Prince George's Community College, where I study Visual Arts to earn my Associate's degree. I also enjoy being an active member and contributor to the Reflections Literary and Arts Magazine club.

I have done a lot of research on Autism Spectrum Disorder so that I can better understand my disability. I know there are many forms of autism; and my form of autism is considered "high functional." My goal is to help other people become more compassionate and aware of the challenges faced by individuals (like myself) with autism by seeing and hearing about that struggles that I have had to overcome. It's difficult achieving anything when you are not recognized as a person for who you are. It's difficult coming out of your comfort zone, making new friends and learning how to experience and find your place in with the "real world." It's also challenging to develop healthy relationships.

I know that life can be complicated and filled with many challenges, which is why it can be difficult to express my true thoughts and feelings without being considered a nobody. Although waking up every day to see what life brings you in the next 24 hours is not easy for me, I will not give up the fight.

I'm a fighter and a survivor. No, I'm not perfect, but nobody's perfect. From experiencing the ups and downs, I'm happy with my life and I couldn't be happier. Sharing my experiences with autism will let people know who I am, and it will help others with disabilities and their families to understand that they're not facing these challenges alone.

With the long road of life ahead, this is just the beginning of my journey. I've been through a series of negative obstacles in my life, but I have managed to survive it all and I am still fighting today! I am very fortunate, being this lucky because one extraordinary and mysterious gift that I have has impacted people's lives and touched people's hearts. In the past, I was known as an outcast, but today I am an inspiration to many people.

With all of that being said, there will still be people who won't understand my world or know what I have been through… but that's life. It's time to prove them wrong! I have people behind me and I will always have love and support. I won't be labeled as an outcast, disabled or broken; I just want to be labeled as DeVante Capers.

Despite being put down by people, at the end, I do not fear my disability. I embrace it because it will not stop me from living my life to the fullest or doing what I love.

DeVante Capers

Monumental Joy x DC Photography

From the "New DC" Collection

DREAM

Deliverance from a state of being.

Reality of what life can be.

Eternity into existence beyond.

Accepting the possibilities to go further.

Means of proving who we are.

Darcelle Battle

DREAMS "R"

Doing

Reflecting

Experiencing

Aspiring

Manifesting

Succeeding

Repeating

I thought and I planned
        I thought and I did
I thought when I swept
        I thought when I washed
I thought when I read
        I thought when I listened
I thought when I learned
        I thought and I succeeded
I thought and I won
        I thought and I lost
I thought and I lived

        -Efflorescent_Child

For My Sister on Her Upcoming Graduation And on her Earning her RN (2017)

Proud of you on your graduation

It's very good to see you rise to the occasion,

while doing something you enjoy and are naturally gifted in alike.

You are very compassionate and careful in how you take care of the patients that are in your care.

I know that Dad is very proud.

If you close your eyes and listen

I'm sure you can hear him say it out loud

This is just One of the many things that you are talented in.

Just stay focused and know that you can WIN, WIN, WIN!

Become F.I.T.

Free

Independent

Thinker

Good Morning Family,

As I ride through the rain, in route to American University for my graduation, I cannot help but to feel an immense amount of gratitude. I thank the Lord for keeping me. I could have been so lost but thanks to his grace- I am finding more and more of me.

I'm thankful for my Dad, my angel, who undoubtedly watches over me each day from his heavenly home. His words, support and work ethic has left a lasting impact on me and has given me the solid foundation and motivation for many of my achievements. Even in his departure, I strive to do my best in his legacy and honor.

I thank my husband for supporting me while going back to school. Becoming my "Daddy Uber" driving me here, there and everywhere. My husband was present each night listening to my essays and research all the while working (full time) in the community, helping to prepare meals, getting the kids clothed and bathed etc. On days where it seemed that I wouldn't make it- he physically carried the weight. I'm so thankful to God for sending me the perfect mate.

I am also thankful for my Mom who has allowed us (my family) to stay in her home after the passing of Dad. She has helped out with the kids and steps in wherever needed. And while thanking her, I would be remiss if I did not thank her "special friend" James, who has been there for her as a friend and companion.

I am thankful for my Mom and Dad Nash who have accepted me and my daughter Zoe (who was 1 at the time) into their home and family. I met the Nash's in 2010- months after my Dad's death so Dad Nash has been a bonus Dad and Grandfather for my daughter Zoe. Thankful that Mom Nash kept our daughter Dana for a few days during each week outside of her normal "working hours" as my husband and I attended work and school respectively.

I am also thankful for my neighborhood daycare Mom, Mrs. Clarice who over the years has looked after me and my girls.

I am thankful for my gainful employment at Prince George's Community College, where over the past 5+ years, I have served the President Dr. Dukes and serve as an Academic and Career Advisor and Adjunct Faculty Member. The College has given me an opportunity to do what I do best- advise, educate, create and learn all the while helping to financially contribute to my family and community.

Lastly, I am thankful to all of the mentors, role models, inspirations, family and close friends who have supported me (mentally and spiritually) and believed in me throughout this journey. This includes my sister who woke up extra early to ensure that my makeup was on point today for graduation day.

I love you all- whether I say it often or not- I'm immensely thankful for you all and for your support during this time.

As we ride through the rain, on our way to American University- I feel an immense amount of gratitude.

And it's because of you!

Grateful. Once was lost. Now found. Planted in faith.

Grateful,
To Almighty God
My Savior Jesus Christ

Because
He saves us
He sacrificed his life

I
One and only
Sole person in life

Once
A time ago
When I didn't know

Was
In the past
Changed my old ways

Lost
Astray and misled
Until I found him

Now
The current time
I Desire to Live

Found
Brought into being
The light in darkness

Planted
In fertile soil
My fathers promised land

In
The midst of
The thick of it

Faith
The light beyond
Cast away all doubts

Overcoming
Prevailing over problems
Moving forward when stuck

Difficult
Challenges can be
But Faithful I remain

Situations
Circumstances only Temporary
Thank you, Jesus!
My Salvation is eternal.

I'm grateful because I once was lost. Now found, planted in faith, overcoming difficult situations.

#NothingisgreaterthanGOD!
#Dontbringyourworryroundhere!!!!
#causeimnotlistening
#Faithofamustardseedmovesmountains!
#Ifyoupraydontworry
#ifyouworrywhypray?

She Survived x Doodle and De-Stress

Survival PLANS Spotlight:

COACH. SPEAKER. ACTRESS. SINGER.
Taundra Noel

Taundra Noel

ACHIEVE SUCCESS

Chasing Dreams & Helping Others to Achieve Success!

Survival PLANS Spotlight:
TAUNDRA NOEL

Passionate. Empowering Coach. Talented. Goal Getter.

> be coachable
> be willing to listen
> be flexible
> be motivated
> be open
> be!

My girl

> Don't let the PROCESS PUNK you out of the PROMISE

My boys

Chasing Dreams & Helping Others to Achieve Success!

Survival PLANS Spotlight:

TAUNDRA NOEL

Passionate. Empowering Coach. Talented. Goal Getter.

Its time for a checkup!

Have you looked at YOU or YOUR brand from the outside?

What are others saying about you and what you represent?

Are your current actions lining up with where you want to be and do?

Are you seated in your purpose and operating effectively?

*Chasing Dreams &
Helping Others to Achieve Success!*

Survival PLANS Spotlight:

TAUNDRA NOEL

Passionate. Empowering Coach. Talented. Goal Getter.

Write Reflections Here

Chasing Dreams & Helping Others to Achieve Success!

Survival PLANS Spotlight:

TAUNDRA NOEL

Passionate. Empowering Coach. Talented. Goal Getter.

What are your physical needs?

What are your needs from relationships you've developed?

What are your needs mentally/emotionally?

Are you conscious and clear on what they are?

Or is it something that you need to think about?

*Chasing Dreams &
Helping Others to Achieve Success!*

Survival PLANS Spotlight:

TAUNDRA NOEL

Passionate. Empowering Coach. Talented. Goal Getter.

Write Reflections Here

_____
_____
_____
_____
_____
_____
_____
_____
_____
_____
_____
_____
_____

Chasing Dreams & Helping Others to Achieve Success!

Survival PLANS Spotlight:

TAUNDRA NOEL

Passionate. Empowering Coach. Talented. Goal Getter.

In order to obtain wealth and true prosperity, you have to SHIFT. But when you don't have it yet, sometimes people don't pay attention to you. So it's possible for them to miss your shifting process and make the accusation that you got money and changed.

*Chasing Dreams &
Helping Others to Achieve Success!*

Doodle and De-Stress: Grace

In The Power of Now

PEACE   TODAY

You are being asked to turn it up…
Turn up your glow…
Shine your love and light…

Today is new day
A new beginning that you are shaping in this moment…
How do you honestly feel right now?
If YOU don't feel like the sun is shining…
I'm telling you that you are that sun
And it's time to turn the light on, in your life…

As you shed the old ways of thinking, living and loving…
Know that you are protected…
Guided…
And literally being taken care of by the all…
You are a divine being…
And it is time to act like it…
Breathe in all that LOVE…
Flowing to you and through you Now..
Exhale a Beam of sunshine…

Today if you stand in your power…
And shine…
You can burn away all that is not serving your higher purpose…
Free yourself from anything that may weigh your heart down…
As you move forward…

Don't be afraid to transform and transmute…
To grow glow and flow…
It is only your destiny when you answer.

Starchild the Urban Unicorn

Master the Paradox

Paradox- a seemingly absurd or self-contradictory statement or proposition that when investigated or explained may prove to be well founded or true.

The format for this piece will be me starting off with 1 statement, then I will give a counter argument that is meant to give clarification to the 1st.

I like sharing my music and other pieces of art with others, but at the same time I prefer being known by only a few people

I hate spending money,

but the whole point of having money is to spend it

Money isn't the most important thing in life,

But it is important

Pennies add up to dollars,

but I really don't care about pennies

1 Dollar isn't a lot

But it is a dollar

20 dollars is a lot,

But not that much

You can't help everyone, but it doesn't mean you shouldn't try to help anyone

You can't care too much about what people say about you,

But it doesn't mean you can't accept constructive criticism

Don't judge a book by its cover,

But if it looks like a dog, barks like a dog, eats dog food, wags its tail, and likes to play fetch, it might be a dog. You decide

Don't put your eggs in one basket

But if u can't carry more than 7 baskets, don't

I might have been glad when my assistant manager was on vacation, but I was also glad when he came back because now I'm more motivated to work harder so I don't get fired.

Learn to be humble,

But don't forget to acknowledge your strengths and accomplishments

Just because you can drive yourself crazy overthinking this stuff,

Doesn't mean you have to

Uchenna Kamalu

** Uchenna Kamalu is one of the student leaders for the Reflections Literary and Arts Magazine, Prince George's Community College (Largo, MD)**

Becoming

Becoming, becoming, changing

Becoming more effective

Becoming mature

Becoming bold. Bold enough to speak true feelings and not take back what I said

Becoming LOUD. Loud with the truth, but soft.

Soft enough to make you lean in, so you can really listen

True development is taking place

What was gray and faint is becoming vivid and clear

Ignition begins, red, yellow, blue flame

Getting bigger

Getting brighter

More and more alive

Becoming spectacular!

Crystal H. Williams

Elemental Forces

Starchild the Urban Unicorn

I'm a lot like Prince Zuko
I tend to get a little heated when I'm mad
Anger and fear sparking flames
But afraid, I am not
Even if I get burned by the flames of the
Fire

But I suppose I could be like Katara too
Calming.
Cool.
Fluid
Flowing through life like…
Water

Unless I call bullshit
Then, I'm more like Toph Beifong
Strong arming and moving mountains
Solid as the
Earth

Having to meditate like Aang
Just to calm down
Inhaling stillness
Appreciating soundless noise
My breathing synchronized with my chest
I exhale
Air

In total balance
One with my powers

I am the Avatar

Uncle Iroh x Doodle and De-Stress

Maintenance required...

"Caring for myself is not self-indulgence. It is self-preservation, and that is an act of political warfare."

-Audre Lorde

Black, American Writer, Poet, Feminist, Activist
2/18/1934-11/17/1992

Why PLAN?

Planning

Lends

Aid

Nurturing

Support

Crowned

Rahim Mitchell

Victory

She never knew her identity, so she could never understand herself
She tried to camouflage into the environment
She wanted to become the one they would pick off a shelf
She wanted to be loved and understood
She did not know that she had a father that already would
She never knew that her true form could not be molded by people
That they could never accept her
That their opinions were feeble
Insecurity caged her in
And shackled her to the cold and rocky ground
The darkness grew deeper within
Nothing seemed to matter, not even her own life
And right at that moment a voice so strong began to speak
"You are my daughter and I will be your strength even when you are weak"
CRACK!
The shackles were no more
And green pastures started to rise from the floor
She finally understood, she was set free
Free from insecurity, acceptance and the feeling of being unloved
Through her Vulnerability He could reach her heart
He Insured her of her status and gave her love like a flood
He Comforted her
He even Treasured her very life
He taught her how to Overcome in strife
He told her to Rest in him because He was all she would need
"You are the head and not the tail, above and not beneath"
He continued, "Through Me you will always have

Victory."

Isis Pree

Isis Pree is a 2019 Hallelujah Anyhow! Scholarship contestant, Prince George's Community College (Largo, MD)

Learning and Leadership

```
                        J
                        G
                        R
                     E  A  H
                     A  D  X
                     C  U  S
                  B  C  A  C  Z
                  S  O  T  H  F
                  W  M  I  O  M
               W  A  P  O  O  I  N
               E  L  L  N  L  N  L
               A  I  I  A  E  F  H
            K  K  F  S  E  C  L  L  P
               W  N  E  H  S  N  U  R  A
               N  E  L  M  N  A  E  E  R
R P J G I G N I H C R A E S X U S O E O D N F A M B I T I O N S G Y S F B R S
  P L E H A W A R E N E S S N C S N N I N C L D T V B H L C E Y G N G T R W
     S T E A D F A S T D N U O F G T T U E E O F E O U H N N R O O S Q
        A V I C T O R Y O M O R A L S N B D C X C P F A O O E I A E T
         H T G N E R T S X D K I E C E A U T O E D N T I N T L U X
            D N E B R E S I L I A N T R T M T N G S T E A S L
               K I N D N E S S J R G N O I J I E E A E M E A
               N S O G A T S G N N I N T M P L N M R T V
                  M R S A R O I I G M A Q I I O I T
                  A P N O D N H P G R M M C F I
                  T I C T C G C L F G R R F N U
                  E R E N E L A H T E E A G C C
                  F A U E S Q E L T V N P D T O
                  O U T O M I J R E O U J I R S N L
                  H L I M T R W D L I G H T E E F D
                  T S O L S E C R U O S E R A F I D
               A G A N H G F M G     M L F J M I D R S
               L E G S V A O         J S X S N E E S
               O F Y O I O              O J A N W E
               M U I E T D              A M C O S U
               E D L H X                Y E P S X
               R A X                       L A M
            A  C  O                         C  Q  W
            A  Y                            B  J
            Q                                  Y
```

WORD LIST:

ABUNDANCE	FAITH	LIGHT	REFLECT
ACCOMPLISHMENTS	FOUND	LOST	RESILIANT
AFFIRMATIONS	GOAL SETTING	LOUD	RESOURCES
AMBITION	GOD	MANIFEST	RISE
ASPIRATIONS	GRADUATION	MENTORS	SCHOOL
ASSESS	GRATEFUL	MERCY	SEARCHING
AWARENESS	GRATITUDE	MILESTONES	STEADFAST
BECOMING	HELP	MINDFUL	STRENGTH
CHANGE	HOPE	MOOD	VALUES
CONFIDENCE	INFLUENCE	MORALS	VICTORY
DETERMINATION	INTENTIONS	OVERCOME	WEAKNESS
DISTANCE	KINDNESS	PARADOX	
DREAMS	LIFE	POWER	
ENERGY	LIFE LONG LEARNING	REACHING	

SURVIVAL PLANS

Creativity Booster:

Write a Poem/Thought/Story or Draw about…

Plans

Word Associations:

Preparation

Goals

Ideas

Intent

Purpose

Blueprint

Strategize

Forecast

Development of One's Self

```
                        V Z
                        M H
                        U R
            K R         P U                         N
              B M       O U H X Y N               O T
                Z A       J V R T B L Y A L P T     S V
                  R A E F E P L O I G M I K R O W  U R
                    O D R O A C A M R O T S G R O W E
                    M C C S E X D M N D W B E T T E R
                    V O E W R V Q O E E D T E A C H E S
                  Y M A B E V F I N R V F R R C B M N R
                    E C A E P F T O L O E U A A G R N D G X
                    N I J Z H A I R A T L H O I H I U D R Q
          R B E V L O V E C T F L C S O M F X T G S T E A C H W T
          F N E V I R D U O P A X H E P N O W M H C P R O M O T E
                    S F D V N M I J A R M E C N A T S I D R
                    F E E S T I T E N P E M E C T L D B E Y
                    K D N W H A H S G A N L P N E Y A V S
                      W H I E E G U E E T A V Q D L O S T
                      F V T H N Z S O W L C N O A O E R
                      O N N L S E W L V O S G N R C A V
                    T A   Q N A S R A R T H C D C I   J A
                  E C       O A E F O L H E E U N     Y T
              I Q             H G E G R S           V E
              Y                 A U                 F W
                                R I
                                N D
                                Q E
```

WORD LIST:

AIM	ELEVATE	LIFE	SUCCESS
BALANCE	EVOLVE	LIVE	SUN
BETTER	FAITH	NOW	TEACH
BRIGHTLY	FAITH	ORDER	TEACHES
CALM	FEAR	OVER	THE
CAN	GOAL	OVERCOME	TO
CHANGE	GOD	PEACE	TRAIN
DAILY	GROW	PLAY	US
DEVELOPMENT	GUIDE	PROMOTE	VOTE
DEVOTION	HARD	PURPOSE	WEALTH
DISTANCE	HEALTH	RENEW	WORK
DO	HOW	RESTORE	
DRIVEN	JESUS	SHINES	
EDUCATION	LEARN	STORM	

LIVING *Legacies*

"All good men and women must take responsibility to create legacies that will take the next generation to a level we could only imagine."

–Jim Rohn

In the Legacy

This poem in honor of the legacy,

The legacy of those men and women who walked a mile… or more before me,

In honor of he and she with names…

and some un-named,

Who made the way for opportunity amidst a world astray,

I'm blessed to say that I have come this way,

Holding my head high and standing on the shoulders of giants,

That's right GIANTS!

Super-human,

Above average individuals,

Individuals who have laid the ground-work,

 For the life that I build up-on today,

Building on blocks of freedom, education, hard work and dedication,

The foundation for all of who wish to achieve,

I'm basking in the hopes, prayers, promises and the DREAMS!

Of those who believed!

I'm being fulfilled by dreams no longer deferred,

Glass ceilings shattered and mountains being moved,

I can shout HALLELUJAH ANYHOW!

As old habits die, fruit matures and flowers bloom,

I'm tap dancing for joy in the spring,

And harvesting food for thought in the fall,

It's because of those before me, that I can do it all!

Because they were not discouraged by barriers set,

Nor did they cower when closed doors and obstacles were met,

I think of those individuals who did not settle for the "status quo,"

Free minded and free thinking is the only way to grow!

You become what you believe!

Her-story tells us so!

I'm living in the legacy of He and Sheros,

Some you may have heard of…

And others you may not know,

I'm following the footsteps that have been placed in the sand,

I'm walking by faith,

Not by sight,

Leaving my fear and worries behind,

Because I know that I walk Pathways,

That have been created by visionaries,

That sight beyond sight,

With insight that starts out like a seed,

It grows and transforms

And even takes flight beyond the sycamore trees

I told yall…

I'm living in the legacy

The legacy of He and Sheros,

Like Dr. Charlene M. Dukes,

And others honorable men and women,

Who you may or may not know,

This poem is in honor of that legacy

And… Prince George's Community College
WE ARE THE LEGACY!!!

Change at PGCC (Prince George's Community College) is...

Change at PGCC Is...
the Culture (so get use to it)!

Change at PGCC is...
the Smoke Free Campus campaign,
It started and became

Change at PGCC is...
Popping up everywhere,
Like Health Sciences, Culinary and Performing Arts Centers

Change at PGCC is...
Institutionally realigning with a mission
To serve our students and the greater community

Change at PGCC is...
Transformative leadership, student centered innovations and economic
viability in our community

Change at PGCC is...
Investing in community wellness, thriving technology, sustainable
opportunities, ballet and other fine arts

Change at PGCC is...
Inclusive and ALL members of the College Community are accountable for
Success!

Wake Up Everyone!

Change at PGCC is...
Happening Here
And its
Happening Now!

In the Living Legacy of David L. Nash

Vigilant. Man. Survivor. Provider. Cool Baller.

My father-in-law, David L. Nash affectionately known as "Dad," is one of the greatest men that I know. His positive outlook on life and vigilant faith has helped him to achieve many extraordinary things throughout his life.

Born on April 3, 1945 in Marianna, Arkansas and raised in St. Louis, Missouri, Dad comes from more than humble and meager beginnings. Being one of twelve children, his home life wasn't easy-and in order to survive, he knew that he would have to do something to become more.

Dad developed a passion for basketball at an early age and seen that and education as his opportunity to get out of the "hood." Dad told me he knew if he was going to make it, he "would have to be educated." He also told me that because he was "hungry," he would practice each and every day- his desire was to go to the NBA.

Upon graduating from Deshawn High School (MO), Dad was accepted to and left St. Louis to play college basketball for Dallas Baptist College (TX). This would lead his opportunity to play for the University of Kansas' Jayhawks. There he met and played with his good friend- former professional basketball player and Olympian, Joseph "JoJo" White. Dad chuckled as he recalled "messing those white boys up" and "hanging from the rim" on the basketball court.

It was 1970, when he left University of Kansas and was drafted by the Chicago Bulls. Dad recalled that they were paying an earnest salary of $29,500.00- I laughed but back then, Dad said that was "good money." It was during his first season with the Bulls that Dad came across an opportunity to join the Harlem Globetrotters- who he played and toured the world with for a couple of seasons.

After a while, Dad decided to move back to Kansas City, turning his sights on settling down a bit and starting a family. During this time, he met and married his first wife, Linda Cloud- and although their union was short lived, Dad reflected on the positive influence that his father-in-law, Mr. Cloud and that his future father in law Mr. Eberra had on him.

Dad met the love of his life, Anita Nash while she was working as a teller at the local bank. She was beautiful but Dad said she was playing "hard to get" and he had to "hound" her just to go out with him. He stated that eventually she "came to her senses…" and it wasn't before long that they began dating and were wed in holy matrimony on June 6, 1980.

Relocating from Kansas City to Baltimore and then to Washington, DC, David and Anita have now been married for 40 years. Their blessed union has produced two daughters, a son, nine granddaughters, one grandson (with one more on the way- David A. Nash III) and three great-granddaughters. Today, Dad still gets around, as an outreach liaison for the National Institutes of Health (NIH) where he has served the government and community for more than 30 years. He is also an active member of several organizations including the retired NBA players association, the Congressional Black Caucus and his church.

At 6'11 and 75 years of age, Dad stands tall in my book, as a great man. One who has had to overcome various obstacles and health challenges (including being a two-time cancer survivor) to achieve success. He has never let anything get him down and this is why he has had so much success and longevity in his life and career.

Takeaways from David "Dad" Nash:

- There is power and healing in a positive attitude/thinking.
- Developing faith in God and in one's self/abilities is necessary to succeed.
- Be hungry and Stay humble.
- Be vigilant in pursuit of success.
- Family first.
- Have integrity.

Featured are some pictures and fond memories from his life and times.

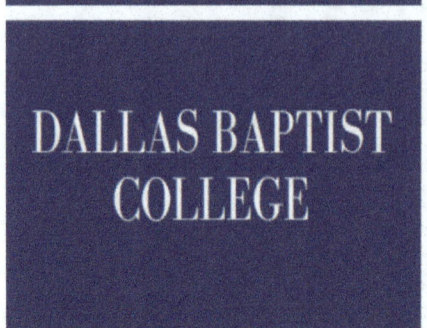

DALLAS BAPTIST COLLEGE

SURVIVAL PLANS

UNIVERSITY OF KANSAS

HARLEM GLOBETROTTERS

Dad,

Thankful that you took time out of your day to speak to my hospitality students at Prince George's Community College in 2016.

Mr. and Mrs. Nash

Est. 1980

Celebrating 40 Years of "Family First"

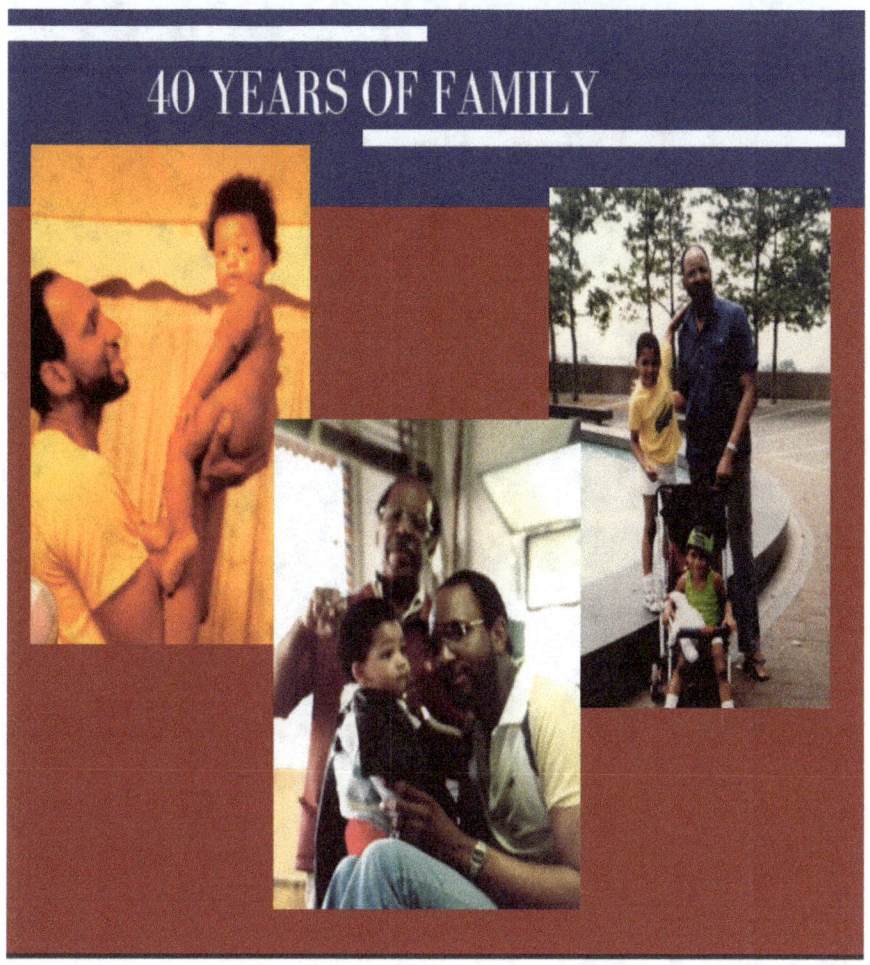

40 YEARS OF FAMILY

Doodle and De-Stress x KNJ

Kayla Nash Jones, Age 12

In the Living Legacy of The Honorable Donna F. Edwards

Courageous Intelligent Determined Committed

Congressional Leader

Takeaways from the Honorable D.F.E. (MD-4)

Having served and worked with the Honorable Donna F. Edwards (personally) as a congressional staffer, I have always admired her strength, courage to speak out or up for what she believed, her determination and her commitment to serve her constituents and causes. Her success as a lawyer, non-profit founder, mother and Congresswoman are nothing short of extraordinary. Being in her presence gave me hope and helped me to further develop the courage that I needed to stand tall in the face of any adversity.

While working for her, I became more community oriented and aware of some of the issues that plagued our community. While working for her, I was given an opportunity to give back, help people and manage community-based projects/events including the Congressional Art Competition. I also had the opportunity to learn more about the political process, leadership and advocacy.

Working for Congresswoman Edwards opened many doors and opportunities for me, both personally and professionally. These opportunities have helped to propel me forward in life.

I am grateful for my experiences working in her office and under her leadership.

It is through this book and service to the community that I keep her legacy (in my life) alive.

Takeaway Tip of the Day

If you want to be successful in life find extraordinary people (in your community) that you can look up to and learn from. If you seek them out, you will find them!

The Legacy Continues...

Survival PLANS

TIPS FOR SELECTING, UTILIZING & HOLDING ELECTED OFFICIALS ACCOUNTABLE FOR THE BETTERMENT OF YOUR COMMUNITY

- Bootstrap/ Fund raise money in your communities to identify your OWN community candidates and support the candidate that you believe in!

- Research ALL Candidates! (don't limit or be blindsided by political affiliation, race, gender or ethnicity)

- Assess Candidates Effectiveness (policies, voting history/patterns, data, background, ability to make change happen and hold people accountable)

- Lookup contact information for your elected officials and reach out to them, if you see where their support is needed.
(Elected officials usually have resources- grants, scholarships, human resources etc)

- Go to/show up at community events- and get to know the youth and elders in your community (this will help you understand the needs of your community members while giving you a visible presence and access.

- Request that Elected officials help foster and leverage relationships between community members and local law enforcement, businesses and support services.

Call to Action:

Now think about your community... How do you engage with your public officials? youth? elders? What are some ways that you can increase your community involvement.

When I grow up...

I want to seem as sweet as my mama

Be as wise as my grandmothers

As classy as Mom Nash

As smart as my Aunts

As free as my sister

Committed to youth in my community like Mrs. Geraldine Lippman

Be a service orientated leader like **Ms. Gail Smith-Howard**

As down to earth and as humble as **Dr. Charlene M. Dukes**

As determined as the **Honorable Donna Edwards**

Know my stuff like Ms. Alonia Sharps

As committed as Ms. Greta Martin

Start a school like Mary Bethune Cookman

Be successful like Oprah Winfrey

Write poetry and advocate like **Nikki Giovanni**

Get deep like Alecia Keys

Cook, bake and entertain (and look pretty doing it) like B Smith

Have more than a million and be as meticulous as my **Aunt Marion**

Sell books like Iyanla Vanzant

Do interviews like Barbara Walters

Be 1 in a Million like Aaliyah

Be a best-selling author like Zadie Smith

When I grow up there's no limit

To what I can be

Thanks to all the women who helped to shape me

"You don't have to reinvent the wheel, But you do have to blaze your own trail."

D. Nash

In the Living Legacy of Gail Smith Howard

6-Word BIO:

Trail-Blazing Woman Professional Motivational Leader

Gail Smith-Howard is a recognized Hotelier and leader in the Hospitality Industry. A passionate trailblazer, teacher and advocate, her 40-year Hyatt career started when she chose the hospitality industry, over the Madison Avenue career she had planned upon graduation from college. That fortuitous change helped set a course for an award-winning career with one of the world's most prestigious hotel chains, the Hyatt Corporation. Today, she serves in a unique position as one of a handful female General Managers working for the Hyatt in the U.S.

From the start, Gail showed passion and talent. Her first position came close to her native town of Montclair, New Jersey, when in 1980 she joined the team of the Grand Hyatt New York, one of Hyatt's flagship hotels, as a Housekeeping Manager. Shortly after, she was promoted to

Hyatt Regency Kansas City where she was awarded Manager of the Year. Following her time in Kansas she become the Executive Housekeeper at the Hyatt Regency Chicago, one of the largest hotels in the company, with over 2000 rooms, where she was recognized as Manager of the Quarter and subsequently promoted to Assistant Director of Rooms. In 1987, she returned to the East Coast as the Rooms Executive at the Hyatt Regency Cambridge, in Massachusetts and later became the Rooms Executive for Hyatt Regency Baltimore (1990-1992) and the Grand Hyatt Washington (1992-1994). Her next role came in 1994, serving as the General Manager of the Hyatt Regency Fair Lakes in Virginia, where she remained for ten years. In 2004, she joined the team of Hyatt Regency Baltimore and since 2014; she leads the team at Hyatt Regency Washington, in our Nation's Capital.

Throughout her career, Gail has received many accolades ranging from Manager of the Quarter awards to Manager of the Year. Since becoming a General Manager, she was nominated for the prestigious "Jay A. Pritzker Award – General Manager of the Year" four times and was awarded this high honor in 2004. She was also recognized as the General Manager of the Year for the cities of Baltimore and Washington, DC. And was selected one of Maryland's Top 100 Women in 2013 and the Baltimore Chamber of Commerce awarded Gail the Women of the Year award. In 2016 she was the recipient of the prestigious Trumpet Award, a recognition highlighting African American accomplishments and contributions. In 2018 Gail was named the WIL Connect Leader of the Year by the Hotel Association of Washington DC, an honor awarded to a female hospitality professional who serves as leaders and role models within the hotel community and the industry.

To contribute to the success of the cities she lives in, Gail has taken on a variety of City-wide leadership roles such as being a member of the Board of the Baltimore Area Convention and Visitors Association, Visit Baltimore, Destination DC, the Downtown DC BID and the Hotel Association of Washington DC. In addition, Gail served on Mayor's

Baltimore Hotel Commission and helped build and promote the Hire-1 Summer Employment and Development opportunity; a Mayoral Initiative to provide young adults ages 16 to 22 with summer job and opportunities in hospitality. Along her career Gail has encouraged and supported many colleagues who are now hold various and diverse leadership roles along Hyatt in other fields. She is a pioneer with her work in Inclusion & Diversity, as one of the first leaders to ignite the conversation and take action for the advancement of Women and People of Color in our industry. Today, she continues work in the city she lives and works in by helping to educate the next generation of hotel leaders through several of Hyatt's Diversity Business Resource groups such as Women@Hyatt, Hyatt B.L.A.C.K, Veterans@Hyatt and HyPride, all chapters she supports and helps grow. Yet, when asked her greatest accomplishments are being a mother to her son Daniyyel and an aunt to her twin nieces.

Reflections of Success

Mrs. ELLA MAE SMITH

I am whom I am because of the foundation of support provided by a loving, caring, intelligent, and strong mother and grandmother. This support also came from my sister, cousins, and other extended family members. My destiny was shaped by my mother and grandmother's belief in God, love, education, faith and honesty. They were of the opinion, that in order to accomplish your goals and realize your dreams; you must prepare yourself for the journey. At a young age, I was encouraged to be, and developed into, an autonomous thinker. Always striving to see those things beyond myself keeping the bigger picture in mind. To love thy neighbor even when they did not look or think like me, and although I may not agree with them to always try to understand things from their perspective and where they are coming from (which has served me well in hospitality). My family's love and support strengthened my self-awareness, self-confidence, and self-acceptance. The importance of education was always stressed, not only because in many ways it is viewed as a great equalizer, but also because it provided one with the necessary knowledge on a larger scale that would allow us to have a foundation upon which to prepare and build future generations.

After graduating Montclair High School in New Jersey I went on to attend the University of Miami. Subsequently transferring to Bloomfield College, where I graduated with degrees in Marketing and Finance. At that time, my Mother was attending Rutgers and my sister was in Seton Hall Law School, both of them were inspirations to me. After graduation, I found a career working for Hyatt, an industry I had absolutely no knowledge of and eventually loved. Now, 40 years later, I still love my career and I am more excited than when I started. Although, this is an industry that is grossly underrepresented in regards to minorities in Leadership and Executive levels, however, I have faith that future generations will break down the barriers that are obstructing this progress.

The Hospitality Industry is an industry that is 24/7, similar to a hospital, where my mother had a career. The key is to find a balance between your family, career, friends and your wellbeing. Taking care of yourself is important, whether it is praying, exercising, or having a hobby or whatever gives you peace of mind. Yes, you can have it all however, I have found just not all at the same time. There will be times you may leave early to attend your child's lacrosse game and then there will be times you will stay late for a V.I.P. event. Your career is a journey not a sprint. We are not Usain Bolt trying to get to the finish line. We must learn to enjoy the journey and take it in. Reflect and grow from it, be grateful and learn to appreciate it. Admittedly, this took me years to understand; however, it will come if you choose to embrace it. In my mind's eye, my mental picture on how my career affected relationships might have been seen differently by my family and friends, so I asked the question… *How did my career affect/impact my relationships with famly and friends? Negatively or positively?*

My Son Daniyyel

First and foremost, my son Daniyyel said I showed him that women in general and more specifically African American women and men can achieve a high level of success regardless of what society has lead people to believe at times.

My nephew Franco said that I created a bridge that has affected generations. That I helped him get to where he is today by giving him the opportunity to grow, having helpful conversations, experiencing life lessons, and as he put it ..."the me watching you and learning from you like a child does from a parent for lessons not being taught. Your compassion for others, the black community, forgiveness, faith, patience, and planning".... Franco is a wonderful young father and has been at times like an older brother to my son for which I am eternally rateful.

With My Friend Diane to my right

My friend Diane, whom I have known since I was 5 years old, said that I inspired her and was a friend that always showed up. ..."*Maybe you could not stay because you had to go to work but you always showed up*". Diane has even more so inspired me. I am often in awe for her, how she balances her career, family and has always been there for me. Ebony magazine did a story on working couples that did not have immediate family around in which my family was featured. In the story, I spoke of how Diane was always there for me when I worked a weekend and needed help with my son Dan. Always appreciate your family and friends and be there for them as well.

My cousin Cheryl, who is the CEO and President of her own engineering firm said *"Your success has positively impacted me and encouraged a determination to succeed throughout my own life. Seeing how you handled being present in our family and balancing the demands of your career helped me define my own personal goals for my immediate family. Our strong family bond and the values instilled in us at an early age, taught us how to interact with others, how to carve out our own paths and make our way in the world. Family is the first group of people you learn to trust. We were fortunate to have a close family dynamic that was, and still is, based on supporting one another's dreams, recognizing each other's strengths and keeping us* grounded. I am inspired by your ability to see beyond the immediate challenge or struggle and how you are able to focus on the bigger picture and not lose sight of your goals."

My Mother, my niece Ella, my son Daniyyel and my niece Elise

My niece Ella said …"As with any demanding job, it takes a lot of time away from family and friends. A large sacrifice in the scheme of things, but most times it is necessary in an industry that never sleeps. It is difficult to count the cost of such a sacrifice, and it is something your family and friends also had to endure, but the opportunity and exposure to great leaders and coworkers within your company and the world is something you had the pleasure of experiencing. You have also been able to provide and assist others through financial means and have been a mentor for the next generation behind you.

So, as one can see, like in any successful career your actions effect people differently, however the overarching goal in my life was to make a positive difference emotionally, mentally and financially. Just as people are affected differently by COVID-19, the pandemic is a disaster for the world; however, I know this too will pass. COVID-19 has had a devastating effect on our industry. I am working less days with less pay as most of my colleagues are. However, what I also see because of the disaster is that people are connecting once again with their family and showing their generosity. We are building and increasing genuine positive relationships. People and companies now have time to really see and pay attention to the injustices in our country and doing something about it. I am taking the time to exercise more when there was not time when working and commuting into DC.

With Jan Duncan

I am even more hopeful for the next generation and have a great amount of respect for them. They are innovators, educated and caring to all people from all walks of life. An example of this is a young woman whose name is Jan Duncan a graduate of Temple University. Jan has and is travelling the world with hospitality advancing in the world of sales. She inspires me with her quest for knowledge and ease at forming connections. If I were to start my career today, I would incorporate moving to different cities around the world and not limit my journey to just within the USA. I would explore, learn, and broaden my overall depth of knowledge about people, different cultures and different ways of thinking.

I say to the next generation to continue to make our industry better and more inclusive. Surround yourself with smart, caring people who believe in the values and goals that you do, but are different from you, so you can get different outlooks. Work hard and smart for what you want to achieve in your career. Find your true north and pursue it with integrity and honesty. Believe in yourself and care about your peers. Work for a company that has your values, such as I did, and believe your career will be fun and you will love your career too. Do not misinterpret my words because words have meaning and are important, and I am not some Pollyanna who says it is easy to advance upward, it is not, but if that is your desire, it is a hard journey, however it is worth it.

Featured are some photos from her Journey:

The Leadership Team of Hyatt Regency Baltimore

Gail and the Leadership Team of Hyatt Regency Washington on Capitol Hill

SURVIVAL PLANS

Top 100 Women Award – (Gail is 5th on second row from the left)

Trumpet Awards

Gail Smith-Howard w/ her former Corporate Management Trainees P. Seward and S. Nash @ Hyatt B.L.A.C.K event 2016

Reflections from S. Nash

When I arrived at Hyatt Regency Baltimore in January 2007 as a "wet behind the ears" Certified Manager Trainee (CMT), I was blessed to have met, worked with, look up to and support the strategic direction of our trail-blazing General Manager,

Mrs. Gail Smith-Howard. Being able to see myself in her (an African American woman) helped me to see and aspire to achieve success. I just knew that I wanted to follow in her footsteps… **Success leaves a trail!**

Years after leaving Hyatt Corporation, I still look up to Ms. Smith-Howard and have enjoyed reaching out to her over the years and taking my Prince George's Community College students to her property at the Hyatt Regency Capitol Hill (on a couple of occasions). I appreciate and am eternally grateful for these opportunities and this relationship.

Mrs. Nash Brings PGCC Hospitality students to Hyatt B.L.A.C.K. Event

Hosted by Hyatt Regency Capitol Hill, Washington DC (2016)

In true transformational leadership style, Ms. Smith-Howard invites Dr. Willie Jolley to #Hyatt B.L.A.C.K event to bring words of encouragement to a diverse group of leaders in hospitality industry

In The Living Legacy Nikki Giovanni

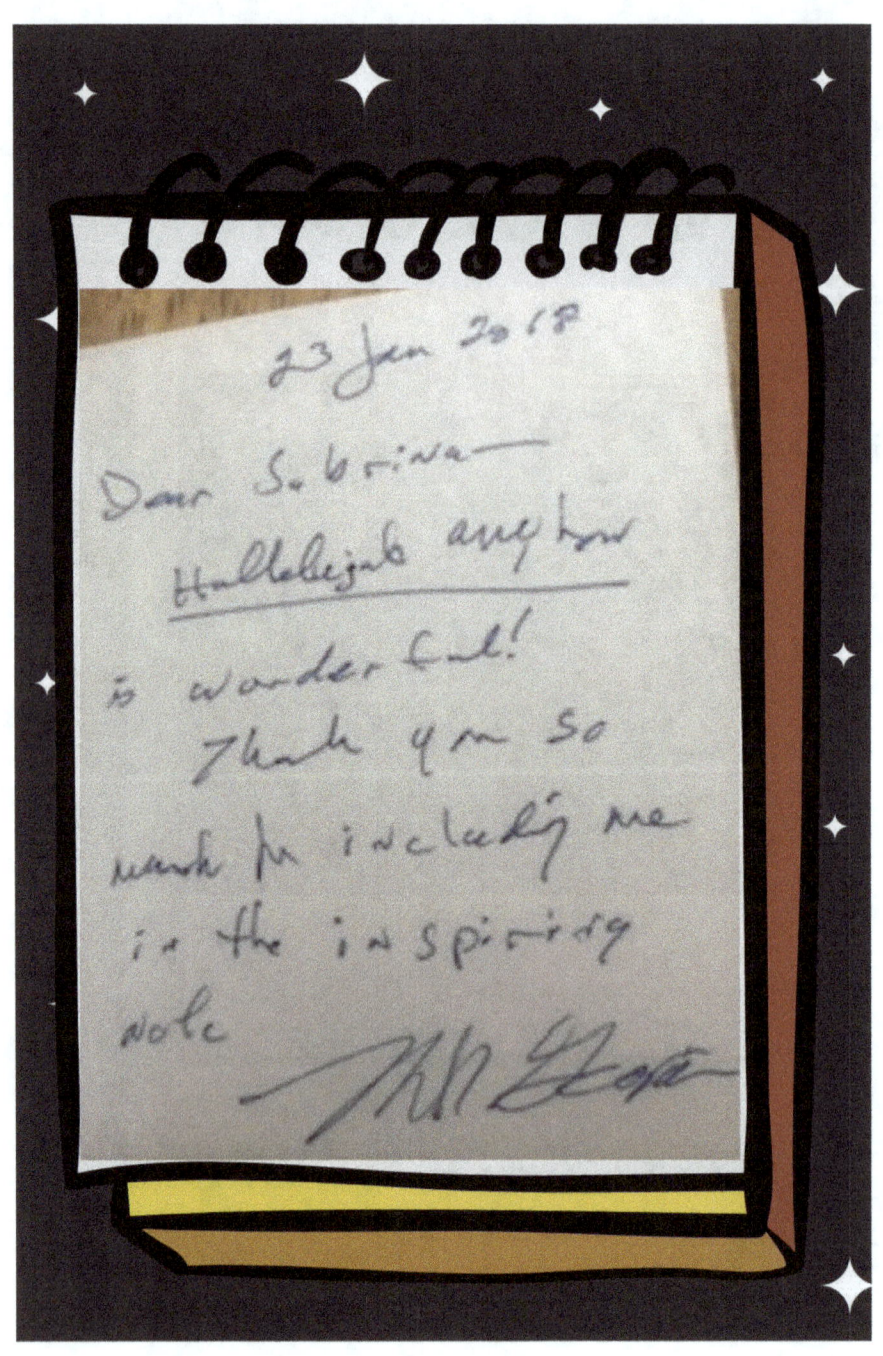

In the Living Legacy of Tuskegee Airman
Major Charles B. Hall

Major Charles B. Hall, WWII Hero, and my Grandfather
By Erica L. Jones

Charles B. Hall made history by being the first African American pilot to shoot down an enemy aircraft in World War II. He was also my grandfather.

Before the civil rights movement of the 1960s, most African-American families of the 1930s were living separate lives than those of white families across the United States. It was a time of separate restrooms and water fountains, job and wage discrimination and segregation.

During a time when many people thought African-Americans lacked intelligence, skill, courage and patriotism, a young black man from Brazil challenged those ideas to become a hero of the skies. His name was Charles B. Hall and he was my grandfather.

My grandfather probably had no idea his service and love of flying would become instrumental in helping his country dominate the air space over foreign lands in World War II and break down the barriers of prejudice at home in America.

Charles B. Hall was born August 25, 1920, in Brazil, Indiana. He attended Brazil High School where he excelled in sports. After his graduation in 1938, he attended Eastern Illinois State Teachers College, where he excelled at track and football while studying premed.

During this time, in anticipation of the United States being drawn into World War II, President Franklin D. Roosevelt implemented a pilot training program to create a reserve of trained civilian fliers in case of national emergency. African-American leaders argued that blacks should share with whites the burden of defending the United States, and Roosevelt soon opened the program to African-Americans. In 1940, the Selective training and Service Act banned racial discrimination, clearing the way for African Americans to be trained for Civilian Air Corps service.

African Americans were sent to Tuskegee Institute, a college founded in Alabama in 1881 by Booker T. Washington, to be trained. My grandfather was one of the first of 43 African Americans to participate in the training. The first fighter pilots graduated on March 7, 1942, forming the 99th Pursuit Fighter Squadron, a part of the 332nd fighter Group.

After training in Tuskegee, Alabama, the 99th shipped out to North Africa in the spring of 1943. Flying out of Tunisia, pilots from the 99th saw their first combat action escorting bombers in Allied operations against the island of Pantelleria in early June.

In 1943, Charles B. Hall became the first African-American fighter pilot to take down an enemy aircraft. The strike on the enemy aircraft happened on July 2, 1943, while my grandfather was a member of the 99th Fighter Squadron. In his P-40 Warhawk, he was on an escort mission of B-25 medium bombers on a raid on Castelvetrano in southwestern Sicily, Italy, when he shot down the Focke-Wulf Fw 190 Würger.

Lt. Charles B. Hall in the cockpit of his P-40 (*U.S. Air Force photo*)

The news of the first African American to take down an enemy plane was covered in detail by the *Courier*, the Baltimore-based *Afro-American*, the *Chicago Defender*, the *New York Amsterdam News*, the *Atlanta Daily World*, and numerous other newspapers nationwide serving the Black community. So you can imagine how significant the events of July 2, 1943 were for a segment of the U.S. population that was fighting for rights and respect in day-to-day life while also playing a critical role in the war effort.

Back in Tunisia, my grandfather received a hero's welcome, and a long-awaited gift. The 99th had saved its last bottle of Coca Cola "for the pilot who put the first notch in his guns," as Ollie Stewart wrote in the *Afro-American*. "Fabulous prices have been offered for the coke and it had to be well guarded. Hall was perhaps the best liked man in his squadron; always smiling and always ready to fly."

While the prized bottle may have been the most meaningful tribute offered up to the victor, that wasn't the extent of the celebration. Gen. Dwight D. Eisenhower and several other high-profile officers, including Gen. Carl "Tooey" Spaatz and Gen. James Doolittle, were on a tour of North African airbases that day. Eisenhower personally congratulated Hall on his feat.

In January 1944, the 99th was on the Italian mainland, supporting operations at the Anzio beachhead, when it was called into action to repel German fighters over a two-day span. Ten different pilots recorded victories on January 27, and the squadron claimed three more kills the following day — two of them by my grandfather who was a Captain at the time. Those victories earned my him the Distinguished Flying Cross, making him the first Black pilot so honored.

My grandfather came home later in 1944 and embarked on a three and a half month-tour to drum up war bond sales. He then returned to Tuskegee to serve as an instructor before leaving the Army Air Forces as a major in 1946.

The Tuskegee Airmen were the first black military aviators in the U.S. Army Air Corps (AAC), a precursor of the U.S. Air Force. Trained at the Tuskegee Army Air Field in Alabama, they flew more than 15,000 individual sorties in Europe and North Africa during World War II. Their impressive performance earned them more than 150 Distinguished Flying Crosses, and helped encourage the eventual integration of the U.S. armed forces.

My grandfather settled in Oklahoma City in 1948, and began working at Tinker Air Force Base in 1949. While working there he met and married my grandmother, Delois Hall. He worked at the base through 1967 before moving on to the Federal Aviation Administration offices in Oklahoma City. He had three children, son Theodore, and daughters, Sherri and Kelli. I am the daughter of Kelli. My grandfather died on November 22, 1971, at 51 years old.

Over time, as the story of the Tuskegee Airmen became more prominent in coverage and commemoration of World War II history, my grandfather's exploits would reach a wider audience.

The Smithsonian Air Space Museum has a display of the Tuskegee Airman featuring my grandfather.

The City of Brazil dedicated a monument to my grandfather in front of the City Hall. They also renamed a street after him on Brazil's north side.

In 2002, the Tinker Heritage Airpark at Tinker Air Force Base was renamed the

Maj. Charles B. Hall Memorial Airpark. Five years later, a life-size bronze statue of Hall, designated to represent the contributions of all the Tuskegee Airmen, went on dispay there.

My grandfather passed before I was born but I believe we are kindred souls connected by our love of flying. Although I'm not a pilot I do work in the airline industry as a flight attendant and l love to fly.

I am so proud to be the granddaughter of WWII hero, Charles B. Hall. It is an honor to share his accomplishments and I hope his story inspires children of all races to follow their dream.

Sherri Hall Harris, Kelli Hall Jones, Erica Jones.

Create a Legacy...

Follow Your Dreams

LEAVING A LEGACY

Leaving a legacy is important. Your children and their children should not have to start from scratch-not if you walked the path of life first.

 Leaving a legacy (to me) is about sharing your story. Helping your children to learn from your mistakes and life experiences. Sharing your books, writings/journals, family history and photos.

Leaving a legacy is working hard to acquire education, land, property, businesses and other tools that help one to develop self-sufficiency. Self-sufficiency is an important skill to develop and pass down.

 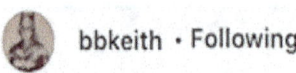 • Following

The Gathering Place

The Living Legacy of the Battle and Burgess Family

(My documented Paternal Family Lineage)

Our research of the Battle's family history is ongoing. We are prayerful that one day we will be able to complete our research of the family starting with our slave ancestors. Currently our family history, documented through the US Census and local county records, starts with our great grandparents.

Isaac and *Penny Jones Battle* were married on December 14, 1874. They were the parents of *William H., Alex Sr., Mattie Battle Avent* and *Isaiah*. The 1880 Census indicated that Isaac was a farm laborer. Penny was a wife and housekeeper. William was the only son in the house during the 1880 Census and he was one year old.

The origin of Isaac's wealth and how he became a land owner is unknown. However, relatives and neighbors have validated that Isaac was a man of wealth during his life. He acquired enough land that when his children reached adulthood, he gave each of them a share of the property. All of his children, except William wanted to move from the area so they sold their land to William Alex Sr. and Mattie purchased property in other areas. Isaiah stayed in the ITA area but there are no records indicating he purchased land or rented during his life time.

William H. Battle married *Mary Wright* on December 13, 1902. Mary was the daughter of *Charles* and *Melissie Wright*. Mary had seven siblings: *Lena Wright Jordan, Lucy Wright Epps, Ella Wright Brinkley, Lee, Junior, Estell Wright Kimbell* and *Charlie*.

By acquiring the land from his siblings, William and Mary became landowners of a considerable amount of land in the ITA community. William like his father was a farmer and Mary was the mother and housekeeper. They were blessed with eight children: ***Pennie Battle Wester, Eugene, Annie Battle Richardson, Alex Jr., Maggie Battle Young, Mable Battle Perry, Beaufort*** and ***William Arthur.***

William, Mary and their children knew the meaning of the phrase "we get more work done before breakfast than the average person does all day." Milking cows, gathering eggs, carrying water from the spring and wood from the woodpile to cook and heat the home were tasks completed before embarking upon a day of field work.

Although William's primary occupation was a Farmer, he was a very skilled and talented man. He was known throughout the community as a skilled basket weaver and the materials he used were harvested from the trees on the land. He also made brooms from straw that was gathered from the land. As a farmer, he grew cane and made his own syrup (molasses) with the cane mill that he owned.

Mary Wright Battle

Mary was known as a skillful negotiator and a crude business woman. She made butter and sold it to the local merchants in Enfield and always got the price she wanted for her goods. She was called on by many in the community and family members when someone was sick. She used different types of roots and leaves harvested from the nearby woods. Although none of her remedies were documented as modern medicine, many of us would not be here today if it was not for her medical intervention. She made clothes for her grandchildren out of feedbags. Her house was always clean and smelled of fresh baked pies and cakes. Her flower garden in front of the house was always in bloom during the spring and fall seasons.

The farmland though plagued with clay and rocks was very fertile. The family depended on the garden and livestock as their basic support for necessities of everyday life. Spring and summer yielded bountiful harvest of fresh vegetables. The garden contained a variety of white potatoes, scallions, leeks, yellow and green squash, hot and sweet peppers, sweet corn, peas, string beans, tomatoes, cabbages, lima beans, butter beans, cantaloupes, cucumbers and watermelons. Watermelons and cantaloupes were often placed in a cool stream in summer and later eaten as a treat. Fall and early winter gardens yielded pumpkins, sweet potatoes, collard greens, turnips, winter cabbages and mustard greens.

Fruits grew wild as well as in an orchard containing a variety of apples, pears, plums, figs, peaches, cherry trees, strawberries, blackberries and grapes. Vegetables and fruits harvested during the season were preserved by canning, air-drying or making preserves for the winter months. Fresh herbs such as sage, catnip, basil, mullein roots were found and used for tea or home remedies for medicine. Doctors were rarely used during these times.

Earning a living required a great deal of physical labor. Livestock and farm animals were used for the heavy work of preparing the land for planting. Cows and pigs were slaughtered for food, steak, pork chops, hand ground sausage and spare ribs. Pork shoulders and hams were often cured in the smokehouse.

Money producing crops for the market were; cotton, tobacco, cucumbers, peanuts, wheat, corn and peppers. The money from the market crops helped sustain the family until the next season of harvest.

After working hard all week, entertainment centered around church, family and community. Music, singing, baseball games, checkers and fish fries would often take place when everyone gathered.

Education was also important to William and Mary. It was said that William donated part of his land to start the ITA School for the colored children of the community. William and Mary's older grandchildren remember staying with them during the week so they could attend school. Their uncle and aunts; Beaufort, Maggie and Mable, helped them with their homework each night before going to bed.

All were called to worship on Sunday and attended the local church. Although the Battles were not noted in the history of the White Oak Missionary Baptist Church, they were instrumental in the organization and support of the church. William and Mary's final resting place are in the White Oak Cemetery. William died on May 24, 1955 of Coronary occlusion and Mary passed on November 22, 1967.

During the life of William and Mary Battle intense physical labor was required to accomplish tasks. Today, with the internet at our fingertips, technology that transmits information in seconds, and the opportunity for higher education, we can accomplish almost anything if we remember the character of the older generation:

" **Confidence**—faith or belief that within (God's Grace) there lay the power and ability to succeed.

¨ **Courage**—mental or moral strength to venture, perseverance to withstand danger, overcome fears and difficulties.

¨ **Determination**—to bring about results, to firmly resolve the issues affecting your circumstances.

The children of William and Mary Wright Battle acquired much of their parents attributes and determination to work hard, honor God and raise their children based on the Word of God. William and Mary had eight children; Eugene, Alex, Beaufort, Arthur, Annie, Mable, Kate and Maggie.

We pray that sharing this small amount of information about our great grandparents and grandparents will assure each of us that we have a rich heritage to be proud of and we should strive each and every day God gives us to continue this legacy for the future generation of this family.

The Ita School

The Burgess Family History

John Burgess and Eveline (last name unknown) had seven children. It was acknowledged that at least some of the children were step children. Since they all carried the same last name, it was assumed that they were all John Burgess' children.

John and Eveline children were; Junious, Cyrus, Albert, Julia, Louisa, Mariah and Eveline.

Daughters; Julia and Louisa married brothers June and James Alston respectively on April 7, 1867 in Warren County and son Cyrus Burgess married Nancy Williams on December 28, 1866.

Most if not all of the Burgess labored as slaves. Junious, Albert, Albert's wife Annie and their three children; Thomas, John and Pierce all were considered the property of Gen. Micajah Thomas Hawkins.

Albert married Anna "Annie" Hawkins on January 01, 1836 and Mintie (Minta) Reevis later. His Cohabitation Certificate with Annie was filed August 20, 1866 in Warren County, North Carolina. Albert and Annie's children were Mary Ann, Zelda/Zella and Waymouth. Zelda was disable and Mary Ann took care of her sister in their later years. Waymouth was a Deacon as well as Church Clerk at Shiloh Baptist Church in Arcola.

Albert's children of his second marriage to Mintie were Cary, born 1921 and Estha/Ester, born 1919 (both in Fishing Creek township according to Warren County Birth records).

Upon his emancipation Albert became a minister of God. Albert was a dark-skinned man, and prior to emancipation worked as a carpenter and body servant of Gen. Hawkins. He is described in a book called "Sketches of Old Warrenton" as "a man of excellent manners, dignified in personal appearance, and of superior intelligence." In Reconstruction days, he was considered an important political figure in the county and instrumental in keeping up kindly relations between the white and colored population. His wife Annie was considered "a woman of a good character. She was very genteel in appearance and very neat and orderly in her home."

The couple were known to the white community of Warrenton as "Uncle" Albert and "Aunt" Annie, terms whereby whites, in those days, could offer a modicum of respect to well thought of blacks without actually bestowing on them the dignity of being referred as "Mister" and Missus."

Albert and Annie lived in a house in Warrenton which was built by Thomas Bragg (well-known architect). "The Constitution of 1868 gave Negroes the right to vote, established a system of public schools, divided counties into townships instead of districts and substituted boards of county commissioners for the old committees of justices. The delegate from Warren County to the constitutional convention was John Hyman, elected by the Republican freedmen."

Many whites did not approved of education black children, much less allowing black men to right to vote and serve public office. The knights of the Ku Klux Klan attempted to intimidate the local colored population by posting "weirdly threatening proclamations and was probably responsible for the digging, before election day, of yawning graves besides the roads leading to the polls. The implied threat did not frighten away the Negroes, who were eager to vote for the first time and who were well organized by Hyman, Burgess and others of their race who had assumed Republican leadership.

In September of 1869, two young Pennsylvania idealists arrived in Warrenton to teach a school for colored children. Despite the supposed "good relations" between the races in Warrenton, the education of colored children was not generally approved of by the local whites and all of the teachers who filled the open positions were from the North. Keep in mind that relationships between northerners and Southerners were not that great either. While the two teachers, Margaret Newbold Thorpe and Elizabeth Pennock were educated, well-dressed and modest, there was no one willing to offer them a home or even a room within a boarding house.

It was considered quite astonishing and unusual when Albert and Annie opened their home to them and rented the teachers certain rooms in their home. In the interest of retaining the teachers for the children of their own race and mindful of the fact that the eyes of the community were upon them. Albert and Annie treated their "guests" in much the same manner as they had treated the family of Micajah Hawkins when working as house servants. They cooked for them and waited on them and avoided any appearance of fraternization. After a few months a white man came to teach in the same schools and while he lived in another place, apparently suffered the same ostracizing for he took his meals at Albert Burgess' home with the two teachers. (Montgomery, Sketches of old Warrenton, pp 274—277 The county of Warren.)

Junious Burgess was born September 15, 1835. As an adult he was described as a tall man, over two hundred pounds and heavy set. He was very light-completed and his race was considered in that class referred to as "mulatto" in the antebellum South. A "mulatto" is technically, a person born of one white parent and one black parent.

Junious labored as a slave, probably in Warren County. On July 10, 1857, he married Almira Williams, daughter of Isril and Malinna Williams. To this union was born five daughters and four sons.

Their firstborn was William "Billy" Burgess, born November 30, 1856. Also born to this union was Levit "LT" Burgess who was born around 1861 (A period of considerable unrest as this was the same year North Carolina seceded from the Union). Levit eventually married Patsey Richardson about 1885.

On April 26, 1865, North Carolina surrendered to the North and entered the Reconstruction period. The newly freed slaves were given the chance to legalize their marriages and on July 4, 1866 in Warren County, Junious and Almira filed a Cohabitation Certificate to recognize their status as man and wife.

In June 1866, the month prior to their filing, Almira gave birth to Cyrus "CC" Burgess their first child born out of slavery. Cyrus eventually married a woman named Bertha.

Junious and Almira's other children included Lillie, born about 1871. She married Jim H. Richardson. Doc F. Burgess born about 1872 married Maria Williams. The names of the other children were; Nelvina "Vine" Burgess born about 1879, Mary Burgess born December 10, 1880, Corine Burgess born about 1886 and married Harry Alston and Lucy Burgess, who did not have a birth year recorded.

Junious Burgess made his living as a farmer probably on a subsistence basis as did many other small farmers in the area. He was one of the first two deacons at Shiloh Church, which started as a bush arbor in Arcola, NC until a log building was erected. Junious' sons William also served at Shiloh in the capacity of Superintendent. William's wife, Candies though not a member, helped organize the first missionary circle.

Junious Burgess died of Bright's Disease on December 16, 1918 in Warren County and was buried in the Shiloh Baptist Church Cemetery. Almira Williams Burgess died a little over two years later on April 24, 1921 of old age and was also buried in the Shiloh Cemetery.

William "Billy" Burgess married Candis Harper in 1880. Candis was born in 1863. Based on the 1910 Census, Warren County, NC, William "Billy" Burgess was 49 and his wife Candis Harper-Burgess was 47. They had five children:

Christana Burgess born 1890—20 years old in 1910

Susana Burgess born 1896—24 years old in 1910

Allie Burgess—The youngest of the five children.

Sidney Burgess—One of the oldest sons

Lady Van Burgess-One of the oldest daughter.

Residing in the home of Willie "William" and Candis during the 1910 Census were Christana's daughter Opheia born 1908 who was 2 years of age; mitt (Mittie) Alston, relationship to family unknown. She was born in 1888 and was age 22 in 1910 and Lowell age 4 born 1907 relationship to family is not know. Speculations are that Lowell is a grandchild of Willie and Candis.

Compiled by:

The Battle and Wright Families

Battle & Burgess FAMILY

The Gathering Place

SURVIVAL PLANS

The Gathering Place

The gathering place
Is where we meet
To share in life
Our family seat

To drink from the same gorge
From one to fifteen
To help one another
To plant, grow and gather seeds

To rise early and feed the chickens
Ride with daddy out to the field to get them ripe pickens
Or a sack of beans
To warm up with mommas most wonderful biscuits

It wasn't much
but it's what we had
On this gathering place
Our family land

We shared love
As warm as our cast iron furnace
Til electricity was strung
And lights were hung

Didn't even know we were poor
With only a biscuit for lunch
Seems like we always had enough
During those cold times and icy winter months

Our three-room timber home
Large enough to hold all fifteen
And our aunts, uncles and cousins when Sunday came.

It wasn't much
but it's what we had
On this gathering place
Our family land

The
Gathering Place

"As for Me and My house, We will Serve the Lord."

Thank You for Sharing Our Joy

This is a tiny message,

But it's written just for you

Who found time in your busy life,

To give us a moment or two

We hope that you can feel

As we, light hearted and gay,

And share with use the magic,

Of this enchanting day

Battle and Burgess Reunion

July 2, 1977

The Gathering Place

Survival Plans Reflection

Aunt Florence Bert

What impact did Daddy & Mom's life and passing have on my life?

My mother had the biggest impact on my life. She was the disciplinary, the training and the teacher in my life. My father was mainly the provider. My mother, not through specific training but by observation, taught me the meaning of saving for a rainy day. Although she never held a public job, she would be the negotiator of every car, tractor and appliance purchased. She had the trust of her husband in that he would work all week and bring his paycheck home and put it in her hands. With only a six grade education, she managed a household of thirteen children, a farm and a husband. Although daddy was the father figure that provided food and shelter for the family, my mother was the glue that held the family together. There was no favoritism among the children, all was treated equally. Although my brother Jessie was the first to die in the family, my mother's passing was the most devastating; the glue was gone. My friend, my every Sunday afternoon phone call was gone and although I tried to fulfill the void with taking care of daddy, he eventually could not live without her and gave up too. Today, even though they both have been with the Lord for many of years, when crisis within the family comes up, I can feel them pushing me. The steps and actions are too specific to be my own and rest doesn't come until I complete the task.

How do I cope with their death?

As with Clinton's death I cope with my parents' death by trusting and believing on the Word of God. I pushed through the fact that

I can't see or talk to them today, but after my life is over here on earth, I will be reunited with then in heaven

Things I would want them to know………

If I could have a conversation with them today, I would let them know that they are loved and missed. I would tell them that we, the children are doing all we can to keep the legacy and their memory that they lived alive. I would let them know we are working hard to keep the home place as a place for gathering and fellowshipping for the family. Lastly, I would let them know that their lives are being manifested through their grandchildren and greatgrandchildren today

Love Your Family

Zoe James-Nash

In the Living Legacy of Clinton Battle

(My Daddy)

Strong   Sound   Hard-working   Man   Provider

Reflections from his Legacy:

Clint,

I remember when you started to write your life story-you were proud to share with me what you had written (as if to meet my approval). I remember smiling and you knew then that it did. As you continued to write in time, I thought that we would publish your memoirs together, this never happened. I am so grateful that our daughter, Sabrina seen a need to let your thoughts be known to ALL in your absence.

You are loved and missed greatly by all who knew you. You touched so many live, especially mine, your loving and caring wife.

-Darcelle Battle (wife)

"My first memories of Dad are of the fishing trips that we use to take. It showed me to have patience. He also instilled in me how to have respect for women and family. He never let me pick on you (Sabrina) even though you would throw my legos around. He taught me equality… he was the first to let me drive in his lap. He would take Clinton and I to a parking lot and would always give me a turn to drive even though I was very small.

At the time of Dad's passing, I was in the military (USAF), stationed in England. I actually was battling an infection from and oral surgery- and actually did the opposite of what I should have done. I didn't attend the funeral- I drank a lot and took medication. My brother Clinton was so upset that I did not come which resulted in us not speaking for years. We are better now- but we both miss him and wish we had more time.

Dad, you did a good job with me with the time that you had. You instilled in me values that I will continue to pass down to my kids."

-Christian Alexander Battle (son)

"From New Jersey to Maryland, people would approach me and tell me about how great my Dad was. I could be walking out of a corner store and someone would tell me about something that he did for them. He gave to everyone. I remember him giving his Dodge Minivan to my ex-girlfriend's mother when her car broke down… Even when our cars broke down, he would wake up early or stay up late to fix them and never complained. A man of few words but I could call him for anything- he would come through.

I was blessed- I remember Dad told me that if I got my license he would get me a car. He kept his word, first letting me have his old Chrysler Lebaron. Then one day out of the blue, he took me down to Carmax and I picked out a new red Mazda 626 which he purchased for me. Many young men my age never had a Dad to do that for them.

He was the type of man that didn't care what job you did, as long as you did it well. He used to tell me that "you could be a street sweeper or garbage man- but if you do that job, do it well and do it to the best of your ability."

A week before Dad passed, I stopped by to see him. I had missed my sister (Sabrina), leaving by minutes- but as soon as I got there, he told me he wanted to take me for a ride. We rode to a trucking lot in Dundalk, MD where his Airgas office was located. On the lot he had a boat and a Mack truck that he had planned to fix up and take down to North Carolina after retirement for relaxation and to start his own trucking business. This was my first time at the lot. Dad had never brought me there in all of my 26 years (of life at the time)- and commented that he wished he would have brought me there sooner- so that we could have driven and started a business together.

Although he worked- he always thought about business and ownership- he took pride in it."

-Anthony Omar Battle (son)

"Although you were a man who said less, my first memory of you is actually of your voice. I remember as a baby you singing/humming "Sabrina lene, Sabrina Lene oh how I love Sabrina Lene." That melody still lingers in my head until this day…

You had your own little way of making us all feel special and connected to you. I remember you waking us up (Anthony, Sierra and I) at the crack of dawn (7:30-8:00 am) on many Saturday mornings to have breakfast with you at the kitchen table. This typically meant that you had something on your mind that you wanted to say to us or share with us. Often times, the message went over our heads but at least I tried to listen…

At some point, I remember that you told me that I earned the "Christianna Battle Award" after your mom- although I can't remember what I had done to be deserving. You would often give me books to read (the autobiographies- Fredrick Douglas, Smokey Robinson and Al Green) were my favorite… and because I was a good reader, you would often ask me to read articles, papers and books out loud for you.

As a teenager, I was full of both good and bad decisions (and opinions). You never hesitated to call me out and check me if I was out of line (even in front of my "friends")- but you also made sure that I had a car and anything else that I needed to work towards autonomy. I never wanted for nothing- and you were always there. You were the first person to actually question and trust me in the same breath. I always wanted to "prove" myself to you.

You were the hardest working person that I have ever met and always gave to others in need. I remember you fixing people's cars, giving people money, taking in family (and extended family) members who needed a place, giving people rides- education, ownership and having a skill was important to you.

At the time of your death, you and I were in a solid good space- I was 23 and we could talk to each other (about just about anything) and even enjoyed each other's company. I reminisce on how I would ask you about "how you and mom met," and stories about your first wife, friendship with Carmelita and your child hood. I was always inquisitive when it came to your life. I appreciated your openness and honesty.

I'd like to think that you were proud of me (but I don't recall those words actually coming from your mouth)- I had graduated from University of MD Eastern Shore, magna cum laude, was working, taking care of my new born baby and my own household bills (never calling you for a handout since I moved out). I remember that I prided myself on being your only child to EVER pay you back after you lent me $1,600 one year earlier, to secure a lawyer needed to save my then boyfriend from facing deportation (but that's whole other story for another book).

Two weeks before your untimely departure, you came to me in a dream. In my dream, I was back at home in my childhood room. My newborn was there with me and you came into my room. You were standing near the window and you looked as if you were in a bright light from the sun. I remember coming towards you in the dream and commenting on "how good you looked." As I got closer to you, I seen a worried look on your face. Terrified I screeched "Daddy, what's wrong?" You took me in your arms and turned me around to see my mother in a hospital bed with a white sheet up to her waist. She was weeping. I remember screaming "what's wrong with mom- oh no, what's wrong with Mom, Dad?

I woke up in tears- not knowing what the dream had meant. I was shook and had the eeriest feeling that I was being prepared for your departure. That weekend, I decided to come and visit you and Mom. It was a good weekend. Relaxed. We talked, laughed rode out and I enjoyed hanging out with Mom. I was reminded of my dream when I came into your room and saw you in a yellow undershirt and khaki shorts. You were resting and you looked "so good." As the words came to my head and out of my mouth, I experienced a flashback of my dream. I became so uneasy and worried that evening, that I confided in Mom about the dream. During our conversation she assured me that I had nothing to worry about.

One week later, I received the call at 5:00 am that would not only rock our foundation to the core but also change my life. Mom crying through the phone "Heee's gonne" – also still lingers in my head.

I left my home in Northern Virginia (NOVA) like a bat out of hell. As I pulled up at Harbor Hospital (Baltimore, MD), I couldn't help but to feel uneasy. I knew that I would have to be there for Mommy and "step up" in whatever capacity that I could.

I came into the room to see you. You looked sleep. You lay on a bed, your skin still warm to the touch, a slight smile on your face- you still looked good… but the reality was that you were gone.

Shortly after your passing- I moved home to be with Mommy. I was now going through a nasty divorce (at 23) and was commuting back and forth to VA for work each day. At home, I made sure that I helped to cook, clean, contribute to the household bills and take care of things that needed to be done. For many months, I would picture you walking through the front door- and sometimes even see your shadow. I went through many stages of grief including shock and depression (which had me drinking brown liquor until I wrecked my new Lexus) to drown out the pain.

When life seemed unbearable- at my darkest hour, I began to pray. I began to literally get my bible, read and pray. I remember getting down on my knees asking the Lord to guide my footsteps and protect me- because I knew I was lost without my Dad.

I would visit your grave and feel like Simba at pride rock connecting with Mufasa- but yearned for your return. Within a few months of your departure the Lord sent me David (my husband) who has been a God send helping to protect and heal me from that trauma.

Today, more than 10 years later, I live in your legacy. I am a walking embodiment (in progress) of what I think you would have wanted and expected from me. I plan to pick up the baton and finish my race called life in your legacy. You don't have to say it… I know you are proud.

-Sabrina C. Nash (daughter)

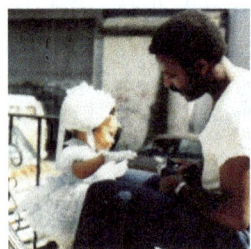

Immortal Love

I remember the day I fell in love with my Dad. I've always loved him as my father, but I can remember the day that I realized, as an adult just what treasure hid beyond that title. Just weeks before his passing, I remember reminiscing about trips to NC hiking through the woods. I remember thinking about just how much time and thought he put into every action… He was a self taught, made man through books and self motivation. He was wise and had a way with words that created movies in your mind... each word manifested like a daydream or a screen play...

He could bump elbows with anyone and everyone... leaving lasting impressions... and changing people's lives for the better... Honest, honorable, and charming... magnetic and humble... I remember thinking how he was "the" Jack of all trades... He could build a house or a car... create every part and troubleshoot anything... like a carpenter... he could Cook... he was clean... a fisherman with hair of wool... Brown eyes... brown skin.

I not only admired and adored him at this point but was inspired and determined to find someone like him because I knew that I would find no greater Love unless it reflected him. It's so clear to me now... I saw the God within him and he always had it shining... Reflecting in thought and in feeling I had realized he was the Sun in my universe, providing Light (knowledge), warmth (love), and security (safe/stability/foundation)... and just like the Sun dependable... he had been a constant in my life that I never had to think twice about...

I was 21 years old when that sun set and I felt it would never rise again. I never knew death until this moment... I never knew what it felt like for someone who was always there to be erased from my present moment and permanently moved into my memories. I remember I was angry... I thought I was mad at the world... this life had been so unfair... to take a man like this seemed careless. I realized eventually it was bigger than I could ever understand... and that I was truly mad with myself... I was ashamed.. I felt so much regret for things not said and done... I spent the next decade doing everything I should have when he was here... My fathers death propelled me through the true cycles of growing pain... that he had already long prepared me for... and for that I am eternally grateful.

My father had instilled a firm foundation for me to grow unshakeable... bending like the bamboo but never breaking under the pressure... His life and death have taught me just how precious every moment is... it taught me how to smell the roses... and as I took it all in.. one day I looked up and realized that he was still here... still a shining light... still planting seeds... still providing this nourishment... this guidance... because one day I looked up and as my eyes met my mirror, these brown eyes of his reflected back to me. I understood in that moment that I was a reflection of Him.. and I fell in love all over again... Literally reciting his words like holy affirmations daily.. A jack of all trades.. creating and troubleshooting, rubbing elbows making lasting impressions... helping all those in my path... clean... doing everything with intention... mindful... empathic and with wisdom that is as gold as the heart beating in my chest... shining my God light for the world to see... like a diamond or a pearl... and my Dad is still my world.

There is no death to mourn over, only this life to celebrate... Revealing the sacred truth of the Immortal Love... for he still lives forever through me... in Peace...

Sierra Yvonne Battle (daughter)
Starchild the Urban Unicorn

First, Clinton was born into a sibling family of thirteen. We all were raised under the disciplinary rules of Christianna Burgess Battle. This meant honoring God, working hard and surviving in this world. It was only after leaving Alex and Christianna's home did Clinton and each of his siblings morph into an adult that the world helped shaped. From my perspective, Clinton became more compassionate about life and people. He shared his home with several of his siblings during their time of need. On his visits to North Carolina, he took time to visit the older generation of people that helped shape his life, often leaving them with gifts, to say he cared. He never hesitated to help when asked, providing financial assistance for daddy's care after mom passed, dividing of the land, heating and air condition unit in the house. I remember a conversation we had when we were dividing the land regarding our brother, Jessie's children. He felted deeply that they should have a share, however due to the structure of the Will, they were excluded. He shared with me that he would give them his share, once completed. There are many more examples of his caring for others that I could give and I can't help but think if he was still here with us, how rich our lives would be to have him around.

When I am forced to think of him not being alive, the emptiness is overwhelming. I ask God, why him? He was one of the good ones. He was one of the younger brothers, they are not supposed to go first, but I realized these are my thoughts, not God. I cope with Clinton's death by trusting and believing on the Word of God. I push through the fact that I can't see or talk to him today, but after my life is over here on earth, I will be reunited with him in heaven. In the meantime, when I have the opportunity to see his wife and children, I am reminded that his living was not in vein; I see his influence and guidance all over of their lives. If I could have a conversation with Clinton today, I would let him know that he is loved and missed. I would tell him not to worry about his family and trust that his training and his leadership as the man of his home is evident in the lives of his family today. I would let him know that in my limited wisdom, his life ended way too soon but I know that God's purpose for his life was fulfilled.

Florence (Battle) Bert (sister)

Happy birthday to my amazing Uncle! Before we moved to NC, Uncle Clinton allowed my family to stay with him in Passaic, NJ from January to June so my brother and I could finish school. He was always there for me personally and making sure I was ok. Even in school, he always challenged me to do my best and his words live with me always. We all were blessed to have him in our lives! He was the quietest of all my uncles but a very strong presence for me personally.

-Anita Williams (niece)

R.I.P , S.I.P, I wish I was old enough to share with me your real estate knowledge, but I do appreciate the times and remember the talks we had as a youth…

-Rahim Mitchell (nephew)

Man, I truly miss Mr. Clint! He was certainly my "bonus dad" and I'm so thankful for that! It's a blessing to have had someone who cared for me just as his own. He was funny too. He loved to joke, but he meant business. I miss hearing him call me "Jess-In-Time," stamped with his southern twang. Miraculously, I was always on time to have dinner at his home. This was my bonus family and I love them as my own. Keeping the Battle family in prayer… They say time heals all things, but I think we just cope with the heartbreak better. Miss you Mr. Clint! Please tell my Daddy that I miss him!

   -Jessica Green (family friend- bonus daughter)

"I met your Dad through your Uncle Otis… He was a kind and loving man but our "situation" just didn't work out." Our union did produce a son, Anthony Omar Battle… I remember that he (Clint) was very attentive, hard-working and that he loved all of his children very much. We remained friends until his death.

             --Carmelita Mathias

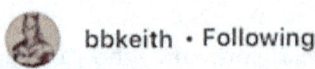 bbkeith • Following

The Red Door. Painting. 2011.

Excerpt from the Journals of Clinton Battle

Airgas has provided a way for me to provide for my family. The truck that I drive every day, has a tag on the front which placed there by the driver who used it before me. He was out of the Suffolk, VA plant and I'm sorry to say that he passed away about a year ago. His sticker reads "money is not everything, but it keeps you in touch with your children." So it goes, I am very thankful to have this job to contribute to the support of my family and friends, as needed.

As I think deeper, what is as equally important (to me) is the people who I work with inside of the Company. I have yet to meet a driver, that I did not like. All have been great, dedicated and hard workers. In which, I consider it to be a great honor to be counted in among this group. Their dedication motivates me to do a better job. They are a hard act to follow. I know this because on the days that I cover their runs for vacation, sick leave etc... the customer's expectations are always high, be it early morning, on time and with safe transfer of the product.

Trust is another motivating factor, Airgas has allowed me to represent them with the delivery of their products and services. This trust was built upon the LaRoche Industries Inc. heritage. I have my own space on a lot, where I am self managed and governed- giving me a freedom to represent the company and myself to the best of my abilities. I feel a special obligation when I go through a Department of Transportation (DOT) inspections to have my equipment in the best working order and to protect the Company's name by not having any violations. I know that this is what management expects, and what they have trusted me to do.

I also feel obligated to be in the best of shape, well rested, and alert when transporting Airgas products on the highways and throughout the cities. This is not a small responsibility, so I know that the Company has placed a great deal of trust in me. At the point of Customer Contact, I present myself in a manner in which Company training and appreciation is represented. My integrity and professionalism has allowed me to fulfill this role.

I am reminded that being a man, gainfully employed has helped me to provide a way for me and my family. I am thankful that I have been able to feed, clothe, purchase property, land, vehicles, education and more as a means to support my wife and children. I am grateful for Airgas...

As I have learned, being able to provide–will help all of us to keep in contact with our children.

Clinton Battle

Unfinished Plans...

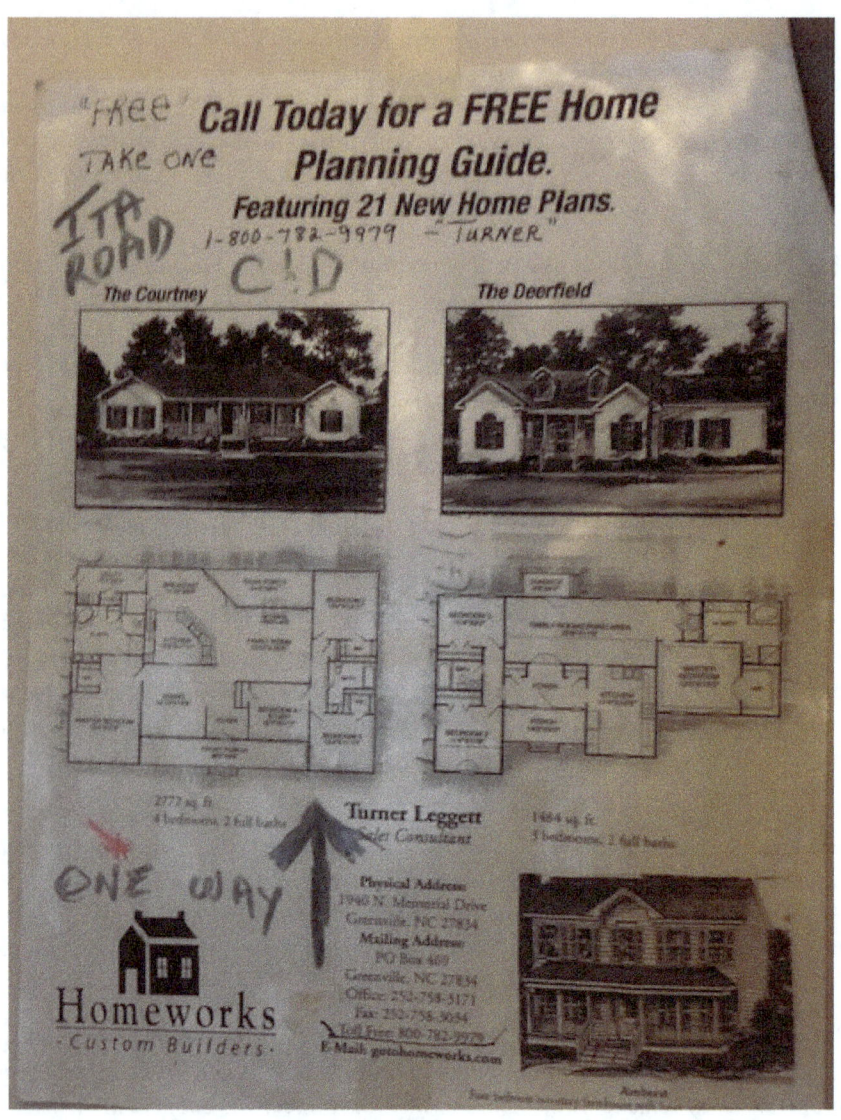

#TheMarathonContinues plans to build a family home in North Carolina by September 2031.

Family Ties

I am committed to you
Deeply committed to you
You are my everything
I give you all of my heart

Me, I'm yours
And yours is mine
Generations will rise
Rise like the sun at dawn

Our love ever growing
Growing and multiplying
Death can't part us
Because love never dies
Our love will live forever
Strengthening our family ties

"The Lord giveth and he taketh away."

Living Legacies x Coke

DAVID A. NASH, III

EST.
9.3.2020

In the Living Legacy of Marion Miller Wood

Obituary

Marion Miller Wood entered eternal rest on September 3, 2020 surrounded by the love of her family. Marion was born in Cumberland, Virginia to the late Perry Davenport and Lucy (Johnson) Davenport. Marion was a woman of God and of great faith. Marion attended school in Cumberland before her family moved to New Jersey. She then moved to Norwalk, CT where she completed her studies in Nursing. Marion's parents raised her and her 8 siblings on the values of faith, love, caring and sharing. Marion was the loving mother of Vincent Terrence Miller and Edwin Gregory Miller. She loved her boys and was very proud of them. Marion believed in instilling strong family values such as hard work, pursuing an education and a career and maintaining a healthy lifestyle.

Marion was well educated, having obtained both a Bachelor and Master's Degree in Nursing from the University of Bridgeport. Marion was a Registered Nurse for Norwalk Hospital for over 25 years, including working in the Emergency Room, until her retirement. Throughout her career and into retirement, family and friends relied and called upon her for medical guidance and expertise. She stayed current in the medical field even after retirement, continuing to support, care for and advise family, friends and loved ones. Marion was a meticulous, knowledgeable and attentive nurse with a very caring and sincere affect in her work. She executed her career calling with passion and excellence. Marion believed in service and giving back. This brought her such joy. Marion enjoyed spending time with her grandchildren and playing cards and board games with them. Marion was also fun and loved to tell jokes. She enjoyed traveling and especially loved fashion. She was classy and enjoyed her suits with matching shoes and exquisite hats. She was simply beautiful inside and out. Marion was devoted to service in the church and served the Lord with gladness and brought many souls to Christ. In Norwalk, she continued her fellowship at Grace Baptist Church. She believed in the power of prayer.
She will be remembered as a person who loved the Lord.

Later in life, Marion married Reverend Dr. Richard Wood and served faithfully as the First Lady at Grace Baptist Church of Norwalk, CT and remained very active in the church alongside her husband. Reverend Dr. Richard Wood and Marion later relocated to Atlanta, GA. Marion was a member of Friendship Baptist Church and served on many boards such as the Health and Wellness Ministry, Member of the Deaconess Board, Tutorial Ministry, Uplifters,
Sunday School Teacher, Intergroup Counseling, Bible Study, Vocational Bible School, Community Outreach and Advocate for Children.

TAKEAWAYS FROM MY AUNT MARION

- Education is imperative

- Health is invaluable

- Stack your coins (save) and invest

- Give back to the youth and your community

- And be fashionable doing it all!

HOW I GOT MY NAME

ONE DAY WHEN I WAS AROUND 12,
I ASKED MY MOM HOW I GOT MY NAME....

SHE TOLD ME THAT THE NAME "SABRINA" WAS ACTUALLY THE NAME THAT HER AUNT MARION WAS GOING TO GIVE TO HER DAUGHTER.

UNFORTUNATELY,
AUNT MARION SUFFERED A MISCARRIAGE—

BUT I WAS NAMED...

"SABRINA"

SABRINA

Straightforward

Angel in disguise

Brutally Honest

Real Friend

Intelligent

Not a cheater

Always loyal

In the Living Legacy of Terrance Sterling

HIS
REMEMBERING
TERRANCE STERLING
LIFE
SEPTEMBER 11

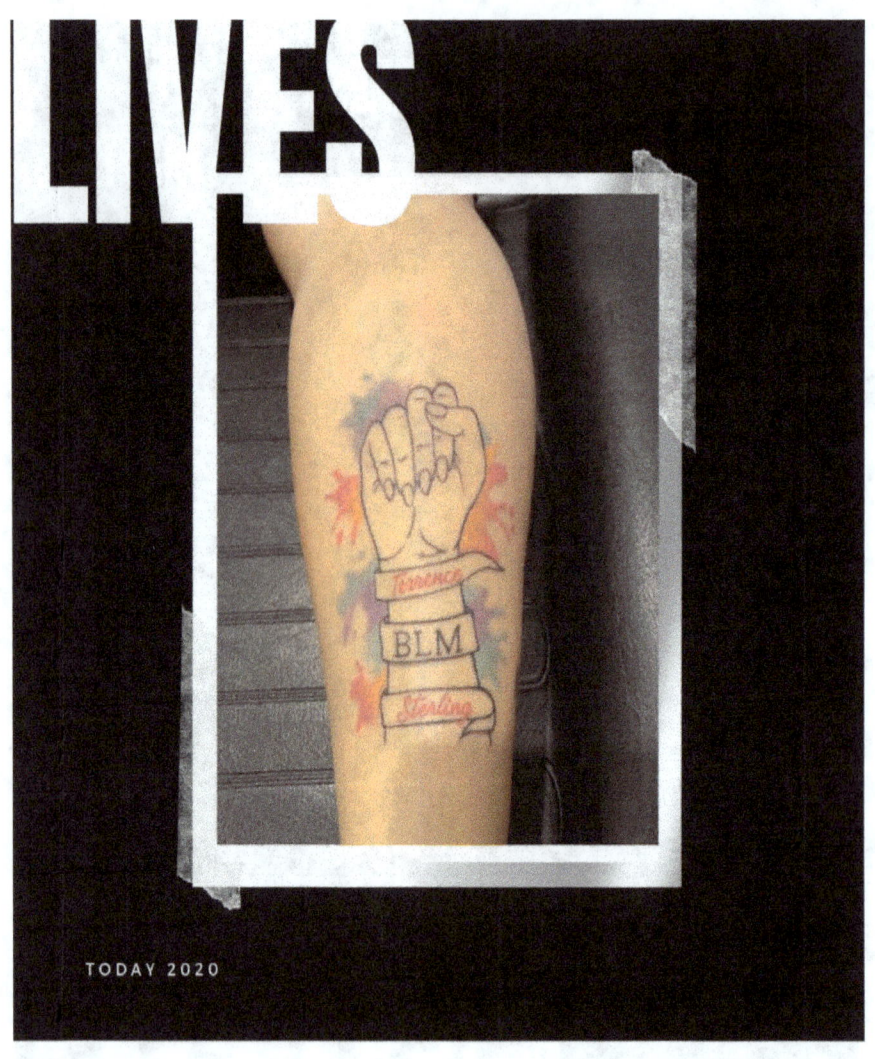

Photos Provided by: Veronica Bert-Jackson

A Journey of Healing through Forgiveness

A great deal has happened since "Hallelujah Anyhow". The hardest lesson throughout this process has been FORGIVENESS. I had been asking God to help me get rid of all this anger and rage I had building up inside of me towards the police officers since Terrence's passing. If I thought or saw anything related to Terrence especially motorcycles, police officers (whether the situation was positive or not), police brutality, racial injustices, or death it would trigger the rage and anger. After praying every day for help, God simply told me I had to forgive the officers, especially Brian Trainer for killing Terrence. I wasn't shocked, but I knew that was going to be very hard for me to do since I didn't want to forgive them at all. I wanted them to suffer the consequences for killing Terrence, who was doing nothing wrong. One day on January 28, 2018 my aunt from Louisiana, sent my parents, my pastor and his wife, and myself a text message saying the following:

"Hello family, I had an encounter with Holy Spirt this morning and He has just released me to share it and with whom. TERRENCE IS AT PEACE!!!! He appeared to me smiling as usual and he and the Holy Spirit took me to a gathering of all of you, Jason, the officers, and the other individuals involved. The officers fell to their knees in front of you all in tears apologizing for what they had done and asking for the family's forgiveness, especially Gene, Florence, and Chrystal. After which, they turned to you, Rev. Dixon and asked for prayer. They confessed that they had not had a moment's peace since it happened. Terrence walked over to them and placed his hands on each of their backs and said, "I FORGIVE YOU!!!" It was then that he appeared to all of you and said, "I LOVE YOU AND I AM GOOD"!!! He said to Gene and Florence, "THANK YOU FOR ALL THAT YOU'VE DONE FOR ME AND CONTINUE TO DO FOR ME" EVEN WHEN YOU DIDN'T THINK I WAS LISTENING, I WAS!!!" To Chrystal he said, "IT'S NOT YOUR FAULT" I LOVE YOU, NOW LET ME GO!!!!!!!" To

Rev. and Mrs. Dixon, he said, "THANK YOU FOR BEING THERE AND FOR ALL THE ADVICE YOU GAVE ME EVEN WHEN I DIDN'T WANT TO HEAR IT!!!!!!!" Afterwards, the Holy Spirit allowed you to feel his presence and there was a SERENE PEACE in the place!!! I KNOW ALL IS WELL WITH ALL OF US!!!! Love you all much and be blessed!!!!!"

This message touched my heart so much and confirmed what God had been telling me to do, FORGIVE THEM!, as well as, let Terrence go and not dwell on the negative of the situation and him passing away, but dwell on all the positive trusting that God will take care of me and give me what I need to get through each day. So, with prayer, counseling, and God's help I have forgiven the police officers. The heavy weight has been lifted and everyday since has gotten better. So, on February 21, 2018, my parents and I had our last FOX 5 News interview after the firing of Brian Trainer. That day I had decided to read a letter and final statement the Lord told me to write for the public, since I had never been vocal in the press and expressing my feelings about what happened. Here is my statement:

"Good Afternoon Everyone! I'm Terrence's sister, Chrystal. And I would just like to first thank everyone that has supported my family and I over the past year and 5 months. It has been hard...but all of your prayers, encouraging words, and acts of kindness and love have helped us get through each day. There is not a day that goes by where I don't think about Terrence. I miss every aspect of his being. And the fact that he was taken from me by Brian Turner and Jordan Palmer. And...Yes! I did say both officers names because they worked together as partners in order for the murder to happen. There will always be void in my heart that will never be filled due to the decisions of these two officers. The fact that U.S. Department of Justice intentionally did not bring us justice in this case is very disappointing. The system that you are to trust to bring justice instead has decided the cover the injustice despite facts and evidence that proves otherwise. Since the U.S. Department of Justice did not do their part, I pray that the Internal Affairs of DC Police Department will hold both officers accountable for their actions. Everyone involved in this case has had the opportunity to make a change, but it's frustrating to know that our justice system as a whole continues to create an atmosphere of division and puts officers that have committed crimes on a higher pedestal, too high to be held accountable. Despite all of this, I am grateful for God's guidance to get us through to this point. Though no amount of money will ever bring Terrence back, the compensation will assist in taking care of his family he has left behind. The settlement does not give me full closure, but a conviction of murder would come close. Despite the rollercoaster of feelings that I've experienced, God and Terrence have been speaking to me. The main themes have been forgiveness and letting go. I've been caring around anger and hatred. With spiritual guidance and prayer, I have come to the point where I can say that I forgive you.... Brian Trainer, Jordan Palmer, and the DC judicial system. I hate the crime that was committed and the decisions of injustice made, but I have to forgive in order to move on. Forgiving gives me control instead of this situation controlling my life in a negative manner. It also allows me to be free and not be bound because I don't have my brother with me. So, on this day I will no longer carry around the burden of your death but of the life and joy Terrence brought to me for 31 years. I'm letting go of the anger, hatred.... all the negative energy related to your death and channeling positive energy into my life...a life full of happiness, joy, and peace which is what I know you would want me to do. I pray Brian Trainer and Jordan Palmer find God and develop a relationship with Him so they repent for the killing of His child, Terrence, and causing pain to our family and friends. I also pray that God continues to let His light shine through my family, myself, and all people who believe in order to spread love and kindness to each other despite race, ethnicity, gender, or religion. We are human and precious in God's sight. Love one another and treat others the way you want to be treated. Thank you for listening and God bless you."

Since the reading of this statement, Brian Trainer was fired, and Jordan Palmer is still working for the Metropolitan Police Department in D.C. I wish I could say that both were fired and found guilty of murder, but I can't. Despite the injustice, my family and I will continue to walk the high road and use this experience as a way to help others. This is why I'm so glad I was obedient by writing and reading my statement. It touched everyone in the room and displayed God's strength within me. It was hard, but I DID IT! And to whomever is reading this, you can too! Forgiveness is not for other party involved in your situation, IT'S FOR YOU! It's the gateway to freedom and not letting other people and situations hold you hostage and control your life. After forgiving I am much stronger than before. God is real, He hears, listens, and will help you with whatever you're going through. This road called life is not easy, but definitely worth it. Terrence wanted me to forgive in order to live a FREE life with more joy than sadness. For those of you who have lost a sibling to police brutality or gun violence, you can't live the rest of your life filled with anger. You have to release the pain, forgive, and then channel your energy in positive ways even if it is anger, channel it positively. Absolutely, this is easier said than done, but it can be accomplished with faith, therapy/counseling, and support of positive and loving family and friends. FORGIVENESS is the pathway to FREEDOM!

God Bless!

Chrystal Sterling

In the Living Legacy of Kayla Ross Perry

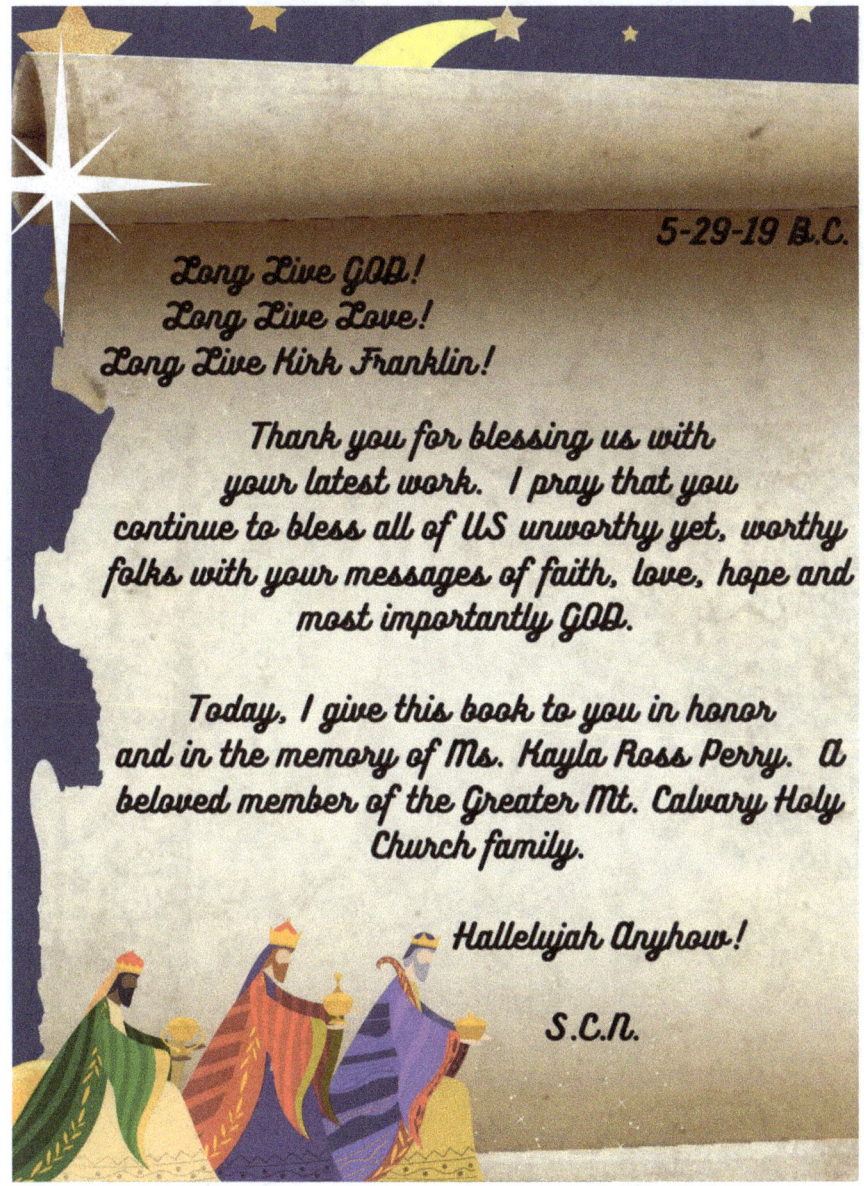

5-29-19 B.C.

Long Live GOD!
Long Live Love!
Long Live Kirk Franklin!

Thank you for blessing us with your latest work. I pray that you continue to bless all of US unworthy yet, worthy folks with your messages of faith, love, hope and most importantly GOD.

Today, I give this book to you in honor and in the memory of Ms. Kayla Ross Perry. A beloved member of the Greater Mt. Calvary Holy Church family.

Hallelujah Anyhow!

S.C.N.

Long Live KRP

KRP Gives Back

Karing, Konnecting, Kommunity x KRP

Legacies never die

Legacies

```
                        U
                      T M J
                    R X O J S
                  E N O F J O A
                A W G I V I N G L
              S E L T T A B A P F L
            U J F F R I E N D S A U O
          R S T N I R P T O O F M N P C
        E T N I R P E U L B N E I I R K A
      S P E T S T O O F X E O C L T E R G T
    A S E C N A T I R E H N I A Y Y P O N R I
  P O R T I O N Z P D W R N T L E T A W Z S O O
R R A C E S R K H K O S A W A P T A R D H V H W N
Y G F A I R R E C E S O N C O V G U E E R N B O A I K
D P E U U C S O U O A P L O P D R N B W F A M P P P R N C
D G Q W N I O R T N T R I B I R S E I I S S H R L I G R E G V
A R Q L O D A N I S T H R T O S S R R V E E A H U E M D T
  C P W P M E E T A T S E I T A E E T G P N S O U C E C
    A L L O T M E N T N U D E P R H A A S R Y N O A S
      K B R O B A L L O M A C H P T R T E C I L D G
        R R D D A V L I E R T X I A J D O O L D J
          T M S N G I T M T B R T G A N N E E H
            R S G A W A O T E I E E T G C N E
              U D D L L R H O X L R I T D I
                S R Z E I N M O I F I O R
                  T A R E H Q B T V W L
                    P W S I U S E M O
                      A E T W Z E O
                        E R J N M
                          L T U
                            D
```

WORD LIST:

- ALLOCATION
- ALLOTMENT
- BATTLES
- BLOOD
- BLUEPRINT
- COLLECTIVE
- CONTRIBUTE
- ENDOWMENT
- ESTATE
- FAIR
- FAMILY
- FOOTPRINTS
- FOOTSTEPS
- FRIENDS
- GATHERING PLACE
- GIFTS
- GIVING
- GROWING
- GUIDE
- HARD WORK
- HEART
- HEIR
- HEIRLOOM
- HERITAGE
- INHERITANCE
- LABOR
- LAND
- LEADERSHIP
- MEMORIES
- MENTORS
- MONEY
- PASS DOWN
- PLAN
- PORTION
- PREPARATION
- PREPARE
- PRESERVATION
- PROTECT
- RACE
- RELATIONSHIPS
- REUNION
- REUNITE
- REWARDS
- SHARE
- STOCK
- SWEAT
- TEARS
- TRADITIONS
- TREASURE
- TRIBUTE
- TRUST
- UNITY
- WILL

SURVIVAL PLANS

Legacies

"Legacies" Crossword Puzzle Clues

Across

4 Hotel Chain headquartered in Chicago- founded by Hyatt Robert von Dehn

7 Anyone who precedes another in office, position ore even a forefather

9 What you are given in recognition of service, effort or achievement

10 Anything handed down from the past from an ancestor or predecessor

12 To be in charge a company, establishment or undertaking; to administer or run

14 Modest attitude towards one's importance

15 American exhibition basketball team, founded in 1926 Harlem, NY

17 A thing or things belonging to or possessed by someone(s)

20 The natural development of increasing in size, changing physically or maturing

21 African American man who was killed while riding his motorcycle by Washington D.C. police officer on September 11, 2016

23 Money earned, wages, profits

24 Firm belief in the reliability, ability or strength in someone or something

25 To be worthy of respect, credit- distinguished

Down

1 First Female President of Prince George's Community College

2 2nd and longest standing African American woman General manager w/ Hyatt Hotels Corporation

3 An experienced and trusted advisor

5 The worth, merit or importance of something

6 Portion of earth's surface not covered by water

8 Legally and/or formally recognizing the union of two individuals

11 A person from whom one is descended

13 To be successful or fortunate

16 Creator of Black, White and Blue documentary

18 Social unit consisting of parents, children and other relatives

19 Serious thought or consideration

22 A thing given willingly to someone without payment. A present.

Works Cited

1. Byron Hord, R. "Curtis Scoon Biography." IMBD.
   https://www.imdb.com/name/nm2933050/bio

2. Cabin The Story (2017). YouTube, uploaded by funzito (2019).
   https://www.youtube.com/watch?v=ue7KiBgtj_c&t=198s

3. "Eastside High School Song (Lean on Me)." YouTube, uploaded by Antoine Vertilus (2016).
   https://www.youtube.com/watch?v=ZYCqebmnhpI

4. *Gil Scott-Heron - Revolution Will Not Be Televised (Official Version)*. YouTube, uploaded by Ace Records, Ltd. Oct. 2, 2013
   https://www.youtube.com/watch?v=vwSRqaZGsPw

5. Gil Scott-Heron- Whitey on The Moon- (Official Audio). YouTube, uploaded by Ace Records, Ltd.
   https://www.youtube.com/watch?v=goh2x_G0ct4

6. Gil Scott Heron- We Almost Lost Detroit. YouTube, uploaded by HoraceIsaac SoWhatSessions, August 18, 2011
   https://www.youtube.com/watch?v=cpNUqNe0U5g

7. Goncalves,D.; McCrary,S. and Olmos, D. WUSA9. "Terrence Sterling: Unarmed &killed by police, his family speaks out." (2017).
   https://www.wusa9.com/article/news/local/fort-washington/terrence-sterling-unarmed-killed-by-police-his-family-speaks-out/65-453167664

8. Jolley, W.J. and Jolley, D.T. *"Make Love, Make Money, Make It Last."* (2017). Jolley Life Publishing. ISBN 978-0-9992731-0-4

9. Kanye West- Follow God. YouTube, uploaded by Kanye West (2019).
   https://www.youtube.com/results?search_query=follow+God

10. *"Kiss of Life-Official-1993."* YouTube, uploaded by Sade (2009)
    https://www.youtube.com/watch?v=MmOau-PMWJk

11. Lorde, Audre. "*Sister Outsider: Essays and Speeches*." Trumansburg, New York: The Crossing Press. 1984. ISBN 978-0-89594-141-1.

12. My Dance Life TV- Devante Capers (Episode 8). YouTube,

uploaded by Digital Mynd, June 28, 2015. https://www.youtube.com/watch?v=IzxQFH9Ovjk

13. Nash, S. *"Hallelujah Anyhow!"(2017)*. FACTS Education, LLC. ISBN 978-0-692-97277-9

14. National Archives. *"The Bill of Rights: What does it say?"* (2020). https://www.archives.gov/founding-docs/bill-of-rights/what-does-it-say#:~:text=The%20Bill%20of%20Rights%20is%20the%20first%2010%20Amendments%20to%20the%20Constitution.&text=It%20guarantees%20civil%20rights%20and,the%20people%20or%20the%20States.

15. Slim, Iceberg. *"Pimp: The Story of My Life."* (1969). ISBN: 978-1-451-61713-9

16. The African American Policy Forum. *"#Sayhername Report."* (2015).https://static1.squarespace.com/static/53f20d90e4b0b80451158d8c/t/5edc95fba357687217b08fb8/1591514635487/SHNReportJuly2015.pdf

17. The W. Edwards Deming Institute. *"Quote by W. Edwards Deming."*(2020) https://quotes.deming.org/authors/W._Edwards_Deming/quote/10141

18. Why Not the Right Thing the First Time- Nikki Giovanni – TEDxHerndon. YouTube uploaded by TedxTalks, June 13, 2017 https://www.youtube.com/watch?v=Ekpw2xzPK2Y

19. Wikipedia. "Million Man March." (2020). https://en.wikipedia.org/wiki/Million_Man_March

20. Wikipedia. "Tuskegee Airmen." (2020). https://en.wikipedia.org/wiki/Tuskegee_Airmen

21. Wisegoals. *"Long Term Dreams- Short Term Goals"* (2019). Worksheet. file:///C:/Users/nashsc/Desktop/Wisegirl%20Long%20term%20Goals%20SP.webp

22. Wisegoals. *"My Main Goal Right Now"* (2019). Worksheet. https://www.wisegoals.com/goal-setting-worksheets.html#twentyyearvisionworksheet

www.ingramcontent.com/pod-product-compliance
Lightning Source LLC
Chambersburg PA
CBHW070041080526
44586CB00013B/873